Herman Schmalenbach

ON SOCIETY AND EXPERIENCE

THE HERITAGE OF SOCIOLOGY

A Series Edited by Morris Janowitz

Herman Schmalenbach

ON

SOCIETY AND EXPERIENCE

Selected Papers

Edited, translated, and with an Introduction

by GÜNTHER LÜSCHEN *and*
GREGORY P. STONE

THE UNIVERSITY OF CHICAGO PRESS

CHICAGO AND LONDON

Günther Lüschen is professor of sociology at the
University of Illinois.
Gregory P. Stone is professor of sociology at the
University of Minnesota.

THE UNIVERSITY OF CHICAGO PRESS, CHICAGO 60637
The University of Chicago Press, Ltd., London

© 1977 by The University of Chicago
All rights reserved. Published 1977
Printed in the United States of America

82 81 80 79 78 9 8 7 6 5 4 3 2 1

Library of Congress Cataloging in Publication Data

Schmalenbach, Herman, 1885–1950.
    Herman Schmalenbach on society and experience.

    (The Heritage of sociology)
    Bibliography: p.
    Includes index.
    1.   Sociology—Addresses, essays, lectures.
I.   Lüschen, Günther, 1930–   II.   Stone, Gregory
Prentice, 1921–   III.   Title.
HM51.S347   1977   301   77-78067
ISBN 0-226-73865-5

Contents

Preface

Herman Schmalenbach represents a unique perspective in sociology and one that has not been widely disseminated even in his native land. We think it is a valuable one, which deserves incorporation in the discourse of sociology. This contribution is clearly in the Chicago tradition.

In the United States, the first reference to Schmalenbach was quite probably made by Edward Shils in an article called "The Study of the Primary Group."[1] There Shils referred in a footnote to Schmalenbach's article on the *Bund* ("communion," translated here in part 1 as "Communion—a Sociological Category") as a "thoughtful essay." Shils, however, deplored the fact that "unfortunately Schmalenbach's work has been entirely passed over by sociological investigators." True, that is deplorable, but quite understandable, as we shall see. The tone of the footnote nevertheless posed a challenge. That long essay had appeared in the German periodical, *Die Dioskuren*, not well known in the United States and difficult to locate. It was finally found at Amherst College. Moreover, the essay demanded a new interpretation of *Gemeinschaft*, an interpretation available nowhere else at that time. At any rate, the essay received its first translation by Gregory Stone, in fulfillment of the language requirement for the Ph.D. degree at the University of Chicago. After two or three years, Erving Goffman mentioned that Kaspar Naegele was working on a condensed version of the essay. The result was a merger of the two translations in an

1. In Daniel Lerner and Harold D. Lasswell (eds.) *The Policy Sciences* (Stanford: Stanford University Press, 1951), pp. 44–69.

abridged form and the first published English translation of Schmalenbach.[2]

An intensive discussion of these efforts by the editors of this volume led to deeper study of Schmalenbach's work. There was a certain resonance with the perspective of the Graz school of *Gestalt-* and *Gegenstandstheorie*, a tradition in the broad realm of structuralism, with which Günther Lüschen had been imbued during his graduate study in Europe. In his phenomenological stance, Schmalenbach could be related in many ways to this type of structuralism and phenomenology, but this very relationship suggested directions for further exploration. Schmalenbach had suffered from undeserved neglect, not only in the United States but also in his native Germany. The historical context of his writing provides some explanation. His work also carries on a tradition of German philosophy—sociology and cultural history—that represents an often unrecognized branch of the social sciences. That tradition receives renewed attention and elaboration in this book.

Acknowledgments

More than any single person, Morris Janowitz has devoted efforts to a revival of the sociological heritage that the University of Chicago at one time had begun to forget. In this vein, he encouraged us to bring together the essays in this volume as part, however small, of maintaining the heritage and continuity of that perduring conversation we call sociology.

A special note of thanks should be given to the family of Herman Schmalenbach, particularly to his son, Professor Werner Schmalenbach, director of art for North Rhine-Westphalia, and to his daughter, Madame Thévenaz of Lausanne.

These good people have also given us help: Immanuel Birnbaum, the late Eberhard Fahrenhorst, Erving Goffman, Kurt Hammerich, Rudolf Heberle, Grete Henry, the late Paul Honigsheim,

2. Kaspar D. Naegele and Gregory P. Stone, translators and editors. Herman Schmalenbach, "The Sociological Category of Communion," in Talcott Parsons, et. al. (eds.), *Theories of Society*, I (Glencoe, Illinois: The Free Press, Inc., 1961), pp. 331–347.

Richard Howe, René König, Michael Landmann, the late Kaspar Naegele, Helmut Plessner, Robert S. Perinbanayagam, Edgar Salin, Hansjörg Salmony, Richard Schacht, Edward Shils, and Sandra Soares.

Thanks are also due to Cläre Lüschen and Susan L. Stone, as well as to the various secretaries and clerks in our respective departments.

Finally, Benita John has labored with, for, and occasionally against us during the entire preparation of this volume.

INTRODUCTION

In what context shall sociology reexamine the contributions of Herman Schmalenbach? First, he probed such fundamental concepts as Tönnies's "community" and "society" and, implicitly, the vast proliferation of bipolar typologies since Tönnies—in Max Weber, for example, and earlier, in Maine. These concepts persist in sociological thought, empirically inadequate and often misunderstood.[1] Variously disguised and emphasized in these typologies, at least five relational dimensions may be discerned: (1) circumstantial relations ("status" in Maine's usage and the sense in which Schmalenbach chooses to apprehend "community" [See "Communion—a Sociological Category," below, part 1]); (2) consensual relations (Louis Wirth's "consensus" and to a certain extent, Durkheim's "mechanical solidarity" and perhaps even Merton's "homophily"); (3) rapport (in particular, Cooley's and Schmalenbach's conception of "communion"); (4) exchange relations (one variety includes certain "contracts," but the interpersonal variant is found in the *do ut des*; the structural variant, precisely in *Gesellschaft* [see ibid.]); (5) symbiotic relations (Durkheim's "organic solidarity," emphasized by Robert Park and most ecologists). Thus, to construe "community" and "society" as opposite poles of a continuum or scale is to encompass far too much. Moreover, to ground such distinctions psychologically and ontologically, as Tönnies did, poses unnecessary difficulties for sociological research.

Schmalenbach, in his "Communion—a Sociological Category," has accomplished a single, long-needed revision in a thoroughgoing manner. Therefore, one major set of the reasons why we present

1

Schmalenbach here includes pointing up the necessity for conceptual refinement in sociology, emphasizing the importance of theoretical continuity in such endeavors,[2] and demonstrating the disciplined effort required to establish continuity. Of course, such careful effort may well result in discarding concepts because we think that the intellectual armamentarium of sociology is, like our military and naval establishments, replete with obsolete equipment. Schmalenbach's tenacious and unyielding attention to the general problem of concept formation exemplifies our point.

A second rationale must take into account the attention given to ethnomethodology and sociolinguistics by sociologists who have drawn on the work of Schütz and Wittgenstein. In recent years phenomenological sociology has become, particularly in England and the United States, a popular sociological method. The danger of phenomenology lies in the acceptance of a sociologically simplified conception of being that ultimately leads to a solipsistic apprehension of world views.[3] Schmalenbach is to be understood as a phenomenologist, but as a very knowledgeable and elusive one who fully understood these pitfalls. He takes his methodology at least beyond Kant's distinction between "phenomena" and "noumena," (the sensual reality experienced in the mind). Toulmin puts it, ". . . on Kant's own confession, there was very little at all that we could *say* about 'noumena,' and still less about the precise relations between 'noumena' and 'phenomena.' "[4] Yet Schmalenbach said a lot, said so much that we have been tempted to call him a "noumenologist" during his early period. Certainly his technique of "categorical intuition" represents an elevation of noumena to a level of scholarly inquiry.

In this he was not unlike Cooley. Moreover, there is here an abiding awareness of the importance of what George H. Mead called "obdurate reality." At a time when sociologists have almost universally recognized what Suzanne Langer, after Ernst Cassirer, has appropriately called the symbolic transformation of human conduct, and have consequently become impressed with the human "power" symbolically to make or break reality, Schmalenbach reminds us of the necessity of a proper understanding of reality and knowledge.

As Schmalenbach develops his methodology, he frequently refers to Husserl but not to Schütz or Wittgenstein, although near the end of his intellectual life he developed a Wittgensteinlike analysis of mind and being, or *Geist und Sein* (parts of which have been translated in this volume; see "On Human Existence," below, part 3). Actually, he came much closer to developing a pure phenomenological approach to sociology than did Schütz himself. Despite Schütz's many acknowledgments to Husserl, one should never underestimate his intellectual grounding in the Viennese school of marginal utility and the influence of the economist von Mises. Thus there is a gold mine here for ethnomethodologists. Phenomenological sociology has much to reclaim from a critical assay of the intellectual territory staked out by Schmalenbach.

Third, there is no question that the formal and historical sociology of Georg Simmel will be better understood in parallel with Schmalenbach's work. Many of the theoretical concerns and substantive topics of Simmel are those of Schmalenbach, although Schmalenbach is ultimately somewhat less empirically oriented.

So much for the context. What of the man and his work?

HERMAN SCHMALENBACH—THE LIFE OF THE SCHOLAR

Herman Schmalenbach was born in 1885 in the town of Breckerfeld in the province of Westphalia. At its zenith, Breckerfeld was a member of the Hanseatic League. Schmalenbach's family owned a small industrial enterprise, quite typical among the industrious people of this region, which was also known for its devout and at times sectarian Protestantism. His family moved from Breckerfeld too soon for anyone to anticipate the notable careers that he and his older brother Eugen (a noted economist), were to have in the academic world.

Schmalenbach studied at the University of Berlin and the University of Jena in such areas as philosophy, sociology, history, art history, and German. At the age of 24 he published his first book on metaphysics,[5] and the following year (1910), he obtained his Dr. phil. at the University of Jena with a thesis on the same topic. In 1920, Schmalenbach received his *venia legendi* as a *Privat-*

Dozent in philosophy and sociology at the University of Göttingen.[6] Only three years later he was promoted to the prestigious position of *Extra-Ordinarius*, an indication of the early success he enjoyed as a teacher and scholar. While in Göttingen, he also taught at the Technical University of Hannover.

In 1931, Schmalenbach accepted a call to the chair of philosophy and history of philosophy at the University of Basel in Switzerland, declining offers made by Königsberg and Prague. He held this position until the end of his life in 1950, and students from all over the world studied with him. It is said that many of those coming from far away intended to stay only for a semester, but then decided to stay on with Schmalenbach to complete their studies and receive their degrees. A number of his students later became university professors themselves in Switzerland, Germany, and other parts of the world.

Schmalenbach was a highly acclaimed teacher. Through his philosophical circle, he exerted strong scholarly and personal influence. His professional and personal contacts included such notable philosophers and sociologists as Martin Buber, Edmund Husserl, Karl Joël, Helmut Plessner, Georg Simmel, Ferdinand Tönnies, Max Weber, the economist Edgar Salin, and the professor of literature, Friedrich Gundolf. Early in Schmalenbach's period as a student, he was close to, although not a member of, the Stefan George circle,[7] a communion of idealistic humanists and literati that foresaw the emergence of a new era and wanted to work for it. In his early work, one notices over and over again Schmalenbach's thoughtful involvement with the sociopolitical issues of his time; it was typical for him to use as a basis for the discussion of future developments not only historical facts but also the hopes and concerns of youth. It is against such a background as well as in the tradition of Plato, German mysticism (as represented, for example, by Meister Eckhart), Leibniz, and Goethe that the inner focus and development of Schmalenbach's work and his motivation throughout his life must be seen. To be sure, the influences of Immanuel Kant are paramount in his philosophy, and shaped, together with those of other scholars, his methodological approach. The former more subjective tradition, however, coupled with a critical religiosity and social concern, better explains his motivation as a scholar and a person. He frequently interpreted Kant in terms of his religiosity and was intrigued more by the speculative than by the substantive contributions of Hegel, Schelling, and (among the neo-Kantians) Nicolai Hartmann or Bergson's *Lebensphilosophie*.

While Schmalenbach's formal responsibility was in philosophy, his social concerns and his search for what he considered the proper sphere of philosophy led him to an extensive and recurring consideration of sociology, its theory, and its methodology. His critical style and comprehensive command of social science problems made him a unique figure who, in his early work, anticipated many later developments in society and also in sociology. Although he held both Tönnies and Max Weber in very high regard, he nevertheless became one of their most fundamental critics.

Schmalenbach is not well known among English-speaking sociologists. Nor was he that much better known in his native Germany, where sociology was deliberately suppressed during the Nazi period. Neither did his cosmopolitan and universal orientation, his true scholarship, qualify him as a philosophical scholar of stature during this dark period of academic history.[8]

PHILOSOPHICAL CONTEXT

One can find in Schmalenbach the major streams of idealistic and humanistic philosophy, covering a broad range of knowledge with considerable attention paid to epistemology and history. Yet it is not easy to assign this original and penetrating mind to a specific school. He himself saw figures like Plato, Leibniz, and Goethe as models of philosophers and scientists—men who, in addition to their scientific contributions, were involved in social and political practice. Yet during the course of his life he withdrew ever more from direct political involvement. Someone concerned with questions of final cause and action to deepen his scientific insight might see Schmalenbach as carrying on the tradition of *Lebensphilosophie*. It is in line with such an interpretation to find him arguing on matters of human experience, practical relevance, and the meaning of life as it relates to a divine will.

Another viable line of thought is present in Schmalenbach's historicism and individualism. Though one might assign him a central place in the idealistic tradition of his time, his sympathy for Hegel, as well as his strong interest in phenomenology and *Gestalt* philosophy, took him beyond the conventional boundaries of idealism. There are also some direct references to pragmatism in his conception of man, oriented as it is to social ethics. Schmalenbach specifically referred to William James, and there are some parallels in his epistemology to that of Charles S. Peirce.[9] Even so, he did not respect positivistic or experimental modes of inquiry. Wundt's philosophy and psychology were not to his liking, although he acknowledged Wundt's vast knowledge. "Know everything, but see nothing" was his dry comment about this "enormous polyhistor."[10] But he was acerbic in his critique of what he called "feuilleton philosophy" as it appeared in the work of Graf Keyserling and in the extreme subjectivism of Ernst Bloch.[11]

While there is no clear statement to that effect in Schmalenbach's work, a personal communication from Hansjörg Salmony, his successor in Basel, states that Schmalenbach considered himself a phenomenologist. He was personally close to Husserl, but he obviously did not follow the transcendental switch that Husserl's conception of phenomenology ultimately took. In the end, Schmalenbach looked for the empirical connections of phenomenological insights, and it may well be that this difference restrained him from absolutely referring to his own work and method as phenomenological. It is on this point of difference that the criticisms he levied against Husserl have to be understood.[12] Schmalenbach appears at times to be closer to the Austrian branch of phenomenology found in the *Gegenstandstheorie* of Alexius von Meinong, together with Husserl the most important student of Franz Brentano.[13]

Schmalenbach's position in phenomenology is also quite akin to modern structuralism. His recognition among French and French-Swiss structuralists and phenomenologists is probably the only clear acknowledgment and understanding of his work (if one disregards his essays on communion and property) outside the circle of his immediate followers and students.[14] A substantive relationship to

Wittgenstein appears in his notion of language philosophy, with which he was familiar owing to the influence of the founder of that approach, Horace de Saussure. Language was for Schmalenbach a reality that begs scientific and substantive analysis.

One might also expect that Schmalenbach would have been influenced by existentialism, but there is no clear evidence for this in his work. There was no rapport between him and Karl Jaspers at Basel. Their one meeting, early in their careers in Heidelberg, ended on a note of incompatibility. Much more obvious is the influence and impact of *Lebensphilosophie*, particularly that of Henri Bergson. This was partially initiated by Eucken and Simmel, and later on by Schmalenbach's friend, Martin Buber.

If one were to look for Schmalenbach's intellectual parentage, one would note that of Georg Simmel, with whom he studied in Berlin and to whom he often referred. Schmalenbach and his students in philosophy and sociology constitute Simmel's most direct followers in Europe.[15]

Actually as strong as the influence of Simmel, although unacknowledged and never mentioned in previous interpretations of Schmalenbach, is the influence of the "activist" idealistic philosophy of Rudolf Eucken, 1908 Nobel Laureate in literature and one-time visiting professor at Harvard (in 1912).[16] Schmalenbach, in his own life history, followed the paths of Eucken. Eucken studied at Berlin and Göttingen, and he taught at Basel and Jena. At one time or another, Schmalenbach studied or taught in exactly the same places. Though Eucken supervised his thesis, Schmalenbach did not refer to him in his work. This is not completely understandable. Quite a few of the philosophical problems and concerns of Eucken reappear in Schmalenbach (metaphysics, religion, idealism, Bergson, James). We can suggest two somewhat obvious explanations for the omission of any reference to Eucken. In Germany, the mere fact that one is someone's student sufficiently acknowledges his indebtedness to his teacher. More likely, Schmalenbach rejected the towering authority figure. While Eucken is no longer well known, in retrospect one should recall that he ranked as the major representative of idealism in this century, and in practical philosophy or *Lebensphilosophie* was an equal of Henri Bergson and William James. He was widely acclaimed in Germany, Britain, and the

United States. Eucken's philosophy was an active social philosophy, dealing with everyday problems of human life and society. In a period of major crisis, he saw considerable hope in practical philosophy, notably that provided by a projective idealistic type. In his logic and epistemology, he took a middle position between idealism and pragmatism and he tried to bridge the gap between sensual apprehension and analytic categorization in science. Above all, Eucken presumed the reality of the spiritual to be a penetrating force in scientific discovery, and there is no doubt that in his distinction of two structural levels, the low and the high, his sympathy was with idealistic thought and humanistic values.[17] Many of his thoughts and his epistemology reemerged in Schmalenbach, who, in his teaching of the noumenon or in his concern for ethics, came very close to Eucken's position.

It may seem that Schmalenbach was merely following the paths of his masters, but these paths only indicate the general context from which he emerged. There is no question that he was very much his own man in his ideas, in a distinctively developing epistemology, and in his personal life. He had no intimate relationship with Jaspers in Basel; he had no close contact with Leonard Nelson, his professional colleague in Göttingen, who was a practical philosopher and the founder of the neo-Friesian school. Instead, despite some philosophical differences in his heritage, Schmalenbach was in a dialogue with and close to Husserl, Joël, and Buber. He was a personal friend of the latter. It was Schmalenbach who carried the offer of a professorship at Giessen to Buber, although Buber declined to accept the offer.[18] Both men frequently exchanged family visits. Yet the influence of Buber, as opposed to that of Joël and Husserl, is unacknowledged in Schmalenbach's writing.

METHODOLOGY AND PHILOSOPHY

Throughout his entire life, Schmalenbach struggled with methodology and the basic problems of epistemology. His continuous involvement with Kant and religion was part of this struggle and culminated in his magnum opus, published just at the start of the

Second World War. Because of the timing, this work never received the recognition that it deserved. *Geist und Sein*[19] poses immediate problems of translation into the English language, because Schmalenbach uses the term *Geist* to connote spirit as well as mind, and ultimately the notion of scientific insight. In this book he states at the outset that for philosophy to begin with consciousness is no longer an appropriate procedure for developing an epistemology related to psychology, because "consciousness is not only the knowing of something but at the same time is a being with it." From here he contends that consciousness must acknowledge its environment, and thus both philosophy and epistemology must deal with man and his existence. The significance of this stems from the fact that consciousness and psychology were both major topics in German philosophy. Consequently, Schmalenbach was involved in such discussions from the beginning of his intellectual career. No doubt psychology provided many suggestions for him, but it is also clear that he like Husserl rejected a conventional, psychologically-based theory of knowledge. On this basis, his methodological castigation of Tönnies, whom he considered as belonging to the nineteenth century and romanticism, for embracing an outmoded epistemology can best be understood.

Schmalenbach pursued his arguments on metaphysics from Plato to Kant and finally to Gestalt theory and phenomenology. In a long chapter entitled "Symbols and Logos," he developed a terminology and quite a few other substantive ideas along the line of Meinong, implying problems of "higher order objects" [*Gegenstände höherer Ordnung*]. While he acknowledged Kant along the way, e.g., by referring to "thinking as creating" [*Denken als Schaffen*], he ultimately developed his own position, contending that objects have a reality as part of the "logos"—the ultimate and irreducible basis of knowledge. It is from the conception of objects as part of logos that the process of scientific observation must proceed. This is a principle of order with respect to which sensual reality is approached. It is not Gestalt. Instead, Gestalt and structure are secondary to it.[20] Parsons may be on the edge of such an understanding, as his synthesizing mind begins to grapple with the relationship between structural linguistics and genetics. In pondering the import of the work of Alfred E. Emerson,[21] Parsons writes: "Emerson's . . . formula was that in the human action fields the symbol is analogous to the gene in the organic field . . . That there is an analogy from the functional point of view of control of the development of individual organisms or social units has been enormously strengthened by the dramatic development of the science of linguistics, again in about the last generation. Symbolic communication through speech utterances is, in the linguistic case, made possible through the operation of what some linguistic scientists call a 'linguistic code' or Chomsky calls 'deep structures.' Such codes are not themselves meaningful utterances at all, but rather the symbolic frame of reference within which meaningful utterances can be formulated. The famous biochemical molecule DNA is looked at by microgeneticists from very much the same point of view: as embodying the genetic code and a more detailed 'program' which regulates the processes of synthesis of the biochemical components of the living cell, notably the proteins."[22] This variety of structuralism and also that of Schmalenbach are more closely tied to an essentialist position than, for example, that of Lévi-Strauss.

In the process of scientific insight, sensual reality is used as a check on the preconceived order. While the object in the sphere of logos is given priority, it may well be given more precise definition if incompatible with sensual reality. The process of generating knowledge starts with the *Meinen* of an object, a reference to a reality in the human mind and existence. The object is part of logos or of the noumenon to which Schmalenbach at other times refers. *Meinen* can be be translated as "opine," although for readability it has been translated as "apprehend" in this volume.

Schmalenbach proceeds from logos and metaphysics in *Geist und Sein* to a philosophy of human existence (with a consideration of play and games, where he shows some obvious affinity to Simmel and Wittgenstein and an adumbration of Caillois's classification of games). He ends with a discussion of ethics and a conception of the dualism in human existence provided by the antinomy of logos and apprehension. The influences of pragmatism appear to be as relevant at this point (and elsewhere) as the affinity to Hegel and dialectics, which Schmalenbach treats in a most refined manner.

In the later sections of *Geist und Sein*, the relation to his former teacher, Georg Simmel, is obvious, although Schmalenbach was ultimately somewhat less concerned with empirical proof than was Simmel. This became clear when he hailed Simmel (in an obituary) for recognizing, besides the physical and the psychological, the "third realm of ideal content."[23] Simmel perceived the scientist as an independent observer of social reality,[24] but Schmalenbach perceived him much more as part of his environment, as performing a role (without, we might add, any consideration of his involvement in or even passive effect on sociopolitical action). Schmalenbach viewed the scientist even more in terms of his very existence, which always encompassed his purely scientific insight.

According to Schmalenbach, Kant rejected metaphysics as a means of scientific insight on the basis of his deep religiosity. But Schmalenbach, because of his personal religious skepticism, was able to turn inward or into the supposedly metaphysical dimension and adopt a phenomenological approach to methodology. Kant had rejected such a switch outright, finding transcendental ideas *ablockend* [seductive] for the mind and *betrügerisch* [deceiving], in his preliminary statements toward any future metaphysic.[25]

Schmalenbach, then, did not go along with Kant's conception of science for science's sake and disregarded Kant's cautions, although not as completely as did Husserl. Schmalenbach did not treat the problem of science and knowledge only by way of a logical examination. Logos, after all, is part of total human existence. In his earlier essay on "Soul—the Emergence of the Concept" (see below, part 2), he sought empirical proof predominantly in history, ethnology, and child development for the analysis of the soul in its noumenal dimensions. These provide a partial basis for the logos, although at times noumenon and logos can be conceived as an antinomy. This provides an introduction to Schmalenbach's phenomenology and to his method. It should provide direct and easy access to Schmalenbach's thought for the nonphilosopher. To be sure, his discussion here is not as rigid and refined as it became in his later life, but on the basis of substantive argument, it does convey a good sense of his line of thought.

In order to understand the noumenon, Schmalenbach drew upon material from the different social sciences, showing considerable knowledge and command of such material. He rejected a sensualistic and positivistic use of the religion of the primitives or of the conception of soul in earlier history. This accounts for his dismissal of both Sir Edward Burnett Tylor and the sensual psychology and ethnology of Wilhelm Wundt. He also rejected what he called the sociologistic interpretation of religion put forth by Durkheim. Instead, he followed the humanistic leads of Dilthey, Driesch, Eduard van Hartmann, and Bergson. He clearly distinguished the natural sciences from the social sciences. For the soul, Schmalenbach contended that a mechanistic interpretation could neither grasp the essence of the concept nor move from there to a deeper insight into human and scientific perception. His phenomenology and methodology subsequently appeared in their fullest development, in a rather involved essay, "Phenomenology of the Sign" (see below, part 3).

This is an epistemological and sociological solution to the problem of the transcendental ego raised by Husserl, namely, whether in the apprehension of reality there can be an ego that exists absolutely. There is no ultimate solution to this problem in Husserl; Schütz remained, by and large, unaware of it.[26] Schmalenbach rejected the notion that the ego existed through the ratification of others by detailing the difficulties posed by positing "psyches of others." Instead, he attempted to resolve the paradox in a merger of theoretical and practical indications. This unity of theory and praxis as epistemology has hardly ever been traced down to its coherent configuration. Probably the Marxists know of it, but do not take it into account. Mannheim certainly had this in mind in his distinction of general from special and total from partial ideologies in *Ideology and Utopia*. At exactly this point, Husserl may be removed from his idealistic base, and Schmalenbach avoids the transcendental switch by explicitly admitting that his earlier contention of noumenal experience was erroneous.

Here we find some resonance with the individualistic pragmatism of James.[27] At the same time, Schmalenbach suggested that the concept of the "other" is not needed. Nevertheless, the "I" and the "me" are still recognizable because situated experience casts the I into the role of the me. Moreover, the conception of practical experience and consequent significant perception do allow the experience of an institutional reality beyond the intention of individual actors. Depending on the context and the action of individual actors, the receiver, because of his own awareness, becomes transformed into something else. For a sociological explanation, the act or acts of individuals may thus well take on the meaning of an institution.[28] Schmalenbach also contended that the I has a tendency to address itself (as, we may add, an asocial self of its own). His argument ended with a demand for an ethical psychology, a position that also reemerged in his *Mind and Being*. In such a way, he raised the sociological problem of norms and values.

Throughout Schmalenbach's intellectual life, problems of ethics interested him, especially as they pertained to a theory of knowledge. He could not accept Kant's position regarding the irrelevance of metaphysics for philosophy, nor was he willing to conceive of philosophy as simply a methodological sounding board for the special sciences that culminated in a science of science. Although he granted Kant considerable credit and was more involved with him than with any other philosopher, he did not respect him as the sorely needed leader of philosophy at the time.[29]

Despite this involvement with Kant and despite a very profound knowledge of his work, Schmalenbach was much more a follower and admirer of Leibniz. In Leibniz he recognized and apprehended the "exorbitant drama of cosmic fantasy." He was also obviously most intrigued by the monadology of Leibniz and his ultimately comprehensive and harmonious world view, despite all its startling paradoxes and seeming biases. Schmalenbach took it upon himself to make this side of Leibniz better known. Overall, he considered Leibniz a paragon of philosophers. In his view, Leibniz had been greatly misunderstood by those who tried to fathom his incorporating of conflicting philosophical systems while simultaneously exerting great influence in politics and several of the sciences. Here was a man who "continuously raised suggestions, was the father of numerous comrades, even forced 'progress' . . . whose ideas, however, bore fruit only after his death. . . ." Leibniz was, in "central essence, what one can call the philosophical Gestalt."[30] The logical fanaticism of Leibniz was also recognized, as were his piety, holiness, and demonic belief in the fantastic, which together were a tribute to his tolerance of contrasting ideas and insights. It is quite obvious that Schmalenbach considered this model to be a guiding influence for his own philosophy and social science, although his interpretation was not unchallenged.

That Schmalenbach himself, despite his seeming involvement with public causes in his relationship to the *Sozialistische Monatshefte* and to the leading circles of social and human change and advancement early in his life in Berlin, did not engage in public issues later on is one of the paradoxes of his life. In part it can be explained by the political turmoil he experienced during most of his lifetime. The 1920s in Germany were quite different from what have popularly been called the "roaring twenties" in the United States. In a certain sense, that decade has been construed as irresponsibly expressive in the United States; in Germany, it might well be termed responsibly, though abortively, revolutionary. Schmalenbach was related to both the socialist and conservative "revolutions" of that period, but neither was realized—"two revolutions that never were," as Rene König has observed.[31] Each was effectively neutralized by Nazism—a third revolution.

Schmalenbach's withdrawal from politics and the public scene flowed from his personal disappointment with the events of this period and certainly with the Third Reich. Some of the terms that he had earlier refined or reformulated, such as *Gemeinschaft* and *Bund*, were incorporated into the Nazi ideology. A few of the persons with whom he had associated joined the ranks of the new political movement, particularly Hans Freyer, who declared the study of *Gemeinschaft* to be the main task of any further sociology in Germany[32] and advocated a revolution of the right.[33] Nor should we omit the fact that his own brother, Eugen, was removed from his chair at Cologne in 1933, the year of the Nazi ascension to power. By 1928 the signs of intransigence were quite visible in German philosophy. In that year the German Philosophical Association spent a whole meeting dealing with the concept of *Gemeinschaft*. Felix Krueger declared, "We must prepare ourselves for new social forms and orders."[34] Schmalenbach's conceptual analysis was no longer in demand. The bulk of the papers on *Gemeinschaft* dealt with the ethical and folk aspects of that term, leading directly to its subsequent transformation as *Volksgemeinschaft*. The utter confusion that must have baffled a humanistic philosopher and sociologist like Schmalenbach is best represented in a book by Hans Naumann that was dedicated to both Stefan George and Hitler.[35] Schmalenbach retreated to the sanctuary of the scientist and removed himself from the pain of political reality. In an unpublished lecture to a Swiss audience before World War II, he dealt with the social structure of neutrality. In his last publication, dealing with Plato's conflict over whether he should opt for politics or philosophy, Schmalenbach obviously rationalized for himself that it was not the philosopher's mission to become personally involved in politics. So far removed was Schmalenbach at that time from the development of contemporary politics in Germany, which had wounded him deeply, that he did not make a single comment on those political events, although it would have been easy for him to use Plato's dilemma as an illustration for his position.[36] Yet this was quite consistent with his understanding of history. He considered history, in true structural perspective, to be paramount. Only in this way might one discover the timeless elements—the social forms.[37]

Schmalenbach's position in sociology is probably best understood as social-historical, phenomenological, and "formal." The sociologist whom he most resembles is, as we have suggested, Georg Simmel. In Schmalenbach, the concept of form is at least implicit in many of his essays, whether they deal with communion, property relations, or individuality. Later on in his life, however, his philosophy becomes increasingly concerned with phenomenological arguments, and his concern for conceptual refinement gives way to the proposal of a mode of insight for the social sciences that refers increasingly to a philosophy of language, meaning, and existence.

The analysis of lonesomeness [See "On Lonesomeness," below, part 2], which ends with the essay on soul [See "Soul—the Emergence of the Concept," below, part 2], marks the earlier period, while the essay on signs [See "Phenomenology of the Sign," below, part 3] marks the later period.

In addition to the implications these works have for "formal" sociology, one should take particular notice of the fact that Schmalenbach was skilled in the sociohistorical analysis of ideas and social movements. On another level, given his concern with epistemology, he contributes to the sociology of knowledge as it is often conceived (or, for that matter, misconceived).[38] He certainly reveals an understanding of the context in which ideas develop and scientists converse by analyzing the existential conditions of scientific thought. Such analyses often become part of his epistemology, which is therefore not only based on logic but also anchored in a logos that encompasses human existence. All this is represented in his *Geist und Sein* as well as in the "Phenomenology of the Sign." True, the scientist apprehends reality, but he grants it a considerable amount of its own integrity and obdurate impact, which will be brought into scientific reasoning as *Verstehen*. Unlike, the frequently cited interpretation of Theodore Abel,[39] *Verstehen*, according to Schmalenbach, is not psychological at all. Although Weber adopted a methodological individualism, Schmalenbach apprehended the individuum as immersed in logos, thus making it subject and object of analysis at the same time.

Sociology

Schmalenbach's sociology focuses on at least four phases of the discipline: (1) problems of methodology; (2) conceptual analysis and formulation; (3) the history of social thought and ideas; and (4) such substantive areas as social movements, religion, knowledge, art, generations, the family, and childhood. None of these foci is clearly distinguished in any one individual essay. Rather, their treatment is intertwined in different configurations featuring different emphases.

Certainly the most elaborate and best known contribution to sociology made by Schmalenbach is provided by his "Communion— A Sociological Category" [See "Communion—a Sociological Category," below, part 1], and we have selected that essay as the primary point of departure for our overall consideration of Schmalenbach. The essay includes: (1) a critique of Tönnies's concepts of "community" [*Gemeinschaft*] and "society" [*Gesellschaft*], particularly the former; (2) a conceptual clarification of community through the revelation that the term encompasses disparate relational categories, circumstance and rapport, thereby reducing the analytic utility of the concept; (3) the proposal of a new concept, "communion" [*Bund*] to supplement Tönnies's twofold scheme; (4) consequently, the destruction of dichotomous conceptualization; (5) a further specification of Tönnies's original intention not to confuse types with concrete, specifically sociohistoric, reality; (6) a view of social forms and historical eras as involving mutual transformations and configurations of the three concepts; (7) a linkage of his reconceptualization with Weber's types of governance; (8) a critique of Weber's typology of conduct, and consequently his methodology. It is well, then, to begin our assessment with a brief review of Tönnies's conceptual formulations and a clear exposition of their intended dialectical relationship—a point often missed in secondary accounts.[40]

Ferdinand Tönnies: Community and Society

In his attempt to describe and explain theoretically the changing modes of social relationships that accompanied the emergence of capitalism in Western civilization, Ferdinand Tönnies proposed the "fundamental concepts," community and society, in his *Gemeinschaft und Gesellschaft*, first published in 1887.[41] Although Tönnies did apply his concepts to the analysis of social change, he was primarily concerned with distinguishing types of social relationships that had no necessary empirical historical reference. Community and society were intended to be applied in either synchronic or diachronic analysis. Moreover, the types, as they were established by Tönnies, were "stripped of their connotation as designating social entities or groups, or even collective or artificial persons."[42] They served as "standards by which 'reality' could be described and recognized."[43] More important, it becomes clear, as the argument proceeds, that the types are not only "standards," but represent social forms that generate antinomial tendencies in any historically concrete instance of social life. Interestingly, this is the case, because Tönnies resorted to a psychological level of analysis, i.e., the level of individual motivation, in his explanation of sociological events.[44]

"Human wills stand in manifold relations to one another. . . . This study will consider as its subject of investigation only the relationships of mutual affirmation."[45] These two introductory sentences state the central unity of inquiry and delimit the scope of Tönnies's major work, *Gemeinschaft und Gesellschaft*. The principal objective of this study was the description and explanation of the ways human wills enter into relationships of mutual affirmation; the study specifically did not cover the whole range of social relationships, which would include, for example, conflict.[46] To realize this objective, Tönnies constructed a dualism that could comprehend all concrete relationships of mutual affirmation as they emphasized one or the other of two theoretically distinct (but not unreservedly antithetical) social forms, community and society. Community was conceived by Tönnies as a real and organic (naturally derived) relationship; society was conceived as an imaginary and mechanical (rationally contrived) structure. Neither concept was intended to have any direct or exclusive empirical reference.

The construction of community as an ideal type proceeded from "the assumption of perfect unity of human wills as an original or natural condition which is preserved in spite of actual separation."[47] Tönnies cited the relationship of the mother to her child, the sexual union of a man and his wife, and the bond that unites brothers and sisters in a family circle. Less exact, in Tönnies's view, was the relationship of the father, in the capacity of an educative and authoritative model, to his children. Other types of relationships approaching the ideal type included kinship, the neighborhood (where the "proximity of habitation [is] supported by well defined habits of reunion and sacred custom"[48]), friendship, authority in the sense of dignity based on courage,[49] and age or wisdom.

All such relationships are premised upon and foster "consensus" in the sense of a "reciprocal, binding sentiment . . . which constitutes . . . the peculiar will of a *Gemeinschaft*."[50] This consensus is reenforced among the members of a community by their "intimate knowledge of each other insofar as this is conditioned and advanced by direct interest of one being in the life of the other, and readiness to take part in his joy and sorrow."[51]

Tönnies expressed the logic of community in terms of three metaphorical laws: (1) Relatives and married couples love each other or easily adjust themselves to each other. They speak together and think along similar lines. Likewise do neighbors and friends. (2) Between people who love each other there is understanding consensus. (3) Those who love and understand each other remain and dwell together and organize their common life.[52]

Community, then, is an ideal construct that abstracts the essence of the organization of the common life among people who share a sympathetic consensus and physical proximity. Moreover, although this condition is most closely approximated in the home or the household, it persists under the impact of such patently disruptive factors as the emergence of distinctions between town and country or between the manor and the village.

It is at this point that Schmalenbach takes critical issue with Tönnies. First, he maintains that Tönnies has violated his own premises in the formulation of the construct, community [See "Communion—a Sociological Category," below, part 1]. Specifically, there is no empirical basis for asserting that membership in such relations as family, marriage, kinship, or neighboring are, in fact, "relationships of mutual affirmation." All such relations manifest countless instances of conflict and animosity. Indeed, communities often conflict with communities [See ibid.]. Consequently, the "intrinsically natural" relations of community must be construed as independent of expressed emotions [See ibid.]. One is a family member or a neighbor regardless of how he feels about it. Community is best viewed, then, as a circumstance. Since we live in communities, we live in worlds we never made, and although we may harbor powerful feelings about such worlds and even about being part of such worlds when their integrity is threatened, these feelings in no way can be drawn upon to account for the establishment of communities or our membership in them [See ibid.].

In contrast to community relationships in which human beings are essentially united despite the presence of ostensibly divisive influences, society relationships are entered into by individuals who are "essentially separated in spite of all uniting factors."[53] It is in this sense that society must always be seen as an artificial, "mechanical," rationally contrived structure of human relationships. For when societal associations are removed—when the artificial structure is destroyed—a residue remains where "everybody is by himself and isolated, and there exists a condition of tension against all others."[54] Society, for Tönnies, is an elaborate superstructure of social relationships precariously erected atop an incipient Hobbesian *bellum omnium in omnes*.[55]

The associations of society are typically contracted in commodity exchange and sealed by promises and "conventions" that are as likely breached as they are fulfilled.[56] Since the basis of society lies in exchange contracts, it follows that its development gains added impetus from the growth of commerce or trade. The agent of commerce is the merchant; just as each contracted relationship of society makes for the realization of the interests of the contracting parties, society, as a whole, is the instrument of the merchant. Tönnies, involved with the socialist causes of the time and the work of Ferdinand Lasalle, viewed the distribution of contracts and commerce as Marx looked at production: "The merchants or capitalists (the owners of money which can be increased by double exchange) are the natural masters and rulers of the *Gesellschaft*. The *Gesellschaft* exists for their sake. It is their tool."[57]

Indeed, it is the essence of society that no social relationship has value in and of itself. It is true that as the growth of society is stimulated by commerce, money emerges as a yardstick of value, but money is never valued intrinsically. On the contrary, "money is desired by nobody for the sake of keeping it but by everybody with a view to getting rid of it."[58] Similarly, contracts are typically entered into with the view of terminating the association concerned as quickly and efficiently as possible. An apparent exception is the credit relationship. When an individual extends credit to another, "the repayment is not really his aim, as he wants to preserve his claim as a constant purpose of always renewed payments by the contracting party."[59] Yet such an aim opposes the goal of the contracting party, who seeks to terminate the relationship in as short a time as possible. Therefore, no relationship in the society is characterized by any inherent stability. Society is a loosely coordinated structure held together, so to speak, by the fortuitous convergence of discrete individual interests. "The *Gesellschaft* can be imagined to be in reality composed of such separate individuals, all of whom are busy for the general *Gesellschaft* inasmuch as they seem to be active in their own interests and are working for their own interests while they seem to be working for the *Gesellschaft*."[60]

Viewed historically, the demands upon the merchant who commands the society are altered with the rise of industry. Early in the development of society, the merchant rules by virtue of his control over the disposition of commodities in commerce. Yet he must consolidate this rule by dominating labor and the retailing of manufactured goods while the production of these goods passes through the phases of "(1) simple cooperation, (2) manufacture, (3) industry based on machinery (real 'large scale' industry)."[61] When the merchant class dominates the commodity market, the labor market, and the retail market, society may be said to have realized itself historically.

In Schmalenbach's view, this confusion of social forms with socioeconomic history is methodologically and empirically untenable [See "Communion—a Sociological Category," below, part 1]. As fas as methodology is concerned, Tönnies has once more violated his own desiderata. Society conceived in this manner hardly constitutes a type "stripped of . . . its . . . connotation as designating social entities or groups, or even collective or artificial persons."[62] Empirically or even analogically, there is no reason to suggest that society is the culmination of a bourgeois domination over markets. Schmalenbach cites the emergence of the Christian church from the early sects as discussed by Weber and Troeltsch, but this is not his primary concern [See "Communion—a Sociological Category," below, part 1]. Relations of affective affinity, still another variant of "psychic bonds," command his theoretical focus. To this extent, he is rather more sympathetic to Tönnies's emphasis upon "will."

A little reflection upon the assumptions that underlie Tönnies's conceptualization of society, as depicted above, suggests the "limiting concepts" or assumptions of classical Ricardian economics. These have been enumerated by Mayo:

1. Natural society consists of a horde of unorganized individuals.
2. Every individual acts in a manner calculated to secure his self-preservation or self-interest.
3. Every individual thinks logically, to the best of his ability, in the service of this aim.[63]

One might speculate that Tönnies was led inexorably by the stern rules of logic to a consideration of individual volition for an explanation, at least, of the genesis of societal relations. Recognizing the fact that his construction of society as an ideal type premised distinct, rational, and self-seeking individuals, Tönnies made the premise explicit and treated it as a theoretical proposition.[64] Societal associations were willed into being by concrete individuals capable of perceiving that such relationships would benefit their own (individual) interests. This explanation of society as a pure product of human will undoubtedly preceded the similar explanation of community in the formulation of Tönnies's theoretical system, since community does not appear logically to require any assertion about the individual volition of its members. Schmalenbach arrived at this conclusion in his critique of Tönnies. [See "Systematic Sociology," below, part 1].

Be that as it may, Tönnies devoted the bulk of his volume to the elaboration and description of two contrasting forms of human will.

The concept of human will, the correct interpretation of which is essential to the subject of this treatise, implies a twofold meaning. Since all mental action involves thinking, I distinguish between the will which includes the thinking and the thinking which encompasses the will. Each represents an inherent whole which unites in itself a multiplicity of feelings, instincts, and desires. This unity should in the first case be understood as a real or natural one; in the second case, as a conceptual or artificial one. The will of the human being in the first form I call natural will (*Wesenwille*); in the second form, rational will (*Kürwille*).[65]

Natural will is conceived by Tönnies as an innate, unified, motivating force that is directly related to activity as a determining agent. Rational will, on the other hand, emerges from experience and is produced out of deliberation. Its identity is maintained in action, because it includes an infinite number of alternatives, most of which are never acted upon by the individual.

While natural and rational will may be distinguished analytically, in reality they are always coexistent and intertwined.

Observation and inference will easily show that no natural will can ever occur empirically without the rational will by which it finds expression, and no rational will without the natural will on which it is based.[66]

The implication for community and society is far-reaching and profound. For it clarifies the reason why the two constructed types are not unreservedly antithetical, or the sense in which Tönnies's theory may be called a dialectic. "*Gemeinschaft* descends from union to association . . . *Gesellschaft* advances from association to union."[67] In short, there is a tendency, rooted in individual will, for every community to become a society, and (what has largely been neglected by sociologists who have based their theories in part upon these distinctions) for every society to become a community. The observation is crucial. If we substitute passion and reason for natural will and rational will, we can observe that when tempers fly in a close relationship, the time has come to calm down, to call for "sweet reasonableness." Conversely, when reason freezes the thought of the intimate other, the time has come to heat up the relationship, to inject temper, to scream!

Even in a single concrete relationship, such as a marriage, the form may take on different contours, depending upon variation in psychic affinities, which are in themselves timeless and may be found in any historically concrete social interaction. For Schmalenbach, however, the twofold construction is inadequate. A third must be added—the communion—particularly to clarify the meaning of Tönnies's community, which indefensibly equates the forms of circumstance and rapport. The analytic application is accomplished, however, in a similar manner. Community, communion, and society coexist in all concrete social reality. Variations in emphasis give interaction a distinctive cast, yet call out opposing emphases. Indeed, the natural history of institutions and even of society may be characterized by the changing configuration of the three forms.

Communion, Community, and Society

In his "Systematic Sociology," Schmalenbach emphasized the importance of "categorical intuitions," as they are developed from "sensual intuitions" and "categorical observations," for the establishment of valid sociological knowledge. At the beginning of his essay on communion, he is favorably inclined toward Tönnies's categorically intuitive development of the concept of community. Yet Schmalenbach also knew that the undisciplined application of categorical intuition, developed on the basis of sensual views, must necessarily lead to what he called "optical intuitions." These optical intuitions may well "mislead their happy discoverer to biased exaggerated pretensions." [See "Systematic Sociology," below, part 1]. Such is the fate of community in Tönnies's sociological framework. This is the case because Tönnies, influenced by Goethe, held strong positive feelings toward community, particularly as that ideal was developed in the age of romanticism when the ideological struggle was initiated against the society of the ascendant bourgeoisie—the "new age." The hopes of youth and the members of Stefan George's circle were also just as inclined toward community, so that the term had again taken on a popular meaning, before and after World War I, that rendered it difficult if not impossible to use in scientific analysis. The term had become saturated with passion, and the concept of society was similarly affected, although in the opposite direction. Society was an object of intense hatred for those who had come to love their image of a benign community. However, society itself was probably an equally inflamed image, even though rationally and logically deduced from Hobbesian premises and those of classical economics.

In a sense, Tönnies did attempt to be impartial. He tried to embrace both romanticism and rationalism in a scientific manner, but his own personal passions inclined him toward the former and he tended to neglect the latter, even though he knew that the romantic community could never be realized. Schmalenbach observes that it was a thought born of sentiment.

Finally, Schmalenbach questions the historical specificity of the concepts. Communities have appeared historically in every epoch. Even "barbarians" (and what is the basis of this image?), fundamentally bound together in communions, shared a community of language. Nor is society merely a creature of bourgeois capitalism.

So the conceptual distinction, in Schmalenbach's view, is fraught with error and imprecision, but his argument focuses on the heterogeneity of the concept of community. For example, Tönnies most frequently referred to family relations in his analogical construction of community—particularly the peasant, rural, or small town family. Sociologically, family members are tied to one another through "natural," "intrinsic," "socially given" conditions. Such conditions transcend the qualities rather than the quantities of space and time. One's brother may be over the ocean, but he is a brother nevertheless, and of course we are tied to other family members of long dead generations. Else why the significance attached to family trees? Nor can we disclaim our ancestry, though we might well attempt to conceal it. All socially operating conditions or facts give rise to communities, independent of us but on which we are dependent. Communities are existentially there, and we existentially belong to them. They are our circumstances. Sir Henry Sumner Maine captured the notion with his term, "status,"[68] and Maine's writing exerted considerable influence on Tönnies's thought.

Tönnies grounded his sociological concepts in psychology. In so doing, according to Schmalenbach (who proclaimed that only a humanistic sociology is interested in psychic elements), Tönnies uncritically adopted the cognitive psychology of his time, which focused on consciousness. This focus was not neglected by interpretive psychologists or phenomenologists interested in the problem of the unconscious. As a partial concession, cognitive psychology did make room for the emotions, or feelings, but such feelings were construed as being in no way contrary to consciousness. Indeed, Tönnies must have been conscious of his love for the impossible community, and then imputed that love to its members. Schmalenbach tellingly reveals the absurdity of that impossible dream by pointing to family wounds that are hardly healed in the comforting bosom of community. In spite of such ruptures, family relations persist—parents remain parents; children, children; brothers, brothers; or sisters, sisters—regardless of feelings.

The formative conditions of community are in the unconscious rather than in the emotions, and at the same time are comprised by objective circumstances. We may consciously accept or reject the community, but it persists in the unconscious. Some "broad" communities—language, ethnicity—may scarcely be noticed, but our unconscious is structured by them all. Indeed, we can never recognize all the communities that intersect and are apprehended in our unconscious. Crisis or antagonism may make us emotionally aware of a particular community, but our antagonistic feelings are directed outward against intruders and strangers. Peasants in particular have emotions, but are uneasy with their expression. Why look to the unexpressive peasant, then, as a prototype? It is true that members of a community have feelings and express them, however reluctantly, but such feelings are not the basis of community. Therefore, the concept of community should be reserved to describe an objectively given, natural, intrinsic circumstance found in the unconscious. As such, it is an inescapable dimension of human existence.

Some try to escape community. Schmalenbach considers such flights from community as the journeyman's years of travel after completing his apprenticeship, but particularly as the wandering of young people as they tear themselves from their families. Such momentary escapees find one another and form genuine communions based on feelings. Schmalenbach notes the religiosity or religious atmosphere that such communions generate. Indeed, the atmosphere verges on the sacred, and Schmalenbach uses the analogy to speculate about religious origins. He finds them in communions, which he construes as asocial, as though specifically to repudiate the "sociologism" of Durkheim.[69] Be that as it may, the problem of religiosity pervades these essays. It is ubiquitous, and not only in the analysis of communion. In that analysis, however, Schmalenbach asserts that communion is built on feelings toward those who are *en rapport*—and also outward toward some greater power, some "felt god." In another unusual thought, Schmalenbach elevates the "basic social [*sic*] relationship to a deity" as communion. One must feel alone [*sic*] before God and this must be accompanied by a "side feeling" of immersion with others [See "Communion—a Sociological Category," below, part 1].

Schmalenbach's discussion of society is less intensive and takes him directly to a critique of Max Weber's methodology and typology of the forms of conduct, a matter we shall consider shortly. Meanwhile, let us note that Schmalenbach concludes by acknowledging that community, communion, and society are best thought of as modes or styles of experience, all of which are interdependent, each setting into motion a transformation of one into another. Here the concern seems to be more with process than with structure. This can be readily comprehended by viewing each style in terms of four dimensions: (1) its emotional quality; (2) its social and experiential basis; (3) persistence; and (4) allegiance. Schmalenbach's primary intention was to remove by analysis the affective dimensions of community from its natural or circumstantial dimensions. Therefore, we begin with a consideration of emotional quality. Then we proceed to respond to the rather more conventional questions of sociology from the perspective of Schmalenbach. How are social relations established? Once established, how do they persist and what agencies are employed to ensure their persistence? How is the person tied to the relationship?

1. *Emotional quality.* Feelings toward community are vague. They may be aroused by and directed outward toward external threats or unfamiliar persons, groups, and events, but they are not

focused inward toward community members. Emotions are constitutive for communion. The emotional quality of society is detachment—a cool reserve.

2. *Social and experiential basis.* Community is always there and at hand. Although it is based on external conditions, it is constituted in the unconscious. The whole is prior to the part. Members are immersed in community. Its prototype is the institution, e.g., marriage and the family construed as institutions. Communion is established and constituted by conscious feelings toward (a) a felt god or any object, even community; and (b) members of the faith. The prototype of communion is friendship or love-in-marriage. The name, "brother," is the designation par excellence that binds comrades to communion, and family love is comprised of pretenses nourished by communion. Society is consciously contrived. It exaggerates rational conduct. Feelings are considered irrational, in contradiction with society. Yet the individual is prior to the whole. Prototypes are the formal economic transaction and the marriage contract.

3. *Persistence.* Just as community exists, so does it persist. It is lasting. The compass of existential will is far-reaching. To some extent, in an interpersonal dimension the *do ut des* of the peasant may contribute to the persistence of community, but only in a noncontractual sense. The fulfillment of obligations, again, is merely taken for granted. In the communion there is no *do ut des*, and above all, no contract. Yet the communion is intrinsically unstable. Emotional ecstasy is fleeting, but its felt impact is deep. Consequently, the psychic bonds require frequent reaffirmation so that their impact can penetrate through to the unconscious, where it can find roots. Revivals, above all, are held to provide such reaffirmations, but when they are successful, they lay seeds for a transition to community. The relations of society are also temporary. They include the interpersonal *do ut des*, but are typically comprised of formal contracts. Once the terms are met, the parties may go their separate ways, which is impossible in the community. Thus, the persistence of society is not based on contract but on the recurrence of those tasks that are contractually accomplished.

4. *Allegiance*. The point at issue here is how the person is tied to which of the styles. In the community, fidelity in marriage and to the church, for example, is again a matter of course. Fidelity is expected and expressed. This can be seen in the case of such far-reaching communities as language, ethnicity, or humanity. Indeed, crimes against humanity are the most abhorrent; they are even inconceivable to many persons. The imposition of an alien language may mean bloodshed, as in South Africa today. Communions guarantee fidelity with oaths of brotherhood or even the literal making of blood vows. Here, however, the seeds of society are sown as oaths, and they begin to resemble contracts. The structure of the Roman Catholic Church is viewed by Schmalenbach as precisely the emergence of a society from an original communion. In the society, fidelity is often contractually sealed (as in promissory notes). Moreover, rationality may be guaranteed in contracts—"I, being of sound mind and body, do hereby . . ." Throughout history, too, we find ritualizations of economic transactions, as in the signing of contracts. One finds the seed of community in the rituals of society. At least, economic affairs come to assume the appearance of community relations.

The interdependence of these styles is nicely established in a pertinent discussion of Simmel's remarks on the vow (society) of eternal (community) love (communion) [See "Communion—a Sociological Category," below, part 1]. Specifically, a love relationship is a communion; a family is a community; and a marriage contract is a society. Once a man and wife have children, their love for one another may be lost and their marriage dissolved, but their community remains.

Implications for the Work of Max Weber

In his earlier period, Schmalenbach was engaged in a critical dialogue with Max Weber. In his "Communion" there are substantively many parallels between Weber's three forms of legitimate governance and the revised social forms of Schmalenbach. In that same essay, however, Schmalenbach's arguments explicitly and implicitly stress major points of methodology, foreshadowing the later critiques of Weber. Particularly in the methodological dialogue with Weber, Schmalenbach argues very much like a phenomenologist, even in this early work.

Schmalenbach finds a precedent for his distinction between community and communion in Max Weber's attempt to differentiate "traditional" and "affective" or emotional conduct, but argues that Weber's methodology is not equipped to comprehend the difference. If that methodology, so infused with rationalism and Protestant asceticism, is carried to its logical extreme, it can only erect an impenetrable barrier between the sociologist and the reality of human existence. It is in this critique, incidentally, that we can best observe Schmalenbach's phenomenology in operation.

Schmalenbach first questions the use of "constructs" for the interpretation of social life. He foresees that inquiries prompted by such constructions can lead into endless empty speculation about the types themselves, rather than about the reality they are presumably designed to elucidate. Indeed, there are many examples of such misplaced concreteness, not only in sociology but in all the social and so-called behavioral sciences, e.g., much of psychology and the psychologistic sociologies. Schmalenbach raises the legitimate question: How can Weber place the subject matter of sociology in constructs and claim at the same time to embrace a sociology of *Verstehen?* The question is mainly rhetorical, and the answer must be a resounding and accusatory negation. Yet Schmalenbach, as seems to be true of many sociologists, did not pay attention to Weber's brilliant discussions of the analytic implementation of such constructions.[70]

Second, Schmalenbach emphasizes the unnecessarily narrow restrictions imposed by Weber's limiting "subjectively intended meaning" to the "conscious import of human conduct." His negative view of Weber's methodology is certainly understandable, given Schmalenbach's own careful and successful attempt to place the roots of the unconscious in the community circumstance, among others. He rejects Weber's "epistemological asceticism," as manifested in his bold, sobersided assertion that a very significant part of sociologically relevant conduct, especially purely traditional action, is treated by Weber as being on the margin of incomprehensibility. Weber himself admits that "broad categories of charisma . . . are almost, but not quite, comprehensible." So what Schmalenbach has tried so effectively to distinguish—community and communion—are barely comprehensible within Weber's methodology, even though Weber, the scholar, was very well informed about traditional and charismatic conduct.

Third, when conceptualizing society, Weber runs into conceptual difficulty in the forced distinction between value-rational and goal (purpose)-rational conduct. The problem is lodged in the simple fact that purposes are always valued to some degree. They may even be endowed with religious value, as Weber so incisively established in his own studies of religion. Moreover, purposes may be formed in value-rational conduct, however "irrational" such purposes may seem to some, e.g., the good intentions of the ideologue, or parental punishment for the child's own good.

Fourth, one must consider the matter of rationality in the selection of means employed. This contention is refuted by Schmalenbach and we shall not reiterate Schmalenbach's critique.

Schmalenbach is gracious at the end. With almost Simmelesque brilliance, he asks the reader to view the two types of rational conduct as agencies of societal transformation. Value-rational conduct transforms society into communion; purpose-rational conduct, by virtue of the value of purpose and the claims of rationality, transforms society into community. This sustains the rationale for separating communion from community as a sociological category. His view is also sustained by Weber's typology of governance as charismatic, traditional, and rational.[71] Rudolf Heberle, in fact, has contended that Weber's typology suggested Schmalenbach's distinction.[72]

In the above manner, Schmalenbach identifies Weber's *Verstehen* with his humanistic [*geisteswissenschaftliche*] sociology, but then rejects Weber's conception of *Verstehen* as too restrictive. His critique focuses specifically on Weber's action theory. Weber's method could only cope with conscious action. Intended meaning in an action puts the individual methodologically into the center of Weber's sociology. Although Weber made reference to Jaspers, Rickert, and Simmel, Schmalenbach holds that Weber's methodology at this point was instead based on a misunderstood Husserl. He does not go into this in any detail; thus we must resort to inference in an effort to assess the validity of Schmalenbach's critique.

When Husserl makes reference to the conscious and to a seemingly psychological individualism as he attempts to understand knowledge and the mundane world [*Alltagswelt*], he uses the individual as a strategic device. Through "bracketing," however, he provides a new meaning to what at first might seem to be merely individual psychology. Actually, Husserl tried to transcend psychology in the process of establishing knowledge. On the basis of Husserl's teaching,[73] we may infer that Schmalenbach wished to assign a more substantive integrity to phenomena under investigation. He realized that the methodological emphasis on conscious individualism would remove major portions of action and conduct from the purview of sociology. Traditional, routine behavior is not usually in a person's consciousness. Schmalenbach asserted that Weber's limited understanding of philosophy and the theory of knowledge led to substantial absurdities in his methodology.

Peter Winch has made criticisms of Weber that are very similar to those of Schmalenbach.[74] Winch holds that an action may be logically complete in itself, so that the frequency distributions of Weber are not needed. Simmel and Weber had disagreed on this matter much earlier. Simmel maintained that a single case may provide an adequate and valid observation for the understanding of social history, whereas Weber rejected that contention outright.[75] Schmalenbach and quite a few others after him consider Weber the more inconsistent of the two, since he employed an individualistic methodology without following it through in all its philosophical consequences. In the view of phenomenology, a single individual may provide many more qualitative insights than Weber could ever acknowledge. Yet the mere study of individual consciousness is hardly adequate, as Schmalenbach made clear. Later on, dealing with the sociology of property, Schmalenbach established conscious and unconscious conduct, in addition to the rationalistic and the irrationalistic that he identified in his encounter with Weber, as legitimate areas of sociological inquiry.

Even so, Schmalenbach fully recognized the brilliance of Weber's sociological insights, despite the methodological shortcomings. He would certainly have concurred with the analysis of Calvinistic and Lutheran strains of Protestantism that Weber conducted in his *Protestant Ethic*. Unlike other critics,[76] Schmalenbach contributed to a further understanding of Weber in his *Middle Ages: Their Meaning and Essence*,[77] and in his essay, "Individuality and Individualism,"[78] which are not included in this volume.

In those works, Schmalenbach elaborates on the emergence of the idea of individualism in the Middle Ages. Following Burckhardt, he does not perceive the roots of individualism as preceding the Renaissance. True, in the poetry and painting of that time, there was much factual individuality, but the consciousness or spirit of individualism was absent. It emerged after the Renaissance and was found in its purest form in the eighteenth century. Luther transformed the religious content of individuality into individualism as a form through the precepts of "religious lonesomeness" and "being alone with God."[79] Here is true individualism. Luther is rescued from his social context by God. This transformation is even more impressive in the case of Calvin, although his views on "mere personality" are terse and must, therefore, be considered a more impoverished concept of individualism. In this matter, Schmalenbach referred to Weber and agreed that even such an impoverished view facilitated economic productivity and success.[80] During the Renaissance and in the teaching of Calvin, individualism existed as a brute fact; in Goethe and the scholars of his period, Schmalenbach observes that individualism became an ideal toward which people strove. This ideal, however, is not as problematic for the individual as the Calvinistic call for individual achievement. The qualitative dimension of individualism, giving each person his own raison d'être, replaced the quantitative dimensions emphasized in the Renaissance and by Calvinism. Schmalenbach found this most notably in Goethe, where the consideration of one's own self and the containment of self were made paramount. It follows from here that only during and after the period of romanticism was humanity able to interpret its own history.

As compared to that of Weber, Schmalenbach's position reflects a stronger emphasis on the dimensions of consciousness and subjectivity. He does not use individualism only as a methodological device for the study of institutions and social action. The individual, for him, is a valid focus of analysis itself. His understanding of action [*Tun*] has, despite its anchorage in human existence and society, a distinctly different quality from that of Weber, and we have therefore translated the term, *Tun*, throughout as "conduct."

The Sociology of Property Relations

In terms of substantive importance besides the essay on communion, one may consider a particular small piece to be Schmalenbach's most special sociological contribution. Hans Linde has hailed "Property, Ownership, and Coalescence" [See "Property, Ownership and Coalescence," below, part 1] as a major and singular contribution to the understanding of the import and structure of material conditions in social relations.[81] This is basic in Marx. Material artifacts were external conditions for Durkheim, and they were also often alluded to, e.g., as means or purpose, by Max Weber. Yet all these writers appear to have less understanding of the unique social quality of property than has Schmalenbach. Weber and (more recently) social system theorists make reference to the psychological context of material artifacts, but Schmalenbach's treatment allows us to recognize such a dimension, and Schmalenbach also gives a distinct and important meaning to property as a social phenomenon beyond its material and nonsocial aspects. Modern sociology in North America, based in all major schools on a conception of interaction, has disregarded such a conception, with the exception of some ecologists and urban sociologists. Likewise, Schmalenbach demands that we seek a more complete understanding of property relations and free our discussions from their ideological bent and their focus solely on politics and power.

Linde nevertheless maintains that Schmalenbach falls short of a full-blown sociological interpretation of property. Whether, in effect, Schmalenbach fell prey to an implicit psychological determinism is not altogether clear.[82] In his later styles, he would certainly have argued the same points in a much more encompassing phenomenological mode. Still, his conception of a sociology of property relations certainly goes beyond materialism and problems of ownership, which he conceives as only one dimension of the whole area. His exemplification of the difference between the ownership of and the symbolic attachment to a valued piece of property, whether owned or not, may appear to be psychologistic, but in phenomenological terms it is not meant that way. His sociology of property also deals with other relations of property—both with those of men to material objects and to their meanings and their intricate interdependencies. Linde pursues such structural elements by distinguishing property relations of *soziale Beziehungen* [social relations] from those of *soziale Verhältnisse* [social conditions].[83] Linde's interpretation to the contrary, the latter type is what Schmalenbach may have ultimately subjected to analysis. Yet his concluding reference to a relationship of community, in order to interpret what we have translated as the coalescence of men with property, invites a psychological interpretation, although it is actually based on set conditions. Schmalenbach's programmatic elaborations remain an overall important sociological essay about the unique social quality of property beyond its mere economic relevance.

Place in Contemporary and American Sociology

As we have said, Schmalenbach's sociological work is tied together by the interlacing of four discernible strands of inquiry: methodology, sociological and philosophical conceptions of social relations (including material dimensions), socioeconomic history and the history of ideas, and the study of symbolism, meaning, and expressive conduct. Essays nominally pursuing a single strand often lead to the further revealing of any or all of the other three. Throughout the essays, too, is found the preoccupation with religion and religiosity that dogged Schmalenbach throughout his scholarly career. The single article on methodology that we have included here, "Systematic Sociology" [below, part 1], has much to say about concepts and history. Those dealing with such concepts as communion [below, part 1], property [below, part 1], lonesomeness [below, part 2], and the soul [below, part 2] shed much light on Schmalenbach's methodology, historical analysis, and apprehension of symbolism and meaning. Finally, the two works on meaning and symbolism—"On Human Existence: Reality, Play, and Seriousness" [below, part 3] and the "Phenomenology of the Sign" [below, part 3]—are also crucial methodological and conceptual contributions.

Schmalenbach distinguished the social sciences from the natural sciences in terms of the argument over causality and dialectics paralleled in the work of Lévi-Strauss.[84] He was, however, more analytic and less inductive than Lévi-Strauss, and his conception of causality would probably be in accord with the discussion of that problem found in the posthumous volume of Roman Ingarden. Ingarden held that cause and effect must be seen as a unity of being and are bound by a principle of coexistence [*Gleichzeitigkeit*].[85] Schmalenbach greatly esteemed Ingarden, who, besides Heidegger, was the most important student of Husserl.

Another affiliate of Husserl, although not his student, was Alfred Schütz, whose phenomenology and sociology have received wide acclaim in the United States by ethnomethodologists and other phenomenological sociologists. In part through the efforts of his student, Thomas Luckmann, Schütz is acknowledged in Western Europe.[86] Schütz was fifteen years younger than Schmalenbach and reached his prime influence, following early acclaim in the 1930s, only after the Second World War. At that time Schmalenbach was in bad health and had only a short period of active scholarly enterprise remaining. Quite possibly, through Husserl, the two men could have known one another.

As their work appears now, Schütz was more concerned with the epistemological problems of sociology as such, while Schmalenbach dealt with these problems in terms of all the humanities and social sciences. However, Schmalenbach explicitly treated many key sociological concepts and subjected them to phenomenological analysis both in a number of essays and in his philosophical work. The position taken by Schütz with regard to concept and theory formation is quite consistent with Schmalenbach's stance.[87] His notion of *Lebenswelt* [world of life] is substantially the same as Schmalenbach's, and the method of "subjective interpretation" is in line with similar formulations, such as "categorical intuition," in Schmalenbach. Where the two differ to a degree is in the duality of scientific inquiry, which is very strong in Schmalenbach and not to be found with the same explicitness in Schütz. Schütz emphasizes the facts of empirical reality, observations that must be incorporated by adequate and logically consistent theories. These observations are both sensual and made against the background of experience. In Schmalenbach, facts are objects that can also be unreal (a parallel to Meinong. They are rooted in the noumena of human existence and play an active part in analysis, although their apprehension [*Meinen*] can and will be modified in and against empirical reality.

While Schütz, reflecting the views of his teacher, von Mises, and his own American experience, seems to refer much more to quantification and shows great respect for American research in social science, Schmalenbach paid more attention to the individual case or to the discovery of a universal singular form, such as the "I," in a set of observations. At times, as Simmel also found, one case may provide the most crucial and penetrating insight, and the concept of social interaction is at best marginal in his methodological approach.

During his early period, Schmalenbach showed a strong idealistic methodology, particularly in his concern for the noumenon. Here there are parallels to Cooley, who was well aware of the noumenon even though he did not call it that. Cooley observes that: Poetry . . . usually refrains from minute description of expression, a thing impossible in words, and strikes for a vivid, if inexact, impression, by the use of such phrases as "a fiery eye," "a liquid eye," and "The poet's eye in a fine frenzy rolling."[88]

Then he invites us to consider G. Stanley Hall's discussion of the fear of (imaginary) eyes in his early study of fear in the *American Journal of Psychology*. Were we to dwell on this, we would find ourselves not far from the "noumenal shudder" and drawn

further into the horror by a *tremendum*—the fascination of fear—
that Schmalenbach so vividly illustrates in his discussion of the
soul [See "Soul—the Emergence of a Concept," below, part 2].
"Persons and society must, then, be studied primarily in the imagination," and ". . . the imaginations which people have of one another are the solid facts of society."[89] "I do not mean merely that
society must be studied *by* the imagination—that is true of all investigations in their higher reaches—but that the *object* of study is
primarily an imaginative idea or group of ideas in the mind, that
we have to imagine imaginations."[90] It does not take any great
stretch of the imagination to see the parallel to Schmalenbach's
techniques of sensual intuition, categorical intuition, and apprehension [*Meinen*], and Schmalenbach specifically refers his methodology to phenomenology rather than to "modern logic." In the later
period of his career, his phenomenological position becomes increasingly more refined, and his earlier idealistic concerns for the
noumenon decrease.

Following Cooley, and pointing up the parallels, we have translated *Bund* as communion. The choice was not an easy one, because Cooley, in his discussion of sympathy or communion as an
aspect of society focused on its "emotionally colorless usage."[91] But
as we know, Cooley viewed sentiments as constitutive of the social
life; combined with his emphasis on ideas, ideals, and mental states,
Cooley's concept does not depart far from Schmalenbach's concept
of the conscious feelings typifying assembled communions. Moreover, Cooley clearly tried to distinguish communion from what
Tönnies had called community. Of course his distinction is not
neat, and in the development of the concept, Cooley includes at
times aspects of community—particularly those, as Schmalenbach
put it, rooted in the unconscious. But Cooley's emphasis moves
slowly and surely toward matters Schmalenbach reserved for communion: friendship, as discussed by Emerson and Goethe; brotherhood; the moods of Carlyle and Job; aesthetic impulses; and
finally, love among men, for God, in God, and the realization of
the self in love. Communion is but an aspect of the whole. For
Schmalenbach, it was a style.

Schmalenbach built his work on and extended phenomenology, but unlike some early American ethnomethodologists, he avoided its solipsistic enticements,[92] and also escaped the solipsism of Cooley.[93] Indeed, both sensual intuition and categorical intuition must always lead into and be affected by sensual and categorical observation when objects are apprehended [*gemeint*]. Yet too great an emphasis upon both categorization and observation may lead to empty concepts or conceptually meaningless aggregations of summated data. For American sociology, Schmalenbach's method most nearly approximates that of analytic induction, a phrase suggested early by Florian Znaniecki, who was trained in Europe. The phrase was applied compellingly by Alfred Lindesmith and Donald R. Cressey in their studies of opiate addiction and embezzlement, and was recently given a thorough exposition by Herbert Blumer in his treatment of the methodology of symbolic interaction.

At times it seems as if Blumer were playing variations on themes by Schmalenbach. Schmalenbach cautions against the blindness of observations without concepts [See "Systematic Sociology," below, part 1]; Blumer bewails a science without concepts.[94] Schmalenbach decries the emptiness of nonobservable concepts [See ibid.]; Blumer argues that "most of the improper usage of the concept in science comes when the concept is set apart from the world of experience, when it is divorced from the perception from which it has arisen and into which it ordinarily ties."[95] Both men are obviously impressed with the dictum of Kant, particularly Blumer: "Perception without conception is blind; conception without perception is empty."[96] Those are almost Schmalenbach's own words.

And are not Blumer's sensitizing concepts the same as Schmalenbach's categorical intuitions? Is not Schmalenbach's program of inquiry requiring the transformation of sensual intuition and observation into categorical intuition and observation for an ultimate apprehension of noumena akin to Blumer's suggested alternative to "variable analysis"?[97] Moreover, both are keenly aware of what has come to be called (after Robert Park) "natural history" and its relevance for science.[98] "The sociological point of view makes its appearance in historical investigation as soon as the historian

turns from the study of "periods" to the study of institutions. . . .
In the process, history becomes natural history, and natural history passes over into natural science. In short, history becomes sociology."[99] In history, Schmalenbach looks for the timeless durations of human existence-styles, or Simmel's forms. Here the method of *Verstehen* is quite appropriate; he applies that method more in the fashion of Dilthey or Driesch than of Max Weber, who, as we have seen, embraced the method with a methodology that rejected it.

So we return to Schmalenbach's styles of association. He characterized periods of history—antiquity, the Middle Ages, modern times, and the late period—in terms of their dominant styles, which were, respectively, communion, community, society, and again communion. But here we have a closed cyclical conception that Schmalenbach would surely renounce, even though he suggested it. Probably he was carried away by the chaos of communions he saw emerging in Germany after World War I [See "Communion—a Sociological Category," below, part 1]. His nagging concern about religion inclined him to hope for a final syncretism of the communions of the twenties that would generate a new faith, just as Christianity had arisen out of the syncretism of communions of antiquity. He writes at the close of that work ". . . the most beautiful stones of Christianity's cathedrals are borrowed from the treasures of antiquity and late antiquity." [See ibid.] We can only observe, with all the brilliance of hindsight, that the erection of the Nazi cathedral somehow obscured the beauty of the stone.

Of major importance, however, is Schmalenbach's recasting of sociological attempts to grasp history as a unidimensional movement over time. Tönnies tried this, but failed, owing to his hatred of *Verbürgerlichung* ["bourgeoisization"], which he identified too much with *Vergesellschaftung* [societalization]. Some American sociologists still speak of the unidirectional historical change in social bonds from rural, folk, sacred, primary, mechanical, consensual (*prope ad infinitum*) communities to urban, civilized, secular, secondary, organic, and symbiotic societies. This is true in spite of the early observations of Robert Park and W. I. Thomas, who called the conceptualization into question, and the subsequent theoretical reformulations occasioned by the research of many contemporary American sociologists after World War II.[100] Within eras, similar contrasts are to be found, as well as internal transformations, as shown in figure 1.

Antiquity	*Middle Ages*
Communion	Community
↗ ↘	↗ ↘
Society ↔ Community	Communion ↔ Society
Modern Times	*Late Period*
Society	Communion
↗ ↘	↗ ↘
Community ↔ Communion	Society ↔ Community

Figure 1. Schmalenbach's Formulation of Dominant Styles in Natural History

Of course, the European observations were there for Schmalenbach to apprehend. We need only mention the work of de Coulanges and Max Weber's study of the city. Schmalenbach himself credits the anthropologist Heinrich Schurtz with analytically distinguishing communion and community. Yet, the essentials were there, and Schmalenbach seized them. In spite of the spate of empirical refutations of the rural-urban continuum in American sociology since the end of World War II, perhaps some American sociologists have not yet incorporated these formulations. This might be because the United States is a nation without an antiquity (or at best with an "alien," indigenous antiquity) or a Middle Age. So for these sociologists, natural history has become history and institutions, periods. The turn in the study of social change in the United States has been away from science. Essentially, this is the lament of symbolic interaction.

Nevertheless, Schmalenbach could never completely move into the perspective of symbolic interaction for two basic reasons. First, there was his phenomenologically based aversion to "sociologism." This is marked by his consistent attempt to find the seeds of the social in the asocial. Second, he often took as given what, in fact, begged explanation. For example, he writes: "As for . . . the capacity of grasping the intention, we can presume that man would not have it if he were not endowed with the very capacity of behaving intentionally, of pursuing his ends, and, in pursuing them, to experience himself as doing so. There is no doubt that he is made this way from the very beginning" [See "Phenomenology of the Sign," below, part 3]. Or ". . . I affirm the existence in man . . . of a primary tendency to 'address himself' without anterior experience of an object to which he addresses himself" [See ibid.].

Phenomenological sociology in the United States has certainly not yet evolved beyond Schmalenbach, but may well be on its way to catching up with him. As for symbolic interaction, George H. Mead satisfactorily explained more than half a century ago what phenomenological sociology presumes. As opposed to the positions of phenomenologists in sociology, that of Schmalenbach would probably have to be ranked as the most essentialist. His concern for the ethos and the totality of human existence puts him close to those in sociology who are engaged in orienting the discipline more toward practice and relevance. Of course, by implicitly denying the possibility of Weber's value-free sociology because Schmalenbach understood logos as part of the totality of human existence, he did not provide an easy route that would lead to immediate practical action. His practical orientation would probably have provided basic insights into our daily life and into a code of values stemming from what he, at times for reasons of simplification, called categorical intuition. In this he referred to the spiritual level of human existence that would allow us to project into the future. Without doubt, while he would have been critical of the demand for a value-free science, he would also have sided with Max Weber's proposal of an ethics of responsibility [*Verantwortungsethik*] over that of conviction [*Gesinnungsethik*].

CONCLUSIONS

If Schmalenbach's work can be construed as significant, why then has it been neglected? For the United States the answer is simple: The work is relatively inaccessible and difficult to decipher. Consequently, aside from Shils's acknowledgment, the Naegele and Stone translation, and empirical studies by Stone and his associates, there is probably no reference to Schmalenbach's endeavors in the United States.[101]

In Europe, there were for a long time only two notable discussions of Schmalenbach's work—those of Theodor Geiger and Ferdinand Tönnies in the *Handwörterbuch für Sozialwissenschaft*, an overall account of German sociology during the first third of this century. Tönnies, however, did not accept the fundamental criticism and redefinition of his own categories of community [*Gemeinschaft*] and society [*Gesellschaft*] to which Schmalenbach had added a third, communion [*Bund*], in order to overcome definitional incompatibilities in the concept of community. Tönnies listed the concept of communion as an example of association, while the concepts of community and society remained for him the only relational terms. Actually, he would have had to include communion within such a categorization. Instead, he avoided such consequences and eliminated by definition the problem of communion as raised by Schmalenbach.[102]

References to Schmalenbach in the introductions to the fifth and sixth editions of *Gemeinschaft und Gesellschaft* attest to the fact that Tönnies did not take Schmalenbach's criticism lightly. Yet Tönnies never revised his fundamental conceptualizations. We find further support for this contention in our interpretation of Rudolf Heberle, student, son-in-law, and follower of Tönnies. Heberle acknowledges the importance of what he calls the "sensual interpretation" of Schmalenbach, lauding it as the first of its kind that needs further elaboration in terms of method. Yet Tönnies, since he defined the concept of community in terms of will and psychology, could easily have incorporated the concept of communion with that of community, because it was a theoretical concept of "pure sociology" [*reine Soziologie*].[103] To be sure, members of Tönnies's camp did not or would not understand the essentially sociological and experiential foundations of community and communion as apprehended by Schmalenbach.[104]

Geiger fully recognized the importance of a distinct understanding of the concept, and referred to it when he interpreted community, communion, and society in terms of Weber's three forms of legitimate governance. However, he was more impressed by Schmalenbach's essay on property relations, from which he expected new insights for sociology.[105] Linde's recent discussion provided exactly that.[106]

There are probably three primary reasons for the general neglect of Schmalenbach in both Europe and the United States:

1. *Time of Life.* Schmalenbach was considerably younger than the "classical" European sociologists. He was not recognized by them as part of the circle, and they hardly ever referred to him. Moreover, he was too old to be one of the younger generation of sociologists that emerged after the Second World War. He died not long after that war.

2. *Nazism.* Schmalenbach remained fairly isolated while teaching in Switzerland during the Nazi period. He himself, most critical of that period in his native land, was obviously not sympathetic to those, like Heidegger in philosophy and Freyer in sociology, who openly or implicitly sided with the Nazis. The actions of Heidegger via his friend, Edmund Husserl, very much upset Schmalenbach; while he had carried on frequent exchanges with Heidegger before the rise of Nazism, their relationship ceased thereafter. Actually, Schmalenbach made no public statement in his writings about this matter, but we interpret his very weak contribution to the *Festschrift* for Ferdinand Tönnies[107] as his way of showing displeasure. Written in 1936, this was Schmalenbach's last publication in Germany. In the Anglo-American world he was perhaps perceived primarily as a German, rather than as a sociologist or philosopher, and as a consequence, was not readily accepted during and immediately after the war.

3. *Intellectual Variance.* Schmalenbach pursued his sociology in the realm of philosophy. Therefore, his penetrating theoretical and

methodological approach did not easily fit with the empiricist practices of sociology in recent history. Nor did he side with Marxian
or critical social theory. Indeed, he would have rejected a preemp-
tion of his position by the adherents of either perspective. Moreover, his particular form of phenomenology, mixed with idealism,
particularly along the lines of Eucken, and pragmatism, in the
manner of James and Peirce, was not at all in demand by European
sociology after World War II.

After a pragmatic period, sociology has now made room for a
greater diversity of approaches. There is an awareness of more
imaginative theorizing in addition to hard-core research.[108] And
there is a growing interest in phenomenological sociology, both in
the United States and in England.[109] So it is quite timely to reintro-
duce the methodology of Schmalenbach as an essential phenomenology. Moreover, both his succinct elaboration of the affective
dimensions of social relations, epitomized by the formulation of
communion as an enduring social form in his confrontation with
Tönnies, and his unique insights into the sociology of property are
reason enough to provide for Schmalenbach's work a position it has
long deserved.

I. Sociology and Social Forms

SYSTEMATIC SOCIOLOGY

Sociology is usually thought of as a young science, and the persistence of such a reputation is more and more disturbing. The implication is false, even if its birth is set at the time it was given (by Auguste Comte in 1838) its present name. Most of the scientific disciplines that have enjoyed academic acclaim for quite a while can hardly boast a longer age. Seen objectively, sociology belongs among the oldest sciences of mankind, and it would be well to point this out consistently, since bearing the flame of eternal youth includes, in this case, disadvantages that far outweigh the few advantages. It is, of course, true that sociology began to detach itself only a few decades ago from a dense quagmire of manifold related disciplines, and became a highly organized, independent discipline. One result of this, intensified by the hope that sociology could never again be deprived of its own raison d'être, was and is a colossal proliferation of methodological endeavors that are especially concerned with delineating sociology from related fields. Unfortunately, such attempts are hampered by the fact that the proponents are not conversant with modern logic, which has

From "Soziologische Systematik," *Weltwirtschaftliches Archiv* 23, no. 1 (1926): 1–15. The initial section of this essay sets forth Schmalenbach's conception of systematic sociology at the time, four years after his publication of "Die soziologische Kategorie des Bundes," included in this volume. Four reviews follow of works by Tönnies, Dunkmann, Sauer, and von Wiese. The development of Schmalenbach's sociology at this stage, however, must be apprehended particularly in the dialogues with Tönnies and, by proxy, Simmel. Over his career, he moved considerably beyond this statement. Thus we omit the brief treatments of Dunkmann and Sauer.

been in a stage of intensive restructuring for some time. Furthermore, there has been an equally extensive proliferation of sociological "systems," the development of which seems to represent the new self-consciousness of sociology very well. All this suggests that one might, first of all, employ the tools of modern logic to clarify the essentials and potentials of every systematic sociology. Yet one has to recognize that these very important developments in modern logic have not even reached a first stage of consolidation at this time. Thus each researcher is obligated to assist in and elaborate on this work, and this, in turn, means essentially a total claim on his competence by the discipline of logic.

The older logic used to make a sharp distinction between concept [*Begriff*] and observation [*Anschauung*]. This is also true of so-called empiricism, where the distinction was revived by contrasting a conception of "concrete" science with "logically constructed" or often "deductive systematic" sociology, so that, at best, an aggregation of discrete, empirical observations became construed as science. However, observations without concepts are blind. So some maintained that only in "systematic" ordering and interrelating of facts is their conceptualization possible. Only in such a way does the rational meaning of each fact emerge so that observations are transformed into viable data rather than persisting as mere "dead" material. In this way, the blindness of observations without concepts was complemented by the emptiness of nonobservable concepts. The logical construction and deductive heights of concepts may indeed be elevated by the most accurate minds. They may think up such scaffolding with a most convincing detachment. Yet, with its distance and estrangement from reality, such a sociology often remains with no consequence for knowledge. The consequences for true knowledge were, by the way, never ascribed to systematic sociology by the older logic. Systematic sociology was understood as a mere quasi-formal comprehensive abridgement of many specific findings, although, on the one hand, these findings served as the basis for an overall system, while, on the other, facts were held to be discovered and discoverable only by the eye-opening revelations bared by discerning the assumptions implied by concepts. Or one understood systematic sociology in a

Kantian manner—as a mere tool for a relatively external control over the material. As a matter of fact, the teachability of a discipline does depend on the development of a systematic construction of thought. Yet each glimpse of true "knowledge" disappears completely in such a theoretical approach, since it belongs neither on the side of plain "hylic sensualism" nor on the side of pure "form" as generating thought. An apparatus of plainly abbreviated control can still fulfill its assigned functions, but what we call true knowledge is not at all provided that way. It appears at this point that the bipolar disjunction of observation and concept is insufficient. Systematic sociology, which appears to us as true knowledge and not only as an agency of orientation, must be constructed by itself out of a most intensive observable concreteness and not merely by stretching the imagination beyond empirical observations.

A fundamental error begins with the last phrase in the above statement. Empirical observations are treated by traditional logic in at least five ways: (1) when it is stated that or if (generally under which factual conditions) some previously analytically determined item, now construed as an empirical item, is actually present or absent; (2) to decide which item of a number of possibilities is really present; (3) an item may be classified as a member of some newly created category within a given system; (4) if the category is newly created, analytic logical synthesis can demonstrate the degree to which that category was established, either in terms of some larger deductive system or by induction; and (5) if the empirical induction, in the context of a given system, is new, it may point the way to a greater differentiation of categories. For all these cases, it is characteristic that either the category to which the objects are referred or at least the general order of potential categories is assumed. To decide whether the "that," "if," or "which" is present, a quick glance will suffice, since it is really determined not by true observation—an attempt devoted to the complete apprehension of the object—but only by presumptive inspection for the purpose of categorization. This holds also for difficult cases and their superficial observation, e.g., for items difficult to differentiate that may require the rebuilding or modification of existing categories. On the most characteristic level, when we deal with "that," "if," "where," or "under what conditions," the intensity of observation is appropriately replaced by increasing the frequency of observations ("how often") for empirical induction.

Completely different is the observation that can be called real, true, or fully "seeing"—a qualitative observation in contrast to the merely presumptive one. Here the object is observed for its own sake, not for its bearing upon a system or from the point of view of a system. Thus it is observed in its complete individuality and originality, in its pristine existence and singularity, as well as in its present fullness and living pervasiveness. In this case the collection of as many cases as possible is of no importance, but the intensive, potentially sensual observation of the specific case is. The categories, which are of course a necessity in order to allow for the communication of the observation (the belief that they are already needed for the observation itself is only half true), will be of lesser importance for the initial, directly sensual observation. This follows because the intention of the communication, made at the completion of presumptive observation, also demands a greater intensification of observation, more intensity, vitality, accuracy, and also greater differentiation. Communication, above all, is not aimed at a specific statement but at verbal evocation. Evocation, however, will appropriately not make use of fixed categories, but of expressions, appropriate to its tenor, which are sensually impressive—saturated observations that are conceptually vague and imprecise. Conceptually imprecise yet evocative expressions may even lend a certain precision to the eye. Subsequent procedure is again oriented toward specific categories. In this, the purpose of the true sensual observation lies in the attempt to discover the categories anew in the light and in the sight of the object, so that the categories are illuminated for the observer by the light cast by the object. In this way, a transformation of sensual observation and sensual intuition to categorical observation and categorical intuition is accomplished.

This discussion cannot, at this point, be referred directly to modern logic. A reference to phenomenology would be appropriate. It has been my intention to distinguish sensual observation from plain presumptive empirical induction. It must also be emphasized that mere presumptive observation is never only "hyletic," but is always some kind of true "knowledge." This goes beyond Husserl.

From the sensual observation, the sensual intuition is transformed continuously toward categorical observation, toward categorical intuition, and beyond, to bring into focus and encompass even the most distant fields of vision. Nowhere in sensual observation are there wholly blind, bald sensations, and in categorical observation there is never plain "thought." The intuition, the "optic," is sustained at the highest levels. In or at the appearance of an observation, categories are formed, or rather, create themselves. A singular experience may always move from a point where it not only speaks for itself but also represents itself as an "example," to a point where it becomes an "exemplified proxy" for a category. As a matter of fact, this does not require viewing additional cases (which can at best lend support through the possibility of comparison). From this one paradigm, experience is "ideationally" recognized as a genetic component. It is of course possible that there may be no other representatives of this category than the one observed. The question of being, or the "that," is always and exclusively determinable from the position of inductive observation. To the eye or intuitively, the apprehension can ultimately encompass the whole range of the object area. This is represented, however, as a unity—not as an additive, summated aggregation, although singular examples appear now in the aggregate and resemble the outcome of inductive observation. Such an appearance is only briefly and fortuitously singular.

In clear distinction from all induction, these evermore encompassing categorical differentiations, orders, and arrangements always transcend developing levels of intuition at lower ranges. These matters of precedence and development must rather be developed by logic, and not at all by an empirical transformation. Essentially an always new and newly emerging observation, intuition can begin as well on the highest level as on any one of the lower levels. Indeed, in contrast to usually implicitly rejected assumptions, the intuitions at lower levels will benefit from supposedly earlier ones at higher levels, and the categories will be developed there. Inasmuch as we labeled erroneous the notion that observations were possible only on the basis of concepts, the eye-opening strength of mere thoughts, not to speak of lively intuitive categories, shall not be denied. In contrast, an all-too-close singular observation can at times stand in its own way, barring its view, as often as it can enrich accompanying observations with greater fullness. This may be asserted without the necessity, from whatever point of view, to prove such general "sensual views" [*Gesichte*] inevitably false. Sensual views can never really be false, because they are the only original basic foundations of all that is called knowledge. The assumption is only that they are really sensual views. When they occur as real, pure optical intuitions and have taken on a larger form of their own kind, these views also tend to mislead their happy discoverer to biased, exaggerated pretensions, shutting his eyes from further related phenomena. Then, in the true sense of the word, these views degenerate. Here is the place to talk, on the one hand, about the importance of categorical observation for all systematic science, and on the other, about the clearly emergent dangers inherent in this procedure.

What has been called fruitful, systematic science was never very fruitful when it was used only to construct some all-encompassing overview. It was only fruitful when it included a claim for true knowledge, which was always necessarily grounded in categorical observation. The building of more encompassing systems should be attempted only in relation to, and supported by, knowledge. Such an attempt—the essence and fate of systematization in general—is not only unprotected from such overriding encompassing pretensions, but also constitutes them and represents them itself. Every systematization is oriented toward completeness. However, completeness is never totally possible in real categorical intuition, nor is it ever absolutely attainable for man. It can never be guaranteed for any or all futures. Every systematic science, even that which is most tightly based on categorical intuition, has therefore given way to other, newer, creative intuitions on which every systematic conceptualization (as distinct from intuition) always depends, or for which it is being replaced, delimited, or expanded. But every systematic science may allow for this in the light of its secondary importance to intuition itself. Systematic science is always secondary in importance to intuition. This holds also when one must supplement the thrust toward systematization from an original intuition that is not determined by a private weakness, or when there is an attempt to build a system of categories that is thought of as somehow desirable, highly regarded as a necessity for the area of teaching, or demanded by some other external conditions. Systematic knowledge is based on every great far-encompassing intuition. One has not only to demand that there shall be systematic knowledge and that it must be based on categorical intuition, but one must emphasize that, from the internal essence of each great categorical intuition, a further urge for expansion and exploitation always emerges in systematic formulations through which intuition reaches its full importance and fertility.

This turn of intuition toward its own systematization occurs in a twofold way. First of all, the "application" of the categories developed in the great intuition is already partially anticipated, partially encompassing the whole range of experience. As this occurs, the intuition internally differentiates itself even more, and the related empirical range of the world is proliferated by even wider ranging and more precise differentiation. Secondly, the categories derived from this most intensive intuition require for the adequacy of their application as well as for themselves (i.e., for their validity), the strict grasp of a precise concept. This concept, however, is never to be considered a single so-called term in the narrow sense, but always in the context of a logically constructed system that can only realize its purest application in the form of specific deductions. Here at last is the place for the dominion of the true concept. Yet it consequently deserves—as does empirical induction—only a secondary position. The collection of factual material, which partially pours into the newly created and also self-determined categories, partially receives its vitality from this. In such a logically constructed system of self-deductive conceptualizations, intuition expresses itself, finding its own clarification and reinforcement. Both factual material and concepts are modes of explication for the basic categorical vision which must precede each of them. This is very important. There can be neither induction nor deduction, as such, without these intuitive elements provided in advance. By themselves, both are actually impossible.

Yet it happens that explicit recognition of intuitive elements has been restricted to a minimum. One can hardly speak of intense sensual observation anymore. Instead, associations with the more or less developed systematic knowledge of other sciences and with the flaunted experiences, opinions, convictions, and prejudices of scientific routine determine the analysis. As a result, the systems built upon these things come to take on the character of qualitative emptiness, whether they appear more as external manifestations of as much empirical material as possible or as deductively derived applications of the concepts. Of course, as must be said, both all true categorical intuition and all primary systematic knowledge are necessarily rare, chance accidents, which cannot be coerced by the mere application of disciplined methodology (such as discussion based on one or the other of the two sides of discursive conceptualization or of factual research). What remains is the wonder of the genius who, in science as well as in other areas, alone lays the ground for leaps into new, so far unexplored, areas.

Ferdinand Tönnies

Ferdinand Tönnies's distinction between community and society has been established for decades as truly fundamental for general sociology. The terms were established in the optical, observational act—in categorical intuition. Vivid experience revealed to Tönnies the radical dualism of all associational forms. Their mutual antagonism was to be found in each associational form. Both forces were anchored in the foundations of the psyche. Finally, the two sides of the dualism contributed to the unique organization and development of the book under discussion.

Now we have a collection added to his world of work—a first collection on which Tönnies hopes to build further in the near future—*Soziologische Studien und Kritiken*[Sociological studies and Critiques; (Jena: Fischer, 1925)], the first five pieces of which belong to the area staked out by his great original masterpiece. Specifically, their initial formulation—much more than a short first draft—was successfully offered by the writer for his habilitation in philosophy at Kiel in 1881. There follow three introductions to the different editions of *Gemeinschaft und Gesellschaft* [community and society], of which the third, to be sure, was never used as such. (That the first two were not printed in subsequent editions at any time is a lack that must forcibly impress anyone who owns whatever edition). Finally, there is a promise of another book, stated as an announcement [*Selbstanzeige*].

The seventh piece, an incomplete article, "Historismus und Rationalismus" [Historicism and rationalism] (1894), and the last, a lecture, "Das Wesen der Soziologie" [The essence of sociology] (1907), also belong in the same context, as does the article, "Herbert Spencers soziologisches Werk" (1889). Less directly related are two reports, the first about the Sociological Congress convened in Paris in 1894 and the second concerning the Sociological Association meeting that took place in London in 1904. Apart from these, there is only the discussion of "Die Anwendung der Deszendenztheorie auf Probleme der sozialen Entwicklung" [The application of the theory of descent to problems of social development]. This actually reviews a set of manuscripts submitted for a competition before the turn of the century and published by Fischer in Jena. Related to these reviews are the polemics the winners employed to defend their contributions. A short article called "Eugenics" (1905), a review of Galton's proposals for social hygiene, and subsequent discussions also fit here.

Since a follow-up series is anticipated, it may be of practical interest and therefore justifiable to reissue these articles, which almost fill 200 pages. Yet the import of the lines of thought in the latter selections, quite correctly questioned by Tönnies (including the question of how they came about in the first place), is so hopelessly marginal and irrelevant, even for those who have dealt with such issues, that I deplore the fact that Tönnies's rich and profound mind has become entangled in it. Objectively his statements are correct, but the question remains whether this was worth the effort.

Quite different are the pieces in the first group. The original plan of *Gemeinschaft und Gesellschaft* makes one wonder, because the development of the sociological concepts, which Tönnies already had in mind in that sketch, is to be found only in the latter third of a mere 33 pages. The preceding sections deal with the general theory of knowledge, the theory of science, and psychological elaborations. For the historian of philosophy these pages are noteworthy even today, though they concern the cultural movements at the beginning of the 1880s. As a basis for his enduring sociological antithesis, however, they are not necessary, and hardly any traces of them are left in the later publication (*Gemeinschaft und Gesellschaft*). Following this general philosophical discussion, the short sociological chapter takes a relatively much more deductive form than one would expect, given the philosophical introduction. In a barely appropriate way, deductions are made that arrive at the opposition (suggested in the preceding sections) of friendly and antagonistic relations embedded in human will. There are still suggestions of this in the subsequent book, yet they are hardly the real bases of the antithesis between community and society. Thus I consider the later outcomes of that ancestry to be erroneous.

One could conclude from all this that the first outline of *Gemeinschaft und Gesellschaft* developed this antithesis only through logically constructed thought based on Tönnies's psychological categories, and consequently not at all from a sociological vision. As a matter of fact, the outline attempts a strictly terminological exposition of what has actually been intuitively conceived, but this first attempt cannot have been the real origin of his knowledge because it simply did not lead to the subsequent results. The very lively examples with which the book starts out in such a suggestive way, and through which the antithesis is immediately given a viable existence, are missing. They definitely provided the real beginning, but the young author did not dare to put them forward at the earlier time. What nevertheless justifies the publication of the outline is the demonstration of the philosophical atmosphere and motivation that always belong to real categorical intuition, even if, as in this case, the conceptualization is at odds with factual observation. In its first edition, the book itself put the philosophical considerations in a shorter and more precise form in the introduction; in its second edition, these considerations were deleted, a fact that the owners of later editions might well regret. The first introduction contains, like the original outline, rather strange speculations, which despite their vulnerability to criticism should be stimulating to the historian of philosophy. We need not go into that here.

Of particular interest is the change that has occurred since the outline was written and is now increasingly evident, namely, that the publication of these general philosophical considerations contributes more to the history of science [than to science itself]. This is even more clear in the article "Historismus und Rationalismus" and particularly in the introduction to the second edition of *Gemeinschaft und Gesellschaft*. Both are keyed toward placing Tönnies's own great insight into its overall history. Tönnies's insight into the two basic forms of all sociality, whose duality is right although neither is right by itself, was really ingenious and, as such, original. At any rate, it stands in a great tradition. The theory of society [*Gesellschaft*] is that of the rationalism of early modern times, where Hobbes (so well investigated by Tönnies) was its most rigid early proponent. The theory of community [*Gemeinschaft*] had blossomed anew in the period of Goethe, in romanticism, and in the historical schools of different sciences stemming from that period. That spiritual world was also the background of Tönnies's great discovery. At first this was driven home to that learned mind almost exclusively by Otto Gierke, who in the latter part of the nineteenth century was also the greatest conservationist of the romantic spirit. Only later did Tönnies investigate, as he did earlier for society, the spiritual background of community in and since romanticism. The pages devoted to that matter belong to the most valuable contributions in the history of philosophy, science, and scientific thought in the nineteenth century, even though at that time Tönnies had not yet established his profound involvement with true romanticism. The dualism of the types of sociality, after all, idealizes the virtues of romanticism. The investigation of the history of ideas, subdued by the mere historical writings about politics, economy, literature, philosophy, and other related sciences from the period of Goethe all through the nineteenth century, remains residual. Once this task is really taken up, then Tönnies's contributions will have to be used. After all, they promote one thing very well—the critical analysis of the diversified structure of theoretical positions and concepts. Here the articles on "historicism and rationalism" and the second introduction find their major task. Even where they do not penetrate to the ultimate roots and where one may see the way to a different conclusion than that reached by Tönnies, they strongly promote knowledge.

The critical analysis of concepts is also the intent of the third introduction (written in the fall of 1918), where Tönnies deals with the concepts of socialism and communism and also with related dogmas. Previously published as an article in the *Neue Zeit* [New time], this introduction derives its major interest from the contemporary movements of the period. Here also one can find much of lasting value that could make an important contribution to the history of philosophy, science, and the history of ideas of the last decades in the manner called for above. Such history would have to refer to Tönnies not only as an author of the subjects to be reviewed, but also as a major influence in the period to be analyzed. The basic import of Tönnies for all sociology (certainly for the distinctly German sociology in Europe) is expressed in the fact alone that leading representatives, such as Simmel, Sombart, and Weber, proceeded in an essential way from Tönnies. That is even more obvious for figures of much smaller stature. Most notably, I refer to Karl Dunkmann's *Kritik der sozialen Vernunft* [Critique of social reason] . . . and the *Grundlagen der Gesellschaft* [Foundations of society] by Wilhelm Sauer. . . .

LEOPOLD VON WIESE

Radically different from the elaborate claims of Dunkmann, Sauer, and others is, of course, Leopold von Wiese's *Allgemeine Soziologie als Lehre von den Beziehungen und Beziehungsgebilden der Menschen* [General sociology as the science of the relations and the relational forms of mankind], of which volume I, dealing with the theory of relations is now available. Wiese's intent is an all-encompassing system, yet one specifically of sociology, "a clearly separated discipline as a tightly knit and consequently systematized special science." Wiese does not create its structure on the basis of an all-encompassing conceptualization of social phenomena accomplished by categorical intuition. It is not that he, like so many others (among them empiricists, because the collection of a mass of data is something quite different), lacks the talent for pure sociological observation. The book contains, in many short characterizations, evidence of true perception, and the author develops sharp insights with his fascinating closeness to life. But his optic is not a categorical optic; at least, his system is not based on such a supposedly all-encompassing approach. Wiese considers "the careful unraveling of a captivating singular problem" (which he erroneously equates with empirical induction) "in the present period of our scientific development" to be less important. Rather, in a really false antithesis, he considers the creation of an airtight theoretical system (even in the form of a relatively empty basic sketch and prospectus) to be the task of the day. I cannot follow him in this suggestion. This analysis of special and (for whatever reasons) important social phenomena, which Simmel very consciously saw as his mission (of course, in his case, grounded in a not all-encompassing but categorical intuition), I would consider to be the leading model for creative sociological work today. This means building a whole structure for which the criteria should be that there be an end to the confusions of sociological with nonsociological phenomena, and that potential sociological facts be arranged in a clear fashion, at least so long as there is no systematic sociology, truly based on categorical intuition, available to us at this time. The system should not be too narrow. That would imply doctrine and dogma, dangers which, as in Othmar Spann's example, are also possible, even in genuine categorical intuition.

Wiese's attempt does not proceed from true knowledge but from necessity. It is the consequence of starting from a minimum of vague, general, and prescientific definitions of the social, by which he is immediately constrained to proceed to a relatively deductive method to derive further constructions. Here his method is not mere formal explication. Another consequence is that his conceptualization, which determines the selection of a material base, results in bare-boned quantification. Of course, Wiese is aware of this, yet he considers that this is the path science must take, although he himself knows that mechanical procedures of quantification are not appropriate for the explanation of what is actually qualitative human behavior. Without doubt, Wiese's own sympathy lies with qualitative rather than quantitative methods.

A result of the mathematical ideal of science is the central position of the conceptualized relation, which Wiese acknowledges as akin to that ideal. Original relations are only to be found between the participants of specific societies, whereas the community type of being never consists of mere relations, because that being is to be found in the total qualification of each community member. On the same basis, one must evaluate the methodological individualism that Wiese is unable to escape, much as he tries to rescue himself. What he says about it is based on methodological errors, in which he also has, of course, Max Weber on his side.

At any rate, this is the basis of Wiese's approach. His methodology remains stuck with outmoded perspectives of philosophical logic, the theory of knowledge, and the theory of science. Wiese knows of modern developments, but the in-depth understanding of their real context has passed him by. This becomes obvious in many ways. It follows from the issues already discussed that Wiese cannot understand the current rejection of the methods of natural science by the humanities and social sciences. Where he accepts *Verstehen* as a method of sociology (in opposition to his own general principles, by the way), he does so in the inadequate meaning given to it by Max Weber. Another erroneous procedure again shared with, or perhaps taken from, Weber is the reduction of sociology to the consideration of human action. Here the rationale for such an approach is mainly to be found in the concern with the confusion of sociology with psychology. That problem should be dealt with in quite a different way. The argumentative process in Wiese is fortunately only rarely disturbed by such concerns, and even then is expressed with a peculiar embarrassment. Psychology, which must, of course, be considered principally on behalf of sociological understanding, includes for him only the psychology of consciousness and perception. The psychic base of community, as distinguished from society and communion, exists as reality in the subconscious. Vierkandt called the phenomenon of communion a community of experience [*Erlebnisgemeinschaft*] in his *Gesell-*

schaftslehre [Theory of society (1923)], yet such a term seems to underestimate the category of communion.

What is laudable in Wiese's attempt at a systematic sociology, despite our all-too-briefly expressed reservations, is threefold. First, we acknowledge the great caution and consideration with which he proceeds in the creation of his structure. This will promote methodological discussion. No question that I would welcome it, if these clarifying discussions were gradually to give way to real sociological work and dedication. In line with his caution and consideration, one finds in Wiese frequent references to the sociological literature. Where there is a dominant categorical intuition, one will frequently not care about the work of others; but there must be a different way to deal with this. The at times exaggerated citations are, in this case, virtues, and Wiese deserves thanks for them. Second, the factual order developed in the first chapter remains fairly unrelated to the organization of the book; he makes many fine and unique observations in his substantive elaborations, which do not relate much to his principles. Thus, regardless of the crude scheme, there are lots of separate sociological accounts that are based on original perception and have a value independent of the system. Third, a final point—which also makes the systematic sociology appear in a different perspective—must be emphasized. However much it is only an externally ordering system, which the author in fact acknowledges but evaluates differently, it can enter only feeble claims to rank as real knowledge based on categorical intuition. Still, behind the attempt to cope with this variety of appearances, there is a great amount of experience. This is the experience of the multiplicity, complexity, and structured character of social phenomena. Here we at least approximate the true sociological optic, even if it is impossible to subdivide the phenomena into great and convincing differentiations. When someone has actually absorbed the specific sociological attitude, this is of merit and must be appreciated.

COMMUNION—A SOCIOLOGICAL CATEGORY

The most important conceptual contribution of recent sociology is the distinction between community [*Gemeinschaft*] and society [*Gesellschaft*] formulated by Ferdinand Tönnies. It has created new perspectives for inquiry in all the cultural sciences (to the extent that they played a part in the true intellectual life of the present time) and given rise to new conceptions. Georg Simmel's *Philosophie des Geldes*, Werner Sombart's *Der moderne Kapitalismus* and Max Weber's profound works are already based upon Tönnies's insights. Recently his book has also become popular in other circles. The term, community, has become a catchword used to designate every possible (as well as the most impossible) delusion of the time. Now and again it primarily represents ideals, thus confusing the original meaning of the term. Clever businessmen are beginning to exploit this term, beloved by youth, for diverse propagandistic ends, and so misuse even its ideal meaning. A "community of interests" is no longer far away from a "community of shareholders."

Moreover, Tönnies's choice of a name for the antithesis of community is not a completely happy one. Tönnies may offer good

From "Die Soziologische Kategorie des Bundes," *Die Dioskuren*: *Jahrbuch für Geisteswissenschaften*, 1 (1922): 35–105. This article has been translated in part by Kaspar D. Naegele and Gregory P. Stone as "The Sociological Category of Communion," in Talcott Parsons, et al. (eds.), *Theories of Society*, Vol. I (New York: The Free Press of Glencoe, Inc., 1961), pp. 331–347. The present translation is complete and is based solely on a translation prepared by Gregory P. Stone for the Department of Sociology, University of Chicago, circa 1955.

reasons for his use of common language and its etymology. Yet it is not only troublesome when the "science of society" distinguishes a specialized meaning of a term from its broader customary meaning; any advantage that may also be gained is endangered by all the risks of ambiguity related to such an extension of meaning.

Meanwhile, in another and more profound sense, Tönnies's own insights have not provided a precise conceptual contribution to the science of sociology. Tönnies's work is, in our opinion, a pioneering achievement, but it is also rooted in the historic past. Beyond the precursors he himself mentioned, there are the experience and knowledge of romanticism—the age of Goethe—which, having provided fertile nourishment for all areas of knowledge, live on in Tönnies's work.

Of course, the bourgeoisie is the stratum-prototype of society, and in the eighteenth century was the status group most determined to control or even replace the aristocracy. This period brought a so-called society-like social structure theoretically into general awareness, and also practically into pervasive existence. It brought about the essential separation of simultaneously united and antagonistically alienated individuals by means of "quantitative individualism," and at the same time it imposed an external mechanical solidarity upon comprehensive, yet merely quantitative or abstract, systems of relations.[1] It is true that the origins of these things are to be found in the early genesis of the new era, and accompany in every aspect the rise of the modern world; nevertheless, certain counterforces had to be neutralized very shortly before 1700, the end of the true baroque period. Only in the eighteenth century is the full impact of the mentality that expresses itself sociologically in the ethos of society realized.

The age of Goethe signaled the first reaction (in the positive rather than the negative sense), or, to put it less negatively, the dawn of a new age. Just as in all other aspects, this occurred also in the sociological sense. The great organic bonds—the *Volk* and the nation, also the family, kinship, and neighborhood groups, village and city, country and countryside—were discovered anew; first, by the *Sturm-und-Drang* movement, and then by romanticism. Even the state no longer had to be the great machinelike Leviathan of Hobbes, created only for the restoration and guarantee of external order. It was instead to be an organism, a "qualitatively individual unity," a "Macroanthropos," as Novalis, Friedrich Schlegel, the elder Fichte, but most of all, Adam Müller and also Savigny and others, asserted endlessly and always with the same emphasis. When A. L. von Schlözer declared, at the extreme end of the eighteenth century, that to understand the state one would best reason "from the analogy of the fire-insurance agency," Adam Müller was enraged saying:

> It would be a sacrilege to regard the state as a worldly association of merchants which is maintained as long as it is convenient and then abandoned when it is apparent that it no longer serves anyone's interests. A state is an association of another kind and has completely different consequences. . . . The state is not a mere domestic manufacturing, dairy farming, or underwriting establishment, nor is it a mercantile association. It is the intimate union of all physical and moral needs, of all physical and moral richness, of all the inner and outer life of a nation, into a great, energetic, vastly dynamic, and living whole . . . [It is a] community in everything that is worthy of note, in everything that is valuable, good, and godly in man. . . . [It is] an alliance of past generations with future generations and vice versa. . . . It is the exalted community, with its roots in the past, of living and emerging generations which weld all into a great and intimate union from life to death.

Romanticism—above all, the age of Goethe—discovered community. To be sure, it seems doubtful whether the interpretation of "eidos" as "ideal"—the actual ideal of the age, and particularly its application to the modern state (every possible modern state)—was not, in a special sense, also romantic. After about 1830, the intellectual and moral world of romanticism collapsed. The nineteenth century reverted to an earlier modern era. Romanticism had given rise to rich achievements and an abundance of diverse creativity in every sphere during the entire nineteenth century, but after 1830 the tendencies of the earlier modern time were resurgent. Realism trod roughshod over the dreams of romanticism. (That there was also much of the unreal in realism has been determined beyond dispute in the meantime. But neo-romanticism, which necessarily arose, is still in large part no less romantic, nor is the old realism.)

Ferdinand Tönnies was the heir of romanticism. He was one of those rare persons of the time who not only incorporated the rich stimulation of romanticism—a consequence that was found everywhere—but who also accepted only very few of the influences coming from the antiromantic, mechanistic spirit. Nevertheless, he experienced a great transformation in his scientific sociological insight.

Romanticism has also been the discoverer of the historical world. The rationalism of the previous era, construing on the basis of naked reason the notions of natural law and natural religion, held that historical deviations from that reason and that nature must be regarded as stark, strange accidents, and absurd, abstruse perversities. In that case, historical knowledge could only be a collection of ridiculous (in any case, foolhardy or even nonsensical) anecdotes or curiosities—at best a doctrine of mere information about the world and men, comprised exclusively of facts. The irrationalism (irrational rationalism) of romanticism recognized reason and nature in what had been considered no more than reality up to that time. Hegel's famous or (with only some justification) infamous thesis—which incidentally had its basis in metaphysics—was the basic tenet of historical study. Yet this thesis provided a justification not only for the things that the older modern time had rejected, but also for the things that were glorified, and which romanticism had scorned in the beginning. For Adam Müller, the mechanistic conception of the state and society is false. One may accept the notion that it was "loathsome" to him (although the frequently attempted separation of that term from "false" is fraught with difficulty). But his theory implied a practical attitude. Tönnies was the first man to see, or at least the first to see clearly, that the acknowledged antithesis of romanticism—mechanical vs. organic—revealed an actual duality, and he decided not to reject either term. Taking sides subjectively was put off or deferred. Community and society both designate types of social bonds.

All this notwithstanding, it can still be asked at what point subjective judgment and objective valuation can be distinguished. And the true meaning of "value-free" (or only "value-relevant") observation still must take into account Max Scheler's contention that love and hate are vehicles of scientific insight. These ideas had been underwritten, incidentally, not only by the absolutism of Franz Brentano; they were also representative of the relativism propounded by Nietzsche. Tönnies's insights are also born of love and hate. It cannot be otherwise, once the deeper realities of such an important conceptualization are bared. Community and society are both recognized types of association. Tönnies remains the heir of romanticism by virtue of the zealous enthusiasm through which he alone saw the phenomena in his heart, which inclined itself lovingly toward community and slighted society. He is only nonromantic in that he regarded community as no longer possible.

This bias remains. Certainly Simmel, Sombart, and, above all, Max Weber have again directed attention to the definitive ethos of society, although for many others the community ethos still matters today. This, according to Max Weber, originated in religion but took on religious meaning only secondarily. But in Max Weber one is never completely sure—much as his heart yearned for Cromwell, for rigor and strength, for dignity—whether he had not blinded himself to the less heroic, but distinctively "society-like," spirit more than to that of community (not to mention the fact that he was understood in that sense to begin with). Neither was Sombart in complete sympathy with the spirit of the bourgeoisie. He did prefer the opposition of the feudal lords, but he favored in a very biased manner the earlier spirit of community-existence. Only in the case of Simmel was the problem more complex. The exercise of caution in making explicit ethical choices had been an absolute necessity for him in the development of pure knowledge. The passion and yearnings of today's youth are much inclined to assert directly: community is good; society, evil. No wonder that every association regarded highly by its members wants to constitute itself as a community. What ends doesn't the tidiness of a clear conception serve!

"Love sharpens vision." Even so, "love creates blindness." And conversely, hate often sharpens vision (observation) and is often blinding. In the case of Tönnies himself (as in romanticism), love alone made scientific insight possible, but at the same time it introduced error. Not only did his passion lead to a negative conception of society, to counteract which it then was necessary slowly to develop a positive counterpart, but it also led to a—it would be false to say too "positive," but nevertheless a "sentimental"—conception of community. Just as the archaic language, part of the charm of the book, is appropriate for insightful feeling, it leads to conceptual ambiguity here and there. And so there is, in the insightful feeling, particularly in Tönnies's melancholic, dejected, foreboding sense of destiny, in that North German acerbity, a sentimentality that is, indeed, often provincial.

These preliminary remarks on the history of scientific ideas seem to me to be necessary for the comprehension of why a third basic sociological category must be introduced into the historically established sequence to supplement "community" and "society". Yet I want to affix my contribution to that of Tönnies, and not only to him but also to the social demands of today's youth.

A Critical Analysis of Community

In its specific sense, the prime example of community that Tönnies decided to introduce (the confusion follows in a later place) is the family, preferably the family of rural or small-town character. Its bases are the natural, genuine, and indeed, physical forms of solidarity: consanguinity and proximity—kinship and neighborhood. Locality also belongs in the realm of natural things. Social units appear, however, as psychic phenomena. The bases mentioned above can only be purely external conditions for the possible emergence of community. By itself, common lineage is never a basis for human association if men are ignorant of it. In response, a metaphysical question might be raised—one which is again appropriate today—whether or not the physical-psychic dichotomy is permissible, but this will not be dealt with here. It will be shown, however, with reference to community, if only to clarify its interpretative meaning, that something may be said about the psychic results of physical conditions, although we acknowledge at the same time that the social has reality only in psychological terms, and that nothing else may possibly be discussed. It will have to suffice to recognize that community is a social relationship that flourishes on the basis of a natural, "intrinsic" [naturhaften] solidarity.

For almost all of our youth, what the language has termed "the entry to life" means that young people tear themselves away from the parental home and parental life style, that they storm out into the free and open spaces of the world, and that they join themselves together in friendship groups, which they themselves like to call "communities" today. Are these communities? The natural innate basis is so little a part of such associations that they rend asunder associations established in childhood, so much so that these are thought to be broken, or at least weakened. But perhaps our conception of the meaning of community contains an unjust limitation. There can be conflict between community and community. The problem, then, is to determine whether the conflict involves the peculiarities of specific associations or is a general characteristic of associations as such.

It need not be demonstrated at this point that to tear oneself away from the parental home and to go out into a strange world in no way reconciles any specific characteristics of the parental home with the conflicting desires of the individual, even if they are expressed in this way. Moreover, it is by no means symptomatic only of the various periods when generations harshly oppose one another. Nor is it a case of various strata of the population being less bound to one another by tradition. The craftsmen always had their wandering years. Or there might also be age groupings and status groups which, more than others, value stable residency. At least, the urge to ramble off is felt by every man by his twentieth year.

Neither is the urge necessarily confined to the unrealistic, romantic high life of a few fleeting years of youth. Nor are the communions, which are formed in this way, of only petty significance. Stefan George, today called the greatest unifier and leader of men toward "community" has taught his disciples:

> This new eminence you are seeking
> Does not come from shield or crown!
> Common and uncommon men alike
> Feel the razor-sharpness of the searching senses;
> As one they express the bold look of the outpost;

Stemless, they grow, in turmoil,
Rare offspring of their own stations in life,
And you know such fellows born together
From the ardor in their gazes.

Furthermore:

This is realm of the spirit: Reflected splendor
Of my realm: Yard and grove.
Everyone here is newly born:
The place of the cradle—the home—
Becomes a sound of fairy tale.
Through a mission and a blessing,
You exchange family, status, and names.
Fathers, mothers are no more.
From filial devotion, cast by lot,
I choose my own masters of the world.

From George one understands that the communion is like a religious association, just as he himself has understood it so often. In their activities, those communions that are taken very seriously seem to have an affinity for religiosity. At any rate, religious associations seem always to start as communions.

That countless friendships of youth are free of religious pretensions does not belie that single asserted affinity. And I would maintain that this is the case wherever communions are taken very seriously. In any event, it is characteristic of today's general worldwide yearning for "community" and also for the "friendship club" of romanticism (and the impetuosity of Klopstock's time), that religious yearnings are closely related to it. Even where this is not completely obvious and apparent, there is something of a religious atmosphere (which I hesitate to call "religion") with respect to which communions take on a profoundly "sacred" character. This occurs whenever these youths take high ideals into their hearts, whenever national youth rallies around a symbol of national honor, or whenever communistic youths offer themselves to one another in the spirit of blissful surrender.

On the other hand, in their origins religious associations seem to be communions to a considerable extent. In a fundamental sense, religion is not a social phenomenon (although there are well-known

theories which hold that to be the case; and although, in another
sense, many strange follies have originated in the churches). It can,
therefore, be neutral toward this kind of sociality as soon as it
becomes social. In contrast to this, the primary religious experience
(the subjective aspect of religion) is probably not a completely
solitary experience in the bare negative sense of each individual
soul's being "alone with its god." True, religious movements often
break out like epidemics. Mystic manifestations of spiritual power
are often experienced by assembled crowds. Also, especially
wherever individuals or small groups are seized with emotion, the
urge to preach, to convert, or to form a congregation seems to be
imminently close to the center. Yet all these things ought not to be
regarded by the exacting and inquiring person as contradictions of
that presumption [of the asocial nature of religion]. For then even
religion becomes social. As history tells us and as appears obvious
when we think about it, it [religion] takes the form that hearts inflamed with blissful indecision and eloquent cries will inflame
others, and exultant souls will merge together. Yet all the natural,
inborn, cohesive elements of human nature are rent asunder by
communions emerging in this way. And if such pious bliss forces
humble piety to offer a new salvation above all to fellow man, then
it follows that he who is conscious of the fact that he has nothing
in common even with his mother, will strongly demand that others
leave their fathers and mothers and follow him; indeed, that bury-
ing a dead father is an affair of the dead.

Max Weber, and following him, Ernst Troeltsch have introduced
an important distinction in the sociology of religion which, in the
history of Christianity, differentiates the "church" from the "sect."
I will return to that: "church" is described by the term, "community"—and even by "society"; a "sect" may be defined as a
pure communion. (Both terms are used in a relative sense.) Max
Weber, on a different occasion, anticipated these distinctions to
free the fundamental concepts of general sociology from the narrow dichotomy proposed by Tönnies and thus prepared it for the
necessary trichotomy. While Tönnies had included what we have
called communion by mere extension from the naturelike association,[2] Weber broke down the community into "traditional" and "af-

fectual" relationships, which he often terms "emotional."[3] In actuality, it is emotional expression, often an ecstatic, bursting flow of love (or hate) from the heart or soul, and mutual exaltation that sustain the communion.

And this is the place where we must determine whether the communion is only a subtype of community or a contrasting form of association, so that both may be contrasted with society.

COMMUNITY RECAST

I have suggested that community is that association which flourishes on the basis of a "natural," "intrinsic" solidarity. But perhaps this is too narrow. Tönnies has already observed that custom and memory, since they must intensify even blood bonds, could give rise to a community without such bonds. And Max Weber in general proposed "traditionalism" as the basis of community (according to him the only basis). Yet these latter things do not at all take blood ties into account, since they can be identified[4] without reference to their establishment in tradition. But they presumably can give rise to community without the ingredient of custom and memory, through which blood ties are bound with tradition, and also without the efficacy of traditional mores. If man had knowledge only of blood ties, then a father, upon returning from afar after decades of absence to find a son born immediately after his departure, would join with him in an exclusive union. There would be no upsurge of emotion. It would obviously represent a community. This would not include the mother in any constitutive way, since she might have died; nor would it require any remembrance of her, although that would seldom actually be the case. Moreover, even the condition of love seems dispensable. A being that generally understands blood ties will under all conditions upon recognition, presumption, or even slight anticipation, respond with something, which one may call "community-consciousness." (I repeat: There need not be any emotional reaction, although one can imagine that emotions might possibly be involved.)

All such things are natural. Community is based upon nature, to which mutually held customs also belong—specifically, those of a village, a province, a countryside—in other words, everything that is mutually inherited, to which one has been born or raised, i.e., common birth and common nurture. It happens that what appears to be a matter of common blood is also a matter of common usage, of a common perspective, etc. As far as these things are concerned, they have no further legitimation than tradition. But even the local neighborhood, some time before this, may have been united and even symbolized as a union of kindred. It need not always have been in existence, although perhaps it has existed as long as one can remember—at least, one might think, since one's childhood, although that of course would condense its "naturality," "objectivity," and the context built on it. One may also grow into a neighborhood community of lesser integration, if one lives a long period of one's adult life in one place. Indeed, a certain community may be formed with the salesman in whose store one makes frequent purchases, even if it appears as a silent thing and without the intrusion of affect; similarly with the silent passerby on the street whom one meets frequently, even though one passes by him without a greeting (at least without a cordial one). As a matter of fact, even the most cursory contact can become the basis of a marginal case of community if only some trace of that contact survives in the self. The fleeting bond lies latent and ready to make an appearance at any time. But in the final analysis, it is only the natural, objectively given conditions upon which this social phenomenon is built. As soon as there is something else, or should something else be a social ferment, this association presumably loses the character of community.

The time dimension is included in the "natural-objective" categories, as is the spatial dimension, so that spatial proximity corresponds to temporal extent. Both dimensions are devoid of any qualitative aspects in matters of theory. The basic assumptions underlying the community construct are only that these qualitative aspects function, not as such, but exclusively as a consequence of the space-time relationship, and that the latter is at least the decisive basis and exclusive condition for the development of qualitative aspects in the emergence of community. It would seem, then, that the significance which is attributed to the qualitative aspect of such "sociation" must be derived from something other than plainly objective natural factors.[5] If one wanted to spell these things out exactly, one would have to say, above all, that in any case there are always objective conditions, or "existential facts." And, vice versa, one may say: All socially operating conditions or facts give rise to community. Perhaps one might also state that these "foundations" are independent of us, while we are dependent on them and can "do" nothing for them. Meanwhile, these remarks are not unshakably certain. And they also point up conditions and foundations that are not completely certain. One can, intentionally or arbitrarily, "do something" about the formation of community by doing something else and then viewing, as its doubtfully anticipated effect, the establishment of or at least the basis for community. Thus one can act with the intention, or at least the hope, that a community will develop on the basis of what has been done.

At any rate, such an act is indirect: one may see the relative justification for such a formulation. However, such conditions and foundations are only seemingly attached. In spite of this, these foundations are, after all, occasionally dependent on us in a certain way. In contrast to this, the communion will tend to take on a completely different character, so that its bases are also independent of us. We cannot intervene in its action—indeed, we must adapt to it as a given. Only the natural and intrinsic bases of community and only community itself remain. Nevertheless, one must interpret these words so that they include a sufficient range of applicability—tradition, custom as nature, etc., although the communion here and there will gain a new interpretation from them or take on a new metaphysical significance (of "true nature").

To restrict the characterization of community to the needed range, something else is important; this establishes at the same time why it seems advisable to me to start from blood bonds as the prototype of its basis. (Tönnies was in the same position, although for different, but related reasons that led him to the country.) I have touched upon the problem of how it is that pure naturalistic or given conditions can form the basis of social relations, since the social has its reality in psychic elements only in the sense that it is a concern of humanistic sociology alone. One must know much more about blood bonds. The fact of their presence can hardly suffice to explain why social phenomena based on them should come into existence. One might, of course, ask whether the unconscious machinations of blood bonds are not sufficient for the formation of community, even if such machinations are unknown. This is all the more the case since they, rather than abstract knowledge of them, are the true uniting elements. This is doubtful indeed. It leads to the possible contention that everything—even the things that may be called natural in a certain sense, such as attraction by mere sympathy—is also a basis of community. Thus, one feels akin to others, one is bound to others by a secret and mysterious bond. ("Ah, you were my sister or my wife in some earlier day!") If this were correct, the distinction between community and communion would blur, and one would be confused with the other. The distinction would lose its analytic utility.

In any case, we have here the bonds of community. Even when they are unconscious, they are nevertheless psychic. Regardless of the place assigned to the concept, "unconscious," in psychological theories, we meet here with something phenomenological. When the unconscious is construed as psychic, it cannot be rendered as a mere physical phenomenon, because we cannot be without consciousness of psychic experience. Nor, at the other extreme, does it suffice to employ the concept of unconsciousness merely in the sense of an auxiliary construct. Eduard von Hartmann apprehended the unconscious more profoundly than did Leibniz and Herbart, and he derived his notions from Fechner. Parallelism, i.e., the notion of an absolute separation between psychic and physical phenomena, was elevated from an originally secondary position by the model of science systematically employed by Fechner as an instrument of analysis. Hartmann, on the other hand, arrived at his more profound conception through direct disavowal of the notion. Yet, on a secondary level and in light of his view that conscious phenomena are psychic, he also concedes to the separation. He fails in his attempt to relegate the unconscious, as an "actual" unconscious, to the physical realm. Moreover, he shows inconsistencies even in doing this. Psychic phenomena, if they also appear unconscious as psychic phenomena, are the basis of community. Little as the objective presence of blood bonds suffices as a condition for community, and much as one must know about it, knowledge of the purely external physical blood relationship would be meaningless for the formation of community if there were no inner psychic apprehension simultaneously present with the external, physical, blood relationship. There must be a psychic blood relationship that, as such, has something of an unconscious quality. One can be aware of it, and perhaps one must be aware of it. But even if one is aware of it, the awareness at best resembles only an inner glow in a clouded stream, which shimmers underneath and which embodies knowledge not at all. This makes it neither clear nor conscious, even if such an awareness should embody a full understanding of it. The unconscious is not the mirror image of the conscious, something referred to by just another index of the condition of consciousness—the same content in a different form. (I refer to Eduard von Hartmann and also to Fechner.) This is extremely important because it follows that, regardless of the unconscious becoming conscious, nothing actually happens to it. It remains generically there, or better, "essentially" the unconscious, although it can be dissolved, distorted, and perhaps reinforced by consciousness. Yet even then, like the total unconscious, it cannot be lifted into consciousness and remain the same.[6]

The formative conditions of community, where they depart from the province of the external physical and consequently become social, belong ordinarily to the unconscious. [These conditions include] not only common blood ties, which disclose themselves here as the "prototype," but also common ancestry of all other kinds, such as the acquisitions of one's personal and more or less awakened life. Even a relatively brief spatial and temporal contact, as such, may have the effect of forming a community, and because of this should leave some trace in the soul. To be sure, we may know about these things, but apart from the fact that such expressed knowledge is by no means an irrelevant matter here, the formulation upon which community rests is frequently not recognition [*Wissen*], but rather a modification which the unconscious has internalized as part of our psychic makeup. Moreover, we may even consciously resist acknowledging community, perhaps by interpreting it as fortuitous, unreal to our nature, and consequently sense-less. Perhaps this also has a certain consequence. First of all, we have, so to speak, surrendered ourselves to our unconscious almost without resistance. The consideration of the psychic substance on which community is based establishes, in a profound sense, the way in which conditions and states that are independent of us, but upon which we depend, actually constitute the foundations for such a relationship. Not only are natural and innate conditions not anti-thetical to psychic conditions, but the unconscious psyche (since the psychic is the essence) is the "innate" itself. The innate is within us, and like, for example, certain plants, also has a clinging mustiness similar to that of mulch.

In the fact that the unconscious is the basis of community, we can consciously apprehend the strongest differentiating quality from communion. In general, one will never regard the community in which he participates as good or bad. Ordinarily, one will not con-sciously recognize it at all. It is merely an existential circumstance or is simply evident. Life in a family or on the farm makes no ex-plicit claims for community. Community is nothing but a fact (al-though a psychic fact). One will scarcely notice his membership in broad communities—a community of language, a racial com-munity, or a community of all humanity. The communities to which we belong stretch into incalculable distances, distances in every dimension. And one can never recognize all of them, since some will always evade the possibility of explicit apprehension. Despite this, we are actually involved in all of them, because our uncon-scious, directly or indirectly, is affected or even structured by them all. As a rule, it is antagonism and crisis that make one aware both of his membership in a community and of its very existence. Even then, such crises do no more than create an awareness. All that one knows about two children of different families is that one be-longs to one, the other to the other—that one belongs either here or there. Here experiential feeling or sentiment is actually lost.

One is inclined today, almost without serious thought—either by following the modern tendency or by opposing certain reactionary circles and therefore taking a stand for community or for feeling (Tönnies's choice of will smacked of Schopenhauer)—to construe the consciousness of community as a feeling. Thus the phrase "consciousness of community" poses a paradox: community owes its psychic existence to the unconscious. In spite of everything, the term (and it should be thought of as nothing more) is vindicated insofar as the psychologist, without wishing or feeling obliged to exclude the unconscious from the total psychic structure, is inclined to speak of psychic matters predominantly as matters of consciousness or awareness in his treatment of certain problems. In part, this is attributable to a methodological polemic; in part, it has a valid basis. More important, this has resulted in a great loss to psychology. Above the "consciousness of community" may be placed the "feeling of community," because feeling may be viewed in a way that allies it more closely to the unconscious. However, that poses a question. Feeling is a phenomenon also related to the sphere of consciousness; at least, that is conceivable.[8] At any rate, feeling is not the definitive basis of community—no more, in any event, than is thinking. If one objects that the term, "consciousness of community," involves the risk of maintaining that society is emergent rather than community, then the argument against [focusing on] "feelings of community" is that one again has not placed community in its true perspective, for it will consequently be confused with communion.

Experiential feeling, at least the experienced feelings that we recognize as proceeding from the sphere of consciousness—if there are similar kinds of psychic events in the conscious as in the unconscious—is just as insignificant for community as cognitive experience. Indeed, such feelings are rare and, as a rule, emerge only in antagonism and crisis. Yet when some danger threatens a community, the response may be only the assumption of defensive measures without further ado. Even when the common life of the community is quite profoundly shaken, as we say (and as we say justly), it may often have an effect only on the unconscious, which then will slowly have to adjust; at least this will be the case if the total event is not wholly unexpected or too much in conflict with the legitimate order. Otherwise, how is it that the peasant, upon the death of his nearest community-associate, if that associate had been well along in years or ill for a long time, perceives (consciously experiences) little more than that he performs the duties to which he is obliged? On the other hand, such situations provide an opportunity for feelings to appear; for example, when the causes or bases are suddenly apprehended or the legitimate order is grossly transgressed. This is particularly the case when the dangerous situation is only threatening and when there is a chance that it can be met or evaded.

If there is absolute trauma for those bound to the community, they will surrender themselves to destiny, and thought is extinguished by emotion and total devotion. Unrestricted affect is unleashed, often in an overwhelming flood. Moreover, it is directed toward the intruder and is of a negative quality, since even in the case of success, wrath, fury, hate, and triumphant feelings are elicited; just as, in defeat, chagrin, rage, bitterness, then grief, and finally, melancholy and regret follow closely upon one another. Much more rarely, in such cases, are positive feelings directed toward the community. These are also reactions to disturbances, particularly when they have been overcome (both in triumph and defeat), or they may be reactions to the mere appearance of a foreigner. Disturbances may also arise from within, as is the case when the young demand passionately to leave the household. Regarding such demands as uncalled for, the father will say, "Here you are, and here you will remain. You belong here." That one belongs inside the group is, again, all that one knows. There is not much feeling of community.

Children's love, even parental love, and finally the love of brother for sister are, for the most part, no more than empty expressions or superficial pretenses that are nourished by the spirit of the communion. We may "belong together" and are usually bound together in a solid, inseparable manner, but one need not feel or think it. Be that as it may, there may be a sudden display of tenderness, happiness, or pride that is positive and oriented toward the community. Still, only in rare instances is such a relationship built entirely on positive grounds and devoid of negative bases. But it is characteristic of the peasant (who can often be used as the typical case of the man firmly bound to a community) to become uneasy at the display of emotions. They are strange to him, just as (although for opposite reasons) they are to the man of community who regards them as irrational and beyond his ken; the former avoids them as phenomena of an all too independent consciousness.

The impoverishment and bitterness of the peasant's life is often mentioned. Moreover, even love for nature is denied him. This notion is now certainly questioned. It has been demonstrated that the peasant merely chooses not to discuss the feeling he has for nature. Actually the peasant only very rarely has the very same thing as a genuinely experienced condition of consciousness. It is not that he is totally unaware of it, but that his conscious experience of such feeling bears no relation to the compact community in which he is unconsciously joined with nature. It is odd that one with such knowledge at his disposal should regard community as it is represented among the rural peasantry, as having been built upon an emotion. It is a sentimentalization of rural life into which the urbanite frequently lapses. History records such idylls as occurring in many periods and in diverse forms. They arise out of the anonymity and isolation of the condition of society and the expression of a desire for a communal belonging that now embraces the rural peasantry and the community, seen as a counterpart of communion just as is "nature." Yet these idylls are directed toward neither a community nor a part of nature, nor do they comprehend the communion.

There are many forms of such sentimentality. One variety is represented in much of the contemporary yearning for community—this yearning is not false (although it is romantic). Even Tönnies made some contribution to it. He empathized with the essence of community so much that we owe entirely to him the permanent acceptance if this conception (the notion of the natural organic bond whose paradigm is the family of the rural peasant). He certainly recognizes disturbances, because "quarrels and controversies must occur in almost every social relationship, because prolonged proximity and frequent contact mean mutual extension and affirmation, as well as mutual restraint and negation—real possibilities and probabilities to a certain degree." Yet he maintains that "only as long as these phenomena predominate, can a relationship be called a genuine community."⁹

Everyone knows that it is not a rare occurrence for two rural neighbors to become mortal enemies when a boundary line is disputed, just as two brothers may become mortal enemies when an inheritance is challenged. What meaning does the lawsuit have for the rural peasantry! Despite this, neighbors and brothers always remain "neighbors" and "brothers." Neighborliness and brotherhood also persist psychically. This relationship is a condition both underlying and transcending hatred, but also being altered in turn. In this kind of relationship, there is certainly something unnatural, though the community as such is not dissolved. Those who oppose one another are not merely enemies. There is probably no better example anywhere to demonstrate how minor a role feelings play as a basis of community.

These observations may suggest that feelings are viewed as belonging to deeper strata of the soul—as being nearer the unconscious—than, for example, thought. Among many contemporaries, feeling (or at least the word, "feeling," and also many varieties of feeling) has understandably lost favor. In essence, however, this has occurred because of the frequent recognition of disguised feelings. A turn of phrase demonstrates this. Emotional functions of the psyche are still considered as very central. Maybe this is fine. Moreover, so-called peripheral thinking originates basically in the unconscious, from which it receives its essential guidance and stimulation, its process, and also the selection and the first arrangement of its content. However, the emotions can only be assessed as psychically more primary because they are seen to be nourished more exclusively by the unconscious. To disregard the parallel: Feeling has its basis in the unconscious (no less than thinking), and emerges or is thrust up from the unconscious. Character and ability are decisive and determinant for the frequency, mode, abundance or emptiness, and possibly other facets of feeling.

Now it is precisely in this context that the fundamental incompatibility between community and communion is to be found. As little as the community owes its psychic reality or even its basis to feelings of whatever kind, its members will experience feelings, especially feelings related to community, such as tender affection for their fellows or for the community as such, joy in the knowledge that they belong, or pride. But the community owes neither its reality nor its basis to these feelings. They are forms of conscious, recognizable aspects of that community, which is really a relationship constituted in the unconscious. Similarly, even if feelings of community were less (relatively) rare and if they were the only experienced index of community, the community itself, as an organic and natural bond, and hence a simple belonging together, would already be present prior to feelings of or about the relationship. They are only expressions subsequently emerging into the sphere of consciousness. They are products or offspring of the already existent, rather than the developing form of, community. And this is said from the point of view not only of interpretive psychology, but also of phenomenology, most appropriate to the analysis of those feelings. Observation of every genuine feeling of community reveals this: At the most, there is implicit a kind of gratitude—gratitude (necessarily) for concessions and grants already present in the relationship. Tender affection, happiness, and pride burst forth from a background of ownership. Moreover, in every other form of feeling found in a community and with regard to those positive or negative ones oriented toward community, their form is based on preexistent conditions, is aware of preexistent conditions, or knows them to be underlying the feelings in question. If one seeks narrowly to relate the reality of community exclusively to the feelings that can be seen to attach to it, then those very feelings are directed toward the basis of community which precedes them.

THE SOCIOLOGY OF COMMUNION

In the case of the communion, it is a radically different thing. Emotional experiences are constitutive in the case of the communion. They are its bases. The jubilant followers who crowd around their leader, chosen in an inspired flood of passionate feeling, do not intend (at least, their feelings do not "mean") to be bound up with

him and with one another on a naturally common basis. They are
bound together by the actually experienced feelings, or at least are
motivated by those affective conditions. However, each one is also
en rapport because of his situation, his character, or whatever kind
of "disposition" is situated in the unconscious. Beyond a doubt, the
budding shoot of the unconscious, when it is not really or at least
not always a direct offshoot, establishes an emotional potential or
at least an emotional set. However, no matter how much the momentary unconscious presumably presupposes each emotion, it does
not contain the conditions of the communion. There are feelings
that have their potential in the unconscious, and it is precisely because of this, because there is a potential in the unconscious, that
an individual is enabled to enter into a communion. Yet the communion is established above the level of unconsciousness. The stuff
of which it is made, the basis of its sustenance, are the actual conscious experiences of feeling.

From another point of view, it may seem that we are laying ourselves open to argument by asserting that feelings are the essential
basis of the communion. What is said to hold together a religious
body is not the feeling of individuals, but the deity they worship.
Without a doubt, the element to which the religious feeling is primarily directed is not the group (or a member, or a collection of
members of the group), but the mystery of spiritual power. But
this mysterious spiritual power, when felt, must be accepted in a
religious spirit so that religion and, above all, a social relationship
can originate. And insofar as the group is "in communion"—which
it is, in the primary stage of religion, as has been demonstrated
earlier—it will be feelings that bind the group together. There
definitely is a "felt" deity, if not a deity. What fosters the counter-
argument is the defense against the fear that religion may merge
completely into the subjective realm. One opposes the discussion
of religious feelings. Feelings have come to be traditionally regarded as merely subjective phenomena. Yet that is wholly false.
Feelings can be intentionally directed, as feelings, toward an object[10] (whether or not anything is decided concerning the existence
or nonexistence of the object). And the primary religious feelings
are intentional. Ultimately, we cannot help but recognize the neces-

sity for the mystery of spiritual power, if religion is to originate, to persist in union with men, and to be experienced by men. (That "experience" is also viewed with aversion, arising understandably out of concern for subjectivity.) The psychic "organs" with which men accomplish this religious relation are, specifically, feelings, whereby purposeful intentionality must be underscored. For the religious, not feelings, but rather the object of these feelings is important. The same sort of thing must be noted by the philosopher of religion, who should be advised to stress a cognitive recognition of religious feelings. The sociologist, not to mention the psychologist, would be guilty of great error in his investigations if he were to exclude religious feelings from his area of inquiry as being nonexistent, or if he failed to notice or observe them as something different from what they apparently are because their "material" is psychic in content. If psychic phenomena were to be scrutinized in an attempt to establish the basis of community, and if they were found to be only unconscious psychic phenomena, pure psychic phenomena could still be the basis of the communion. However, the psychic phenomena related to the rise of religious events are not to be construed sociologically as deities, but as phenomena whose (presumed or actual) reality is psychic, that is, "objectively psychic," in the sense of psychic phenomena as objects of study. If the sociologist is concerned with the study of religion, he is also concerned with the subjective side of life. It may be seen, by the conception of an original religious experience as bursting forth from a "psychically real" god into the souls of men, that God also has a subjectively psychic existence, and this is certainly of concern to the sociologist. I leave this aside. To avoid complications, I will henceforth restrict myself only to the discussion of earthly social relationships. Most important, the general picture would not be changed by the references made here. The basic social relationship to a deity is a communion.

The sociology of the communion can in any case benefit positively from the study of the intentionality of primary religious feelings. Earlier I represented the social emergence of fundamental religious events in this way: that the soul, in the case of the most central religious experience, is altogether lonesome, "alone with its god," and that it is not joined with others in an earlier religious relationship even after it returns from that experience with be-dazzled eyes. In any case, the soul is in such a state of fascination that what now emerges as a social phenomenon can only begin as a communion. (Originally, this was the same in the odd cases of Calvinist and Jesuit religious experience.) It is not always neces-sary that the social emergence of developing religiosity occur in two successive steps. Together with the lonesomeness of the soul in its ultimate conversion to God, there is very frequently a sense of closeness, a "side feeling" experienced by one who is immersed in the presence of others. Often he is transfixed in a realm of emo-tion, if not drowned in a sea of emotion deriving from his associa-tion with others. Many times the individual is transported only by the tumultuous surging of a large throng, although ultimately he has to leave these exalting forces behind. I have also referred to these phenomena earlier. In this case, mundane social conditions take on a logically secondary position in the core of fundamental religiosity. But insofar as they are there, feelings form a basic con-dition of the communion, and the communion is constituted solely by them.

What the sociology of the communion has to learn here is that the basic feelings of the communion need not directly comprehend its members. The youths who cluster around some high ideal held in common are "fired up" in a communion, even if they do not de-liberately turn to one another. In a diffuse way there is a felt con-sciousness of those feelings of solidarity. Similarly, friends will embrace one another with inspired affection, just as will those of a common religious faith.

COMMUNITY AND COMMUNION COMPARED

At this point one could renew an earlier objection with increased forcefulness. In the case of community, the feelings of community that are occasionally found there should make reference to the pre-ceding facts of community as their constituency. The religious com-munion rests upon its makers' collective conception of God. He is, then, a "condition." He is a thing to which new feelings must adjust as being recognizably "there," if the religiosity is to become social. This is assumed to occur in two successive steps. But, if the given is not psychic and in any case not social, then "god" is a "given condition." Insofar as he is a given condition, there certainly must be a "felt god" in the formative stages of religiosity. That feeling is thus always present. Likewise, that psychic fact is always manifest. In that case—at least to begin with, I will have to present it in such an unambiguous, arbitrary manner—the condition is never (mundanely) social. Those to whom the experience of God is "given," individually in the beginning, will not be emotionally bound together by that first religious experience. The communion emerges among them as soon as those confronting each other after being "touched" perceive the common bent of their feelings and excite one another on this basis. The communion does not emerge before this instant. It emerges out of a new feeling that is now a communion of feeling, now social for the first time.

As far as community is concerned, I had to emphasize the contrast. The community is already there when it is manifestly felt, that is, when feelings of community appear. Not only are the requisites for the potential conscious experience of association already there, but the community itself is already there. As opposed to this, the communion is established through the actual cognitive experience of communion feeling. Now it is not clear whether this communion feeling has occurred as a simultaneous (if only concomitant) event of the central religious feeling, or as a successive act. There is another possibility, namely, that the common character of the religious feeling, which was at first presumed to be dispersed among individuals although even then it was a parallel experience, may not have been only a mere correspondence, as we say, but also something social. It is this indeed. But then the social is also a given. By the coincidence of initially separate emotions and the certainty of their union, which is presented even here as being at hand, and by the allegedly simple correspondence as a preexisting social constituent of the act, the social character of the event is presumed or preexistent. In this view, the social phenomenon is not representative of a communion, but of a community. There must be other manifestations of community, in terms of which it is often difficult to differentiate the communion, but on the basis of which one can know that the initial conditions are purely correspondences, and that the community is created at first by acknowledging them. Through this it has only become observable. Community "appears."

Citizens meeting one another in a foreign land do not have to establish a communion first. They greet one another as such, because they already "belong together." It can be the same in the case of persons belonging to the same religious faith. Of course, this is more often the case among established religions. The more or less ecstatic and orgiastic character of fundamentalist religions (in their inchoate phases) provides us with a historical example which demonstrates, as well as any example can, that, at a meeting of members of the faith who are not yet known to one another and in the interest of their already existent union (which is, therefore, a community as such), the opportunity will be seized to permit quite another communion to emerge on the basis of the community-like sense of belonging together already at hand. Understandably then, one can be in a community and, in addition, because it is something different and new, become deeply involved in a communion with a few members (or with all the members, or with the community itself). This is a point to which I shall return. Moreover, brothers can be close friends, even though a basic conflict between the different social images they have of each other may interfere. Only where, as in the case of a recently established religion, the communitylike sense of belonging together is not deeply rooted, will there be even greater opportunities for a communion to spring up on that basis, i.e., on the basis of reviving a fundamental religious feeling that is still glowing. Be that as it may—and one may recognize on that basis the radical difference between the community and the communion, if the latter is built on the basis of a community already at hand—it is conceivable that very mature men, who meet one another as members of the same recently established religion and, as such, become acquainted, may sometimes permit only the community at hand to assume any reality; since their behavior is oriented exclusively to the fact of such union, a communion is not formed. The orientation of behavior toward the community may occur consciously in that case, but more often it takes place in the unconscious and emerges out of the unconscious. This is all the more true if the sensation of the unconscious is dependent on the cognitive recognition of this relationship. Then the unconscious orientation of self to the community is a response such that a direct bond is imagined to exist on the basis of analogous modifications of the unconscious—I say "imagined" with complete justification. It becomes all the more complete the more the conditions of the community present in the unconscious are there naturally. An intrusion upon the unconscious and its subsequent alteration ought to have occurred during such great experiences as those of primary religiosity. Nevertheless, there is a greater likelihood that the basic core emotions of religiosity will have been reawakened, and in that event a communion will develop. In any case, a social bond is established through the actual cognitive experience of an emotional state.

However, with the observation that every experience of communion may become a cause to form a community because of the fact that the unconscious is simultaneously modified through that experience, another side of the argument appears. These phenomena as such produce no difficulties at all. But they do give us reason to recall that the communion can be welded together in the emotions whose central attitude is not directed toward communion members but toward some kind of god or some other kind of external manifestation. In that case, the feelings on which the communion has been formed should emerge only as collateral feelings. I have even maintained that they may be characterized only as diffuse, hollow residues. One could, moreover, regard these events as unconscious phenomena. They are not. They are conscious experiences deviating in a certain way from the relevant core experiences. Also, here the difference between community and communion is absolute. Advocates of the communion could now claim that the members of any religious sect who are passionately devoted to one another enter into that relationship unconditionally and unconsciously, with their innermost essence and being. In point of fact, a merely superficial emotional upheaval, since there are also central and peripheral layers of consciousness, produces a merely superficial communion, although it is still a communion. Such superficiality, moreover, even though there are other reasons, may eventuate in the fact that the emotions are not rooted so deeply in the unconscious, or at any rate may produce the result that they have inconsequential effects on the deep core of the unconscious. This is so because, beyond all doubt, the emotions are expressed in the latter way and are manifested in terms of their depth. The communion will be the more heartfelt and sincere, the more the formative feelings affect the unconscious. In addition, the conscious experience of the feelings is primary to the extent that such emotions, in turn, inflame the unconscious (also if they are potentially rooted in the unconscious).

Only feelings constitute the communion. However, these effects on the unconscious give rise to community along with the communion. Yet it does follow from this that the deeply rooted communion, or the communion insofar as it is more deeply entrenched, must resemble a community at the same time. This will always be the case—or rather, could be the case—should one disregard communion. In any event, it could become the case to as great an extent as is possible. Nevertheless, this possibility is limited. Because the impulses of the unconscious manifest as feelings may actually unearth deeply rooted emotions, only in such a case can they give rise to deeply rooted communion. They are only impulses of the unconscious and not outgrowths of it. Such impulses tend to break out again and again into actual feelings and can become equally as important as the feelings themselves. Even when these impulses are dormant—one can also say extinguished—they may become "outgrowths," and a basis for community is established. Herein is the real reason why, in the case of new religions, there is a greater probability that a communion will be established upon subsequent encounters of those who were originally separately excited than that a pure community will arise. When I said a short time ago that mutual belonging is not so deeply rooted in the unconscious, but is only exhibited as an unconscious impulse, I did not mean to say that such impulses cannot penetrate deeply. The advocates of communion should not fail to understand that the community established as an outgrowth of the unconscious manifests the characteristic of depth at the very time it has arrived at a position of (relative) rest—certainly at a position of permanence. In that case, it has taken a course which the communion and its advocates usually do not prefer. This touches upon a theme that I can treat better in another context.

Here some agreement should have been reached upon a mattter that was admittedly passed over earlier. Now the matter may be easily resolved. I have stressed that the central formative sentiments of the communion may be focused upon a god, a hero, a master, or a high ideal, if they also embrace at that time the members of the communion. Both are surely bound together when the object of the emotion is a community. That is also possible, whether one is himself a part of the community or is not. I spoke earlier of community feelings, which of course are not essential to the community, but which sometimes flourish there, and then, as I said before, become the more conscious forms of community. They allude to these feelings gratefully (also with the corresponding negatives), just as they do to those that are already present. Although this is so genuine and basic, something new is established at the same time. Those experiencing this feeling are joined with the community as such, which is already existent, and they also join in a communion relationship (with the community itself or with its separate members). In this connection, the latent basis of the profound conflict between community and communion may be found in the fact that those who have grown up in a community easily come to mistrust such communions, while the advocates of communion come to prefer that relationship to the community. Perhaps it is also noteworthy that the communion may be proposed to a community by someone who is not part of the community. This is often the case in much of the contemporary yearning for community in which, instead of a yearning for a particular community, there is a diffuse yearning for community-in-general. Sometimes entering into a truly unique generality is yearned for, not to mention the fact that this imposes a false meaning upon the word "community." However, when it is understood correctly, it may be seen that most of those who think in this way would not be able to endure a full and exclusive realization of their wishes. As men with a severely curtailed consciousness, particularly consciousness of feelings, they would be incapable from the outset of realizing anything from the community.

In the context of the closely related contingencies of community and communion lies the further problem that previously obscured the sharp distinction between those radically different social units. This must be allowed to dissolve. We "feel that we are attracted to someone," "feel akin," "bound together by some secret bond." Is that basically different from feeling the genuine ties of blood, or is it merely a matter of degree? In any case, it does not at all appear to be community. It is communion. Now, whenever one feels sympathy, the decisive condition of the communion has been realized. Is it not different, when one feels blood-ties? Inasmuch as they are steeped in true feelings, there is not only a true ongoing community, but also a communion has been formed. But we have a difference. The feelings that emerge out of the context of blood relationships "feel" the organic, natural, ongoing community, and this dominates the situation. These feelings are relatively meaningless. Whoever feels drawn to someone, feels at the same time a given conciliation and thus a community. But he may take this opportunity to permit a communion to emerge in the situation. Not the community that is there but the communion that is emerging becomes the major point here. As always, there may be marginal cases where the opposite also holds. "Sympathic communities," which are almost unnoticed and scarcely felt, may manifest themselves only in concrete conduct. They are then only gradually different in conduct from blood relationships. However, the fundamental isolation of the classes is not impaired.

These last remarks may appear trite to many readers. The well-intentioned ones have probably protested against my repeated assertion of the absolute difference between community and communion as impractical in reality. True differences might be there. They may also be so profound that it is essential to differentiate the concepts ideally and radically. But that was only the business of terms. Theirs is the burden of proof. Of course, they must square with experience. But experience would also show that ideal distinctions could provide merely secondary and auxiliary aids for clarifying reality in response to our cognitive needs. In truth, ideal distinctions were always and are everywhere mixed with experience—true reality. One should not press these artificial distinctions to the extent that he no longer recognizes subtleties of meaning. The demand for exclusive distinctions ("either-or-ness") would also require an inadmissable "scholastic" conception of reality.

There is one general, if brief, answer to such a general protest. This necessitates turning once more to that great notion—the Platonic ideal, the Eidos—which was rediscovered by a new philosophy associated predominantly with the name of Edmund Husserl. This is not the place to embark upon the logical demonstration of these claims. But classifications, as they are truly called although with a misleading and overcharged expression, are by no means only accidental auxiliary devices for the fortuitous ordering of reality. Nor are they to be viewed apart from that experience, which would deny them any recognition. But here the fundamental differences are revealed in the pure eidetic sphere. Reality can obey (again a distorted word) without question nothing other than these types. It is indeed true that we cannot always easily recognize their exact boundaries in empirical reality, but to treat them as subtle differences is only permitted, in a sense, where they are ideally acknowledged.

SOCIETY, COMMUNITY, AND COMMUNION

I have attempted—I hope that justification of the related method will be spared me here—to distinguish between two great types of social phenomena, community and communion, because of their customary confusion, and I have indicated the exact point where their radical differences arise. The distinction becomes more important, and perhaps more clear for many, when I place the two categories together with a third that belongs here—society. When all three fundamental sociological categories are considered together, it can be demonstrated with full penetrating force that the principal difference between community and communion is not of less consequence, but of exactly the same consequence as the difference between those two concepts and society. I want to observe particularly the general justification for their interrelatedness after the phenomenon itself has been distinguished and after the delimitation of the society's distinguishing character has, in the main, been accomplished. This look permits the assertion that I am restricting myself deliberately here to undisciplined allusions.

As opposed to community, society derives its central character from the fact that the individual is prior to the relationship. The bond is merely subsequent, while in the community the members find themselves in the organic whole from the start. It may well be known that there never is and never can be that independence of the detached individual which has primacy in the society. The society is a concrete relational form that presupposes the actual separateness of individuals. They can do nothing other than enter into relationships. And these are only possibilities (necessities at the most), which, above all, will be realized as secondary situations. The old antithesis between the priority of the whole and the priority of the part is what basically differentiates community from society. Together with this contrast, a further qualification must be made with reference to both categories. The concrete separateness of the individual is maintained in the society. Individuals who enter into these relationships, and by so doing recognize the possibility of and even the necessity from the outset of joining associations, realize this. As frequently as they do join associations, they remain essentially separate. There remains some distance between them that may be shortened only by single links, i.e., relationships. These remain clearly visible at a glance and consequently rational, just as the wholeness of the society relationship is only relational. The ethos of cool reservation is the spirit that inspires society.

The members of every community are originally united with one another; the parts of society are essentially separated from one another. The comrades of communion have nothing at all to do with one another in the beginning. The communion is originally established when they meet each other (also after a community has already been established). The experiences that give rise to communion are individual experiences. While it appears here that the communion is closer to society, it approaches community after it has been established. The friend is an alter ego. We feel his joy and his sorrow as our own. The weakening of such a communion stirs up our very souls. Indeed one cannot speak of coalescence; one should call it fusion—perhaps a more intense statement. Certainly it appears in different degrees. Still, actual separation completely vanishes in the communion.

In this view, if the communion may be placed somewhere in the middle between community and society, it may be placed over and against both from another point of view, so that they belong together when opposed to the communion. In any case, one can establish a sequence from society to community to communion, just as one can also establish a sequence from community to society to communion (naturally, both may be reversed).

It is characteristic of the society that the relationships of which it consists have their basis in the *Do ut des*.[11] Every action generally takes place on behalf of some counteraction and in the expectation of such. The contract has a representative significance here. The contract is basically foreign to community. The members of a family are not bound to one another merely by contract. The contract is here a variety or, from another point of view, a subcategory. In any case, it can thenceforth control the consciousness. Thus the "thinking" of the peasant—no one will doubt that it is only "thinking"—takes place specifically in the manner of *Do ut des*. Nothing is more foreign to the communion than to think in such a manner. Absolute surrender, sacrifice, ceaseless and unremitting concessions, not only of goods but of the self, are demanded and maintained, at least in extreme cases; other cases are only slightly and gradually distinguished from these.

In addition to the relationship of the part or the link of a member to the whole, just as the contract is characteristic of the society, so is enduring association characteristic of the community. The bonds of community are by nature such that they endure. They are constituted as enduring. They may be loosened with time, but that changes nothing of their original intrinsic tendency to endure. Moreover, only the simplest and totally external suggestion is needed to revive the ostensibly exhausted community. In contrast, society relations are always placed upon a momentary, fixed, and solitary basis. As soon as the business is settled, the individuals concerned go their separate ways. But the tasks, the reasons why individuals came together, are recurrent. If no barrier intervenes, they may desire to resume once more their previously established relationship. This can ultimately assume a certain aspect of duration, although the bond is always established on the basis of separate acts. However, some external basis is necessary to thwart this secondary endurance.

Instability from within is ultimately symptomatic of the communion. As long as it persists, it persists only in separate discrete acts and never outside those acts. Therein lies the basis of our contention: not coalescence but surely—or at least—fusion. Yet the more or less ecstatic flood of emotion that sustains the communion and in which it survives is, by its very nature, a fleeting thing. It may, to be sure, well up deep within our souls. It may be capable of canceling out humanity completely and of driving us into madness or death. But it is not enduring. The delirium passes. The affections of consciousness become pale and are supplanted by other things.

All these fundamental modes of differentiating community, society, and communion, as may easily be seen (although I may have omitted detailed proof here), flow directly from the qualities that constitute the central essences of each category. The differences are explained legitimately in diverse ways. As soon as new questions are formulated, new foci of investigations will be disclosed.

Even so, not only because of empirical realities, but also because it is necessarily evident, communion always shows a tendency to become transformed into community or society. The reason for this is the last-mentioned attribute of the communion, instability, which is fatal to it again and again. A phrase that was once viewed humorously in the past may have the same effect here by expressing the inner contradiction, as we say, of communion, and also the remedy one applies to the contradiction. It is the vow of eternal love. On the one hand, as a vow, it applies the mainsprings of a societylike social organization or content; on the other, when it expresses a degree of intensity through a word that implies endurance, it lays claim to possession by the world of community. In this way, it counteracts both in its true meaning.

Historical Transformations of Fidelity and Substantive Forms

Universally, the communion attempts to overcome its intrinsic instability by fostering an acceptance of the ethos of fidelity, thereby adopting in reality part of the ethos of society and part of the ethos of community. The meaning of fidelity in the old Germanic system of knighthood is noteworthy, one of the most outstanding examples of communion relationships. (It is by no means solely Germanic, nor even characteristic of the German tribes, as the historians—not to speak of others who have their private motives—would have us believe, but a pervasive form found in every corresponding type of culture.) In those eras, where sociality is so unusually defined as a phenomenon of the communion, an enhanced valuation of fidelity is needed to provide solidarity in such relationships. Today this may be seen in every segment of the population in that most powerful communion of our times (how and to what extent it is a communion will be seen later): Every marriage has instituted a solemn oath of fidelity, sworn before everyone. As a complete institution and as an arrangement of monogamy and patrimony, marriage has succeeded historically, first of all because a dutiful fidelity was recognized as binding. Moreover, religion actually imposed this. Children already grown into the community of religion, when they enter an adolescence distinguished by desires for communion, are expected not only to enter into a communion relationship with their inherited ascribed religion, but to promise fidelity (confirmation). The religious association is of course primarily a communion, but it also runs all the risks of a communion.

Fidelity, therefore, is actually and precisely to be understood as a substitute for love, as Simmel has so appropriately observed. As long as one loves, he need not necessarily be faithful. Love is its own guarantee. Through fidelity and its pledge, love becomes a communion that is based upon the actual, conscious experience of that emotion and endures in it, partially transformed into community and partially permeated with the marks of societylike social organization.

Fidelity is also significant in the society. Thus, fidelity to the contract is plainly the virtue of society. Contracts that are concluded after long delays require a guarantee that the parties who entered into the contract freely and of their own accord, thereby limiting their freedom, will not abrogate their obligations. The original form of the contract is the promise. That is to say, the abstract promise, the general promise, is truly a pledge of fidelity. Every promise avows fidelity, namely, to be faithful to what has been promised. The general pledge of fidelity is merely a promise with no specific content, or better, without a single, avowed content (this certainly bespeaks a spirit approximating that of communion). Only persons who are substantially free, unhindered, and not involved in irrational ties with others can conclude contracts and make promises. Otherwise they would be led into incalculable conflicts, since the one who stands upon such agreements himself ought to expect that a man detached from all irrational commitments would promise and contract nothing unless he were in a position to fulfill it in the light of other agreements, all of which must be calculable. Only those persons who remain substantially free, who have not subsequently been subdued by any of those mysterious powers of irrational factors (who have disregarded higher authority for such requirements), can make promises and guarantee contracts. The bonds in which they are voluntarily joined must have some foreseeable duration; from that point, they are merely relations. One is amazed at the manner in which fidelity already has a societylike character.

In periods of prevailing societylike social structure, this [fidelity] is a matter of course. And only where it is a matter of course can all the related sociality take on the character of society. We are accustomed to speak only of such conditions of society. Thus it is important, insofar as we wish to examine these central sociological categories meticulously, to examine their vestiges in every cultural manifestation. It would seem that an approximation of society is to be found in all economic and legal transactions, but principally in all such things that are basic structures and firmly cemented; those things that have not only become autarchical but ordered, whether in communities or communions. In these cases, the forms of society require special guarantees against the influence of irrational factors, and also guarantees that they can rid individuals of them. In such a way, people are enabled to enter into commitments in a truly liberal and lasting manner. Hence the extensive pomp, the ceremony with which all legal and even economic affairs were endowed in earlier times. Yet even in these instances, societylike forms are twisted into communitylike forms. Mankind is not so far developed that the forms of society are accepted in and by themselves. People are not free to the extent that they are totally independent of irrational factors. So one surrounds legal and even economic transactions with a special dignity that impresses them upon the memory and makes them appear to the participants as forms of community. The communion is similarly transformed, through the vehicle of the oath with which comrades pledge loyalty to one another, on the one hand, into a society, and on the other, into a community. Among these forms one finds some that show this with enhanced clarity. Now comrades seal blood communions by drinking a few drops of one another's blood, and presume to establish a community as cohesive as blood bonds. Up to the final weakening, the name, "brother" (communion brother), is the designation par excellence that binds comrades to the communion.

Wherever communions endure for long or should endure, they take on, partly intrinsically and partly intentionally, the character of society on the one hand and community on the other. That is specifically the case in religions, the culminations of communion relations. The history of Christianity provides an outstanding example. To become stationary [permanent] it had to become statutory, just as every club develops a set of formal rules, which are hardly needed for an outing (nor can anything happen beyond that moment without agreement). The institutions of a religion certainly have an originally religious meaning. Yet they maintain themselves socially, establishing a society at the same time, and running the risk of spiritless stagnation. Moreover, the regimented arrangements of Rome in connection with the Catholic Church were established right from the beginning. But all this was transformed, because of the enduring and matter-of-course character it assumed, into factors that establish community. This is especially the case for later generations for whom the structured association is a given, grown into the unconscious. In infant baptism, the transformation of the religious communion into a religious community is an exclusive and special expressive symbol.

Again and again, religion takes care to recollect that neither society nor community, but the communion, is the sole suitable association for its basic nature. Again and again, Christianity extols love in place of the reasonable, measured, societylike relations of mankind. Again and again, genuine religious people will not become immersed in community. This is the social meaning, tightly bound up with the religious meaning, of enforced celibacy for the priests and priestesses and, in Catholicism, for the monastic orders.

The way in which the nature of the communion is basically at variance with that of society and that of community is made most evident by the example of Christianity. In such things may be found the essential sociological difference between church and sect. The sect is the social form in which, over and over again, the source of religious communion is awakened in individual emotional experience, so that the diffuse self-evidence of community, like the clever coolness of society, is burned up by seething emotion. Love communion and adult baptism are symptomatic precisely of this. And just as the source of religion, in its social aspect, is communionlike, so is it necessary again and again to achieve religious renewal through sectarian movements. As is always the case, the diffuseness of the sect gains its configuration only through elements of society, and it always persists in an enduring pattern as community. The theological and philosophical meaning of "original" religion should not be equated here with "empirical" religion. In every respect, I would like to repudiate any intention of making value judgments.

The communion, when contrasted with fidelity, occasionally suggests its own true nature. Fidelity is then called "mere" fidelity and "cold" fidelity. Indeed, on the basis of these menacing dangers of community and society, the communion can feel so strongly antagonistic that it extols its own weakness of instability as a countermeasure, and in any case accepts it consciously. It may also be considered proper, as an extreme communionlike tactic, always to remain open to the formation of eternal communions. The antipathy of some artists to the humdrum existence of the petite bourgoisie and the heartlessness of the grande bourgoisie is symptomatic of the communion mentality. They charge that community manifests a remote and superficial provincialism, and existence in it, a sham. They charge that society is computerized modernization. The consequence is that the uncertainty, vagueness, and stability of the existence of the communion is imbued by them with positive value, although the communion may seem remote in the light of new, beckoning adventures, new, seductive inspirations, and consequently, new, impassioned communions of love and friendship.

The categories community, society, and communion are essential to the systematic development of sociology, above all because they are universal and modal categories. They are not classes of, so to speak, substantive social forms, such as the peasantry, the bourgeoisie, the aristocracy, or the family and the clan. They are rather modes, styles of existence in which, above all, each substantive form can exist as this, that, or the other.

This does not hold without qualification. Many specific substantive social forms, as I have asserted was the case with early religious associations in the context of communion, at least manifest a certain affinity for one, the other, or the third of these modalities. Thus, legal and economic relations essentially manifest a societylike character, which is seldom expressed in feudal and small-town situations or among friends, lovers, and religious associations, since the opposing conditions preponderate, and this character stands first and foremost in the determination of such units as economic and legal associations. The economic and legal structures are used only as means in a secondary, superficial way. Moreover, it is not unusual in such units that they experience conflict with these alien structures. In contrast, the family tends essentially toward community. Occasionally a family appears that has the aspect of a communion and seems "moved" and "exalted." Organically growing families, which have no sympathy for the unusual ethos of the communion, regard such instances as contrived and false. Such cases seem odd to them, and comic at best. But in families whose members relate to one another distantly in the style of society, genuine family cohesion seems to be lacking. In the case of such controversies as those involving inheritance, which could efficaciously be placed before a court of justice for an essential and unambiguous decision, they will consider such a move as more of a profound family disturbance than quarrels lasting for years. Like the family, the status groups of farmers or the petite bourgoisie tend to be organized along community lines.

As far as communion is concerned, I have designated original religious associations as having a special affinity to such a mode. Perhaps I could have substituted the association of warriors or the cameraderie of the military. However, the simplest pattern of the communion is friendship, just as legal and economic relationships are critical instances of society, and the family, of community. Even so, there are occupational friendships in which goodwill and sincere affection are blended. But the occupational and political links are always basic. The term "friendship" always seems misused in the case of these associations. Genuine friendships stem from long and abundant contacts in community. Nor are these associations devoid of distress. Occasional separations are recommended. But if it is apparent, upon meeting again, that the community only—not the friendship—lives on, one becomes sad and disappointed.

All these examples should show how substantive social forms are neutral toward the three modalities within certain limits and how, in spite of this, many of them have a special affinity for one, the other, or the third of these fundamental sociological categories. But these are fundamentally independent of one another. They are ideally and essentially independent. Essential analysis will show where medleys and passages of reality (in a certain sense, only seemingly so) appear. In any case, they will necessarily occur, just as I demonstrated was the case with communion with regard to its instability. Similarly, but in an opposite manner, pure community and pure society produce, at least among human beings, an effect that ultimately breaks out explosively in a desire for a communion. Thus, community empties into society, and society is transposed into community at the same time. At any rate, the three modal forms are reciprocally qualified by one another. Neither society nor communion is conceivable without at least supplementary, community-related bases, e.g., linguistic, customary, and epochal relationships, or whatever additional commonalities must be provided by nature, by means of which society or communion relationships are facilitated. And neither community nor communion can exist without society-related structural factors. Finally, community is built upon communion just as much as upon society.

I have designated these absolutely inevitable, original, legal, and economic relations as the earliest to entail a preliminary indication of the society mentality in the context of the community and the communion. However, I have also emphasized how they require built-in communitylike anchorages in order to become firmly established in such circumstances. I might also have been able to suggest earlier how they persist simultaneously through the sentiments of communion (for the most part, religious), the sentiments of ceremony and dignity which alone provide them with enhanced and impressive status. Meanwhile, wherever the specific society has become autarchical and has emerged as the paramount social structure of an era, the communion is its provenance. In that case, the society, in its culminating, pure form, by no means proceeds continuously out of an era of community. A specific ethos stands behind it. And that same ethos, wherever it is still original, requires a communion association. The rise of capitalism and the modern state also entailed heroic periods. Looting and military expeditions as well as religious inspirations have brought society into existence. Only when the ethos as ethos was slowly—again, not continuously —observed to be incompatible with the content of that ethos, did the true society gradually take form. And there still lives on in every enterprise much of the communion spirit.

Love, Marriage, and the Family

The case of community is no different. Its paradigmatic form, the family, has itself sprung up from conditions of the communion. I have said already that the monogamous patrimonial family, especially in its capacity as an institution, implies that it originated as a communion. Moreover, every contemporary family was formed out of such beginnings. At first the family is a marriage. New marriages are certainly not real marriages right away, and they are certainly not "families." Enduring childless marriages reveal a kind of incompleteness. With children, the couple really grows together. Nevertheless, the marriage is necessarily the beginning of the family. It was always naturally this way, and matriarchal law is no exception.

Marriage can, at the time of its consummation, be strongly communitylike. And it is always entered into in a more or less communitylike manner. The prospective spouses are courting only within relatively homogeneous social circles circumscribed by world and life perspectives—primarily modes of thought, customs, "connections," and the like. Just as in the case of individuals or even whole groups, and at times entire status groupings and strata (in such a case, on the basis of a powerful, living communion ethos among them) the sphere of potential choice may be displaced straightaway by preference to some remote and distant place, so that there is another kind of marginal case in which the clan alone predisposes two mates to one another. Yet in other respects, the demands and requirements appropriate to the status group are involved, just as are economic considerations, which are also only the surface manifestation of a community spirit. There are, nevertheless, marriages contracted in the pure form of society. These are entered into by means of professional intermediaries, newspaper advertisements, and the like. Yet they too must first grow together in terms of community to become proper marriages and mature families—indeed, to succeed at all. In any case, such a marriage conceals its origin and perceives something amiss in the relationship: a contradiction to the essence of the marriage and the family had been established. Community was missing.

This conflict, however, is also experienced when the marriage takes place exclusively on the basis of community, just as there seems to be something amiss in the marriage consummated as a pure artifact of society when the married pair does not find itself in communion. In every age, marriage based on romantic love has been valued as the true, more or less real, genuine ideal. Perhaps this is a misunderstanding that has risen through the propagation of communion spirit into areas where it really does not belong. At times youth thinks that marriage appears somewhat profane and prosaic in contrast to love and the related communion. In fact, there are indeed many experiences which demonstrate that love— "love" in its specific sense as an actual affective emotion—dies in marriage. It is at times painful to "love" because this can resist the transformation of the relationship into community. Love marriages do not always become "happy," because in day-to-day living together, marriage—even the family—is by necessity what it is: a naturally evolved community. Indeed, its characteristics presuppose the foregone conclusion. However, this is often the way feelings antagonistic to the ethos of the communion arise in the marriage: by the foregone conclusion, the everyday routine, the dullness and boredom of reciprocal relations. Even that which here appears in such a negative way has a positive value for community, whose obvious, certain cohesion means first of all productiveness and maturity.

Each conflict between communion and community in the marriage, and each recognition that the marriage—the core of the family—is a community like others and that only as a community can it have any relatively significant permanence, still do not permit reason to blink away the fact that the highest ideal of marriage in every age has been the communion, the love marriage. To be sure it was always known that community must emerge from it, and factors always used to be at hand for the establishment of such an association. However, the marriage that was a pure form of marital communion was always valued highly. Whoever tenaciously held on to that other attitude usually claimed that love was still the important element, and that usually meant—especially with respect to the preparation often experienced among young people —that love would "in due time" be awakened. Thus, even in the case of societylike marriage contracts, a final decision was withheld unless there was at least sympathy.

Here again is the place to recommend the third fundamental sociological category, the communion, for a place alongside community and society in the context of modern research. A reputable work of ethnological sociology, Heinrich Schurtz's book on age categories and male bonds [*Altersklassen und Männerbünde*][12] has correctly disclosed the category of communion.

Schurtz proceeded from the observation of empirical data. At the start, he was far removed from higher aspirations. What interested him, first of all, were the appearances of bachelor and male quarters, living establishments in which young unmarried men in primitive societies—this is at least the first import of the arrangement—would assemble for hunting and warfare, but above all for worship. They formed communions in this manner, with characteristic ways of life that were kept closely concealed from the outside world under penalty of sanctions. These were, therefore, secret societies from which all women and children were excluded. Married men did not, as a rule, take part. Occasionally, they had their own (although inadequate) male quarters. In such a way a man always lives, whether successively or concurrently, in two wholly disparate relationships: in the family, to which he belongs at least as a child, and again later, in his own communion. In between, he belongs to something else which without a doubt has that social character we have called communionlike in this essay. The arrangement, whether clearly or obscurely and with innumerable specifications, is found all over the face of the earth, not only among the primitives, but also among the rest of us, including lower class people whose diverse customs give evidence of this. This duality, which has been illustrated by Schurtz with many examples, even appears again and again among the bourgoisie.

From that point on, Schurtz arrives at the recognition of two basic forms of society. He recognized only two forms because he was as little acquainted with the actual society, in the narrower sense, as he was with its distinction from community. It seems that Schurtz never encountered the name of Tönnies. This brings into even greater prominence the fact that Schurtz perceived the dichotomy of community and communion in the relationship that Tönnies designated as community. Certainly, except for that, the main point of the difference has not been apprehended.

Schurtz regarded the battle between the sexes as the basis of the antithesis. So long as one knows only two fundamental sociological categories, this appears to be acceptable. Moreover, Tönnies conceived his dichotomy between society and community as one within which male and female were brought together. In the case of Schurtz, it is a different dichotomy, between community and communion (if I may introduce these terms at this time), which polarizes female and male.

This is so because women and maidens were first of all excluded from the male communion—just as was the case with children firmly bound to community. To be sure, they then make their own attempts to establish women's and maidens' communions. But they are unsuccessful with their feeble imitation. For woman, as Schurtz plausibly explains, sex is of predominant importance and pervades her entire social existence. Just as woman, by virtue of her sex, is intimately related to "Mother Nature," so, deduces Schurtz, is her social life predominantly of a community character. Since women bear and rear children, they provide indispensable protection for them during their first years of life. Moreover, Tönnies places this representation of community—relationship between mother and child—in the context of blood ties and permanence. Children, and ultimately fathers, are included with mothers in the community. However, on the part of women, there has been from early times until today a natural hostility toward male communion that has provided the materials for many an amusing tale.

These circumstances were altered by the fact that boys succeeded in entering the men's communions upon reaching puberty. Thus, these communions were organized on the basis of sex more than anything else. Now, among all primitive peoples—and here Schurtz uses firsthand observations, although they are mixed with error—men fear sex, which can make them ill at ease. To be sure it is central to their thoughts and feelings, although shyness is just as predominant. Thus a decision ensued for the male communion, which would be disturbed in its functions by complaisance with respect to sex. The ethos became hostile to maiden friends and to women, a notion which still lives on among the rest of us, however much we usually regard the customs of primitives as unnatural. It follows that long-term membership in the men's communion (which was required as a rule and which alone could give to such units the import that they certainly still have for the rise of higher cultures) makes it necessary for young men to postpone marriage for a long time. Often the primitive was not married before the age of forty.

These things imposed upon the youth the necessity for entering into "irregular" sexual relations, i.e., such that no families, no communities were formed. These were often organized, and for the most part molded into stable forms, so that one can speak of general prostitution, which repeatedly has had a religious significance. Whether within this situation, related to it, or without it, love communions arose in such enormous number that these relations, as Schurtz indicates, which actually only preceded marriage, became more highly visible. They gave rise, mistakenly, to the "promiscuity theory."

Even in the protest against this, in the insistence inherited by Schurtz from modern anthropology that monogamous, and as is usually asserted, basically patrimonial marriage was the original form, the phenomenon of matriarchy was viewed then as a temporary decline of the family, which, according to Schurtz, was brought about by male communions. Even in that contention, the seeds of error were implanted in Schurtz's social theory. Whatever it has to do with monogamous and patrimonial marriage, however, it concerns the primary or secondary character of matriarchal law. Besides these laws and in exception to them, there is at times an even predominantly appearing abundance of free-love communions among the youth, with reference to which one may wish to speak in the same manner as Schurtz, although not in such an exclusively focused sense, of a certain promiscuity.

Consequently, the maidens belong to the communion relationships among the unmarried men. They are in no way only limited to the family or to the futile efforts to establish communions among maidens. There are tendencies, to be sure, to keep them out of the true male communions, and these are strengthened by familial forces to claim them as sole and exclusive members, or by feeble attempts at maidens' communions. The consequence is always a demand for the sexual chastity of the maiden. Thus it is either through prostitution, as common among primitive peoples as among the higher cultures, that women win entrance into the universe of the male communion, or through their "ruin" by virtue of early wed-lock.

Wherever there are male communions, young maidens and older women take part in some way. Naturally they perform different functions (often suppressed and subordinated) from those per-formed by the men. Nevertheless, they are bound just as are the men either to the communion or to individual males in communion-like liaisons. Since free-love relations are communions, they are sexual, comprehending the sexes. At the same time, they are emo-tional-affective communions. The distinction between the sexes has nothing to do with the distinction between community and com-munion. At times it certainly appears to, since the genuine male society is per se an especially differentiated clear form of pure communion with respect to which a woman is denied absolute com-munion-parity because of her sex. But the very profound notion found in the fact that the wife role is said to be primarily courtesan-like contradicts even this, because that courtesan character is both more central and more communionlike. Even in contemporary mar-riage, the communion attitude of the woman, no less than that of the man, must be maintained despite the monotony of mere com-munion.

However, I am not exploring the sociology of the sexes. Besides, that presumes a metaphysic of the sexes, a metaphysic of male and female and their differences, which can probe the matter in its essence. Even though it is certain that this is completely and basi-cally a fundamentally structured contrast and is of central socio-logical importance, I prefer to offer no opinion concerning whether or how this matter has significance for the three basic sociological categories.

There remains nothing in Schurtz's theory but the analysis of the family as community and communion. Only the claim that this has a sexual basis is untenable.[13]

MAX WEBER RECONSIDERED

Tönnies's distinction between community and society treated the communion in the first place as a sublimation, so to speak, of com-munion. This further distinction had no place in Tönnies's psychology. (In accordance with his adopted perspective, he placed the principle of community simultaneously in a naturalistic, organic— namely, an unconscious—nexus and in pure instinct or pleasure.[14] This principle, in fact, also bound mother and child together in the manner of a communion.) But because of empirical observations, progress from that point led to the more precise analyses of Max Weber, setting traditional bonds apart from affective, and particularly emotional bonds within community. That Max Weber came in this case to an abrupt halt is explained by his biased insistence upon locating the subject matter of sociology in social action, i.e., exclusively in the manifestations and ideal-typical constructions of social existence, rather than in the social forms (essences) or in social existence (concrete reality) as such. He defines what I have called humanistic sociology as the sociology of *Verstehen*, the sense of the meaning given to *Verstehen* by Dilthey. In reference to Jaspers and also to Simmel and Rickert, he restricts *Verstehen* to such an extent that only acts of consciousness can be understood. Both misconstructions are similar in the attitude they propound, by virtue of which subjectively intended meaning, in the sense of the conscious import of social action, is alone construed as comprehensible. A misunderstanding of Husserl seems to have produced this confusion. The consequence is that "a very significant part of sociologically relevant conduct, especially purely traditional action, is treated as being on the margin" of incomprehensibility, because it is reaction—no longer bound to a subjectively intended meaning.[15]

The absurdity of epistemological asceticism (in which Max Weber's strivings for methodological precision in these matters demonstrate that his philosophizing was not always trenchant) means that the pure and genuine community should, in its essence, be interpreted as unanalyzable not only in spite of its sociological relevance but also in spite of the wealth of knowledge that Max Weber himself had of that social form. Only aspects manifested explicitly in consciousness can be known. This, however, is already derived from a consciousness of feeling, and it abstracts through feeling its understandable meaning in Weber's sense. Consequently, the distinction between the traditional—insofar as it is still understandable—and the affective-emotional, between community and communion is blurred. One can compare here *Wirtschaft und Gesellschaft.*

> Predominantly traditional conduct—just as that which is merely imitative response—stands wholly and absolutely on the border-line of, and often beyond, that which can be called a "meaning-fully" oriented action, because it is very frequently only a hollow response in the direction of a long and firmly established attitude of resigned reaction to a customary stimulus. The bulk of all long established daily routine approaches this type, which be-longs in the theoretical system not only as a marginal case, [. . . then he is entirely a marginal case here! . . .] but also because the tie to customary ways of doing things can be preserved in different degrees and senses. (First §2)

In this case, this type approaches that of affective conduct. Therefore, there is a transition between these things, because Max Weber's position on the conscious takes community into considera-tion only at that point where there is an understandable meaning and where community becomes simultaneously communion-like. Indeed, Weber knows that even his "meaning of social action," and in truth even an "understandable meaning," often lie largely in the "unconscious":

> Pretended "motives" and "repressions" often directly disguise the real context of the determinance of his action for the actor himself. . . . In this case sociology is confronted with the task of defining, explaining, and confirming the context whether or not it has entirely or in part been raised into consciousness. (§1, 16).

As a matter of fact, the entire methodology of Max Weber breaks down at this "marginal instance of the interpretation of meaning." And it leads at the same time to a point where central social phenomena are excluded from possible observation. "All traditional actions and broad categories of Charisma"—I will treat that eventually—"are composed of fragments that are almost but not quite comprehensible" (§1, 10).

The following sentence demonstrates that Max Weber himself was not entirely satisfied with the matter. Chapter I. I. 9 shows, above all, which premises led to the restriction; yet this does permit alternative conclusions about these things. But see:

> Actual conduct is carried on in the large part of its manifestation in semi-consciousness or unconsciousness of its "intended meaning." The actor feels the meaning in an indeterminate way, and, not knowing it, acts mostly instinctually or habitually. Only rarely, and only by a few in collective action, will a meaning (whether rational or irrational) of an act emerge into consciousness. Genuinely affective, meaningful action that is wholly and clearly apprehended is in reality always only a marginal case. Every historical and sociological observation will always have to take these considerations into account in analyzing reality. However, that should not preclude the fact that sociology forms its concepts through the classification of objectively possible intended meaning, *as if conduct were carried on consciously in a meaningfully oriented manner.* (§1, 11)

This last statement (underlining is mine) permits the speculation that the consequences are already suspect for Weber. Surely the concepts must have the breadth to comprehend all objectively possible reality. Observations ought never establish "exceptions," but always only "special cases." Max Weber did not heed his own prescription at all, at least not completely. Concepts like "affective," "emotional," or "rational" are not at all "derived from the classification of intended meaning," but are types of psychic "acts" (they are acts in themselves, not in their meaning)! The phrase "intended meaning" is the place, in principle, where misunderstanding Husserl has produced confusion. I am so close to the perspective of Weber's "*verstehende* sociology" that I deplore the fact that I cannot discuss this any further. The concept "intended meaning" is exceedingly ambiguous. Max Weber's "consciousness of meaning" comprehends it only slightly if at all. This distinction may belong to logic, but it doesn't belong in sociology, where Weber has put it. But, how sociological it is indeed! Weber tries at last to exclude the most fundamental social phenomena from the concept of "social action," cf §I, II 4, also II 3. Also "individualism" (§I,I 9), the doctrine of "social relevance" as pure "chance" (§3), and the failure to comprehend "universalism" have their

roots in methodological errors. Finally, there is even the consequence that Max Weber's *"verstehende* sociology"—*nolens volens*
—is rationalistic! Weber has various hunches about "irrational un-
derstandings" and "irrational meaning." However, see §2:

> Predominantly affective behavior belongs also . . . (like "tradi-
> tional") . . . on the border and often outside that which is con-
> sciously meaningfully oriented; it can be an impulsive response
> to an unusual stimulus. It is a sublimation when affectively con-
> ditioned behavior erupts as a conscious discharge of a feeling-
> state. For then it is already on the way (not always) to *ration-
> alization.* (Part of the emphasis is mine.)

In fact an "intended meaning," in the sense of "conscious-mean-
ing" employed by Weber, precludes the irrational even in the case
of affective behavior. An inquiry in terms of intended meaning
must always either fail in answering its purpose or rationalize its
operation after the fact in an artificial manner. Certainly, all such
rational motivation must be insulated against the irrational in the
final analysis. Therefore, there is no final solution. The examples
of Weber §1, I 5 are *entirely* rational and *entirely* irrational in their
basic motive. What can be more rational than to counteract irri-
tability by chopping wood! What is more irrational than striving
for relaxation! What Weber really has in mind is the "meaning of
the act," and his "opinion of the acts." Consciousness is completely
irrelevant to these acts. And the entire position is altered by this
realization. Moreover, it has ramifications in completely different
directions. Rationalism impressed Weber conclusively and in a
completely positive way, when he said that "all irrational, affectively conditioned meaningful contexts of conduct are most clearly
represented and studied as 'deviations' from a constructed purely
rational purposeful course!" Even if reality is preponderantly irrational, the method of *"verstehende* sociology" shall be "rationalistic" in the construction of concepts! (§1, I 3, cf. also I 6.)

It is worthwhile corroboration to note that Max Weber, simply
acknowledging the potential phenomenon of communion, at least
recognized a tendency toward differentiation in spite of the encum-
brances of his methodology.

By virtue of another theory of Max Weber, there arises a dichotomy of social action within the rational society. I doubt whether what he calls value-rational and rational-purposeful may legitimately provide a parallel dichotomy within community—or indeed any dichotomy at all. The philosopher will mistrust the new distinction conceptually. Value and purpose are closely related. Purpose assumes value wherever there is ultimate purpose or self-purpose, and many freely convert one into the other. At least in the case of ultimate purpose, therefore, the irrational and value penetrate the rational-purposeful act. Accordingly, it must necessarily be indicated that rational-purposeful action is always dependent upon them, referring beyond itself to external matters. As opposed to this, value-rational action should be characterized in such a way that—seen in the perspective of purpose which is dissipated in the act—it can be disregarded completely, because purpose is truly tied to value, but value is not truly tied to purpose. Consequently, Weber's terminology is vindicated here. Rational-purposeful refers, first of all, to purpose; value-rational to unmediated value. But the former is also valued and, therefore, irrational. If value-rational action has value in itself, then it may be asked whether this constitutes anything more than a difference in degree. Irrational and externally given preferred, demanded value is indispensable whether it is affixed only to purpose and consequently to results, or whether to the intrinsic value of the action regardless of the consequences. Beyond this, however, as has been uniquely demonstrated earlier by Weber himself, that which he called rational-purposeful likewise has its own unique value—in this case, in the action itself. In this instance, value is not in the content of the act, which, as in the value-rational, is only indirectly significant here, but in rationality—rationality as such—which is, consequently, really an irrational value. Moreover, in the case of rational-purposeful activities, the purpose is neither the essential nor the only source of value, and in such cases the purpose, as well as the results, can even be highly insignificant. This can be seen by assessing the good intentions in so many theoretical as well as practical moral systems of rational-purposeful modes of thought. Those whose aspirations are good are not censured. Their failure results only in chagrin. Even a rational, painstaking attempt to achieve a purpose whose value seems imprudent or unintelligible to a rational-purposeful critic is rejected only as odd or foolish or droll or, ultimately, as mad, while an act not really rational meets up with ethical aversion. In all of these cases there is certainly a difference between value-rational and rational-purposeful activity. The rationally-purposeful act is that which I have called "autarchic" rationality. One can even call the difference absolute. However, the contrary case of nonautarchic rationality means precisely that which is not totally uninhibited, whether it be community or communion. And instead of a category there is a mixed type. Like all such categories of the kind discussed earlier, these must be anticipated rather than thought of as questionable.

Nowhere are rational-purposeful and value-rational acts to be separated conceptually. Only in one respect may a basic difference be stated, if not conceived conceptually; nor are we speaking only of a mixed type—this is within the category society. This is accomplished by virtue of the fact that the irrational, whose rationality is always necessarily required, can be given and legitimated emotionally-affectively or traditionally—or better, naturally (comprehending the traditional act). With only an imperceptible nuance, Weber's terms (to be sure, he is always truly difficult to understand) may be applied to the actual difference. Purposes, therefore, are present in value-rational activities, and above all, these as such are irrational rationality. They are, themselves, emotional-affective. Thus they are there in collective experience as values of action. In rational-purposeful acts, purposes and the claims and precepts of rationality are, in any case, traditional and natural. Consequently, they are unemphasized and taken for granted. There is no gainsaying the fact that Max Weber's exposition did not propose this distinction rather than the distinction discussed earlier. However, it appears that that which was surely perceived by him, although it was certainly confused when it was perceived, implies the conceptualization we are about to make with respect to yet another distinction, if and so far as the distinction is more than a merely relative one, and especially if it is, in accordance with his position, seen to be even reciprocal. Max Weber emphasized such reciprocity, at least with regard to the first dichotomy. In this view, rational-purposeful and value-rational acts, insofar as their distinction can have lasting significance, are both merely agencies by which society is transformed in one instance into community; in the other, into communion. They are not merely mixed forms, but distinctive agencies of transformation, just as each of the other two categories has that same quality vis à vis the other. It follows that the distinction between community and communion and the vastly different dichotomy of rational action are not subject to question, because in each of the rational and irrational "hemispheres" (as one might say) there is a duality and consequently a fourfold overall classification. In actuality, rational action, together with irrational, does not comprise both hemispheres, but when considered along with emotional action and the unconscious it forms a trichotomy, in which one can include both areas of consciousness as well as, perhaps, both areas of irrational action. This actually exhibits again, by its own resistance to manipulation, an all the more weighty justification for the separation of community and communion.

Weber's strange terse statements about "value-rational" and "rational-purposeful" action, *loc. cit.*, chapter I, §2, are obviously not completely clear to him: cf. the closing sentence of paragraph 3. However, he saw at least that the irrational, in its relationship to purpose, does permeate rational-purposeful action: "action, therefore, is rationally-purposeful only in the means employed." To be sure there are purposes "simply as given subjective regnant necessities," which Weber appeared to regard as admittedly not rational, but neither did he regard them as irrational. He never made up his mind. But in the end he did say that "absolute rationally purposeful action" is "in reality only one constructed, marginal case." Actually it is not even that. As opposed to value-rational action, it should be manifested as rational only in the attitude adopted to the consideration of means for accomplishing purposes. In any case, that is the impression conveyed by all the examples of the type proffered by Weber in §2. But then, value-rational action is included with that action plainly designated "rationally-purposeful—only in its means," and consequently, all rational-purposeful action may be included with it! In truth, with respect to that which

Weber *abstractly* asserts to be the essence of "value-rational" action, one is not led to the attainment of purposes at least, not at first—to ascertain the value of such action. Furthermore, it is not necessary to take purposes into account to ascertain the rationality of acts. To meet a specified number of obligations is a wholly "purpose"-less value-rational action (there should be no begging, no sought-for affirmations; only pure gratitude can be imagined in fulfilling obligations). Still, §2 is not concerned with such examples. Whether there can be complete freedom of purpose in autarkic rationality, which corresponds fundamentally to Weber's ration-purposeful action, remains perhaps in doubt. But there are instances of autarchic rationality which seldom imply an "end in view": often in formal bureaucratic reports, filing and tabulation, classification of all kinds, also in many military drills, and, for the scholar, in his mania for filing data; stamp collecting is another example of "autarchic rationality devoid of purpose"; many children's games belong here, as do most forms of nonsensical play. In the case of "dedicated" rational-purposeful action, it is not necessary to place a value upon the end in view and its accomplishment. In other respects, one might well speak of autarchic rationality as a constructed marginal case in a certain sense, but never "in a substantive sense," instead of the precise empirical meaning of the concept. However Weber's distinction is of still another kind. Thus, he gives those ends of an "action that is only rationally-purposeful in its choice of means" a value-rationality over against those long-established ends that are "given simply as regnant subjective necessities." These latter obviously do not appear more rational to him, but "more commensurate with rationality" (thus, he develops superficial concern over their logical impossibility). They are simply impossible. But such impressions *can* appear, because these "ends in view" are "self-evident" to us. Moreover, the examples given by M. Weber indicate that this is decisive. Yet Weber must certainly have realized that "self-evidence" is something very subjective and has an entirely different meaning for one person than another and for one culture rather than another. Self-evidence is always only "evidence to which we have become accustomed." And rational-purposeful action is, therefore, only an aspect of rationality transformed by community. However, if there were universal self-evidence of a "natural" kind, then it is fitting to allude to Weber's "regnant subjective necessities" as a part of nature; otherwise they would be included by him in the narrower sense of natural as "traditional." Economic efficiency, which Weber cites most frequently as the example of a purely rational-purposeful end, has certainly been shown earlier by Weber to be in no way self-evident in all eras. Economics is, as I have pointed out, only coincident with rationalism as such. Rationalism as such, however, was not always self-evident. It had its "heroic" and communion era. Only afterward did rationalism become self-evident. I refer to Weber! The state of Puritanism—already characterized by "autarchic rationality"—is regarded by him, and justly so, as a prime example of value-rational activity.

Be that as it may, interpretation is needed here. In a later part of his systematic book, where the resistance offered by methodological distortions and the related distortions of concept formation had become less impenetrable, Max Weber arrived at a special, yet very important, social phenomenon simply by glancing at that which appeared by itself in the direct apprehension of the trichotomy of the fundamental sociological categories—the "types of governance":[16] "There are three pure types of legitimate governance. Their legitimate validity can primarily be: 1) rational in character . . . 2) traditional in character . . . 3) charismatic in character; on the basis of unusual devotion to the sacredness, the heroic power, or the mimesis of a person and the order revealed or created by his (charismatic governance)."

That which Weber emphasized above all was the unusual character of the latter, with reference to which he exhibited, in a fundamental respect and in a first-rate manner, the abrupt contrasts with rational governance on the one hand and traditional governance on the other (both are specifically everyday forms of governance). Still, Weber realized that the charismatic governing relationship is above all an emotional *Vergemeinschaftung*. Beyond its unusual character, he notes further that charismatic governance is intrinsically transitory. To overcome this fact, "charismatic governance, which so to speak, occurs in its ideal type form only *in statu nascendi*, must alter its essential character: it becomes traditionalized or rationalized." Et cetera. I will add nothing more.[17]

THE TRANSFORMATIONAL ANALYSIS OF EPOCHS

I have been able only à propos of examples and only suggestively to consider the relationship of the categories, community, society, and communion to the status groups, classes, and professions, to the sexes and the age grades. However, one more thing that belongs in this context should be treated at the close, if only briefly and somewhat more systematically. It leads us back again to the actual problem of time: the relationship of the three categories to the typical epochs of history.

It is disputed, to be sure, whether there is such a thing as a universal epoch of history. Indeed, the debate appears (or appeared a short time ago) to have been negatively resolved: history did not follow universal laws. There can be no doubt that the historian as we know him, in most instances does not direct his interests to "laws" even if they should be available, but to the unique configuration of historical events. And the legitimacy of merely idiographic historical writing is thereby asserted. Eventual laws interest him only incidentally; but they must sooner or later, because they are absolutely and necessarily expedient for him. Thus there must be laws, if only as a premise of possible historical knowledge, which, in its turn, is empirical. Actually, no one denies that there are historical laws. Only a theory oriented toward a *Weltanschauung* and a position formulated in the nineteenth century to defend historical interests have managed, for a time, to proffer a seeming disavowal of historical laws or regularities.

If there are typical emergent phases of religious and political forms, then it is not clear why there should not also be typical forms of process. And if these are found to pertain to single cultural areas, then there can at least be some for entire cultures. Oswald Spengler, with exorbitant disregard for competent scholarship to the point of error in method as well as in regard for facts, has become unjustly known for his unique scientific contributions, to the extent that metaphysical, ethical, and logical critics have all the more heaped up blame upon themselves. He built his significant position badly, just as in all his writings, through his unmitigated impetuosity in every regard as well as by his gross errors. For example, his argument for the mutual impenetrability of cultures is an exaggeration of the notion of organism that does not apply even to plants. Rather, the disturbances of typical entities is the rule.

Eduard Meyer introduced freedom of will into the arena, opposing Lamprecht and Breysig. As in similar instances, this had already happened before, and it is happening today in opposition to Spengler. Eduard Meyer, for example, still spoke of the Middle Ages as "antiquity."

Antiquity, the Middle Ages, modern times: those are the stages ordinarily used in the classification of typical epochs of history. Spengler is certainly incomprehensible where this is concerned. If we limit ourselves to the examples of antiquity and the Christian culture of Western Europe, we are left not only with an induction from two cases, but we observe a parallelism of centuries with countless analogous periods, courses of events, and analogies— therefore, of the entire period. However, in antiquity, the "later period" merged into the "modern period" in Italy only after certain very long preparations, which first began in a definitive way at the end of the second century of the Caesars; in the East, however, a radically altered structure—the "late period"—had emerged much earlier. The elementary beginnings of the period for which we are already preparing ourselves today appear at first in a seemingly remote distance. Pessimism is no argument, especially not here. The result of the "late period" of antiquity is also Christianity; above all, our Middle Ages, indeed, our culture, were built on the heritage of late antiquity.

Antiquity

That is the age when peoples still wandered, migrated nomadically over the earth. That is also the age when the perennial summer content of life occurs, at least for youngsters, in the forms of military expeditions and raids; when community relations of any agreed upon permanence cannot be established; when the epitome of vassalage is the predominant social condition; when all existence is carried on by everyone in a religious manner; when religion is pregnant with events, although customs still waver and change easily. The sociality of every ancient age—and sociality is not the only peculiarity, although one of the most important by which typical epochs of history are characterized—is communionlike. The early period of contemporary West European peoples presents—from the functional point of view, which is certainly not substantive— the same picture as that which one must imagine represented the original period of the Aeolian Homer.

Middle Ages

There the people have become sedentary. They have been assembling in homelands in smaller and more stable associations, in ordered habits of daily life. Custom develops its commanding power. Thinking is traditionalistic, as are domestic arrangements and affairs of the market. When one lives in permanent dwellings, there is now more than the next day or the next week which can be anticipated and scheduled. In any event, [one can plan for] a year. Moreover, religion is settled; the "church" has emerged; or a certain centralization of cult locales, oracular speech, regular Olympiads, and a unification and stabilization of myth or dogma. However, the communion spirit is still active throughout. Precipitous agitations spread through the populace. Corybantic religiosity breaks out. Sectarian inflammations spread. And the distance beckons: to the crusades and the expedition to Rome by the medieval German emperors, to colonial expansion. However, the annual feud becomes, just like a tournament and contest, merely a festive game for an exclusive social status group. There the communion has at least given rise to status groups. Status groups of rejecting errants disregard the social structure that is formed. The work day becomes supreme, commanding all ecstatic activity. Organically derived community is at the basis of all these things.

Modern Period

The transition to the modern period required centuries of a peculiar quality, centuries accorded the highest glory in antiquity as well as today. However, the actual modern period is thoroughly different. This is all the more true because its seeds were already sown in those past centuries. And the social structure of the modern period is society. The specific system of society was formed precisely in the specifically modern period, theoretically as well as practically. The recent inquiries of Tönnies, Sombart, Weber, and earlier, of Marx, on the one hand, and Gierke, on the other, have conceived the essence of society on the whole in the society of the modern period. In revolt against the society of the modern period, the demand for other, qualitatively different nonsociety sociality broke out in the age of Goethe, the romantic period from Herder to Hegel; this in part suggested, in part already recognized, and in part imagined modern times. If one reckons that the Renaissance, up to the seventeenth century, did not lead immediately to the actual modern period but was an epoch of transition to it, then the period, which in the antiquity of the early so-called Alexandrian centuries (the currently conventional word, Hellenism, is used too often to include the later period in an encompassing sense) stretches from the Diadochi to the Roman empire (Neither Alexander, in Spengler's meaning, nor, for that matter, Napoleon is the "renaissance" in the final analysis), corresponds to our modern period. What Calvinism signifies to us—certainly not the basis of rationalism (which is already derived from the Renaissance but which made it practicable for all classes of then progressive people)—is the stoicism of antiquity. However, the societylike modern period was clarified and formed out of a world that had a completely different kind of social structure. The society of the modern period evolved, not suddenly but throughout the centuries, from the community of the Middle Ages, whose manifest communionlike essence is so pristinely clear from afar, that, in this regard, its mere suggestion suffices. Yet the ethos of these communions soon tends toward society. The necessary conditions, which have led from the community of the Middle Ages through the communion culture of what we call the Renaissance to the society of the modern period, are still and have always been a great enigma in spite of trenchant and thorough study.

Late Period

The late period ultimately follows the modern period. The modern period is very gradually (again, not continuously) transformed into it. Only the most outstanding of its earliest marks evidence to us its emergence. Yet antiquity provides the insights.

The political structures, principally the administrative, juristic, and economic structures which the age of society has erected, will endure for many centuries. They are formed now, in the world economy and the world trade of world empire, into their wholly gigantic dimensions, and at the same time into an enormous bureaucracy organized in every increasingly subtle detail. Certainly the precise functioning of this gigantic system is disturbed by repeated eruptions. This is because the masses of men, inwardly acquiescing to the prevailing mechanization of their collective daily existence, seek to burst it open periodically by often repeated disturbances. However, tired of this, they permit these political and economic arrangements (which provide at least an external security) to persist, even at times manifesting a collective gratitude. What is released in these eruptions is more than the pressure of mechanization; it is basically psychic dynamite. The world economy and world trade of the world empire, for which the age of society has provided the formative conditions, have meanwhile meshed together in greater and greater degree all the peoples of the earth. Torn from every mothering environment, individuals wander homelessly through the cities of the world: the amorphous mass of a chaotic amalgam of people formed out of atomized, pulverized individuals, who, however, are held together less and less by the society code of honor and who are set against one another in cold isolation. Moreover, they are uprooted mentally and psychically, no longer satisfied by the rationality of the systems, driven along by their boredom from their desperate frustrations to "something else," which manifests itself in avid religious desires. Nor is there rooted stability here. One reaches out for the distant and the exotic, for the very old and the very new. A principled exoticism and an arbitrary modernism are combined, and the mishmash is brewed as a religious syncretism from whose bubbling syrups and vapors the thirsty souls drink overhastily, without permanently slaking their thirst. In this way, hearts are merged in the blissful sobbing of salvation found in brotherhoods and cults of all kinds, frequently to be reduced in a short time to flotsam and cast out in other directions—where they find other similarly harassed souls in this over-populated world with whom they can join together in other communions.

The intellectuals who wandered through the metropolises of the East and West as philosophers are also bearers of this mentality—particularly since neo-Pythagorism and neo-Platonism replaced Stoicism. They are the academic proletariat, which seeks its bread, sometimes here, sometimes there, and usually finds it in abundance or in scarcity, however it appears. Yet despite the lesser education that was different in degree throughout all strata at those times, the metropolitan proletariat of today is related to it in a mental similarity. The actual metropolitan proletariat, housed in confined quarters, coming from all countries, a crowd of individuals quickly merged and connected in a spate of separate alliances which endure only temporarily over the years in free-love communions—also as marriages, whose offspring (often very early, otherwise late in adolescence) are separated from the parents—take to the gutters, and stagger through life again and again in faltering, glowing communion associations. The organized working class of our day does not have that appearance. This is to be found in the *Lumpenproletariat*, hated so much by Kautsky and beloved by Mühsam. Yet there are many similarities to *panem et circenses*.

Finally, there is licentious soldiering. Mercenaries are recruited from one end of the empire to the other, and from all the peoples of the earth. They are hard, disciplined legions when it pays, but otherwise unrestrained, brawling bands who can murder their field commanders at one time or extol them as emperors at another. However, they (including the generals) were permeated at the same time with religious excitement and passion, erecting alters to Mithras on the Rhine, believing in and eager for miracles, prepared for all outward and inward excesses. In none of these things are the appurtenances of status anywhere permanent. Upward and downward mobility alternates from generation to generation. The father may be a slave, while the son is already an emperor, whose son, in turn, may be a tramp. Status groups are split asunder. The people are mixed together as they experience the highest raptures of the heart, uplifting inspiration, and sacrificial surrender, even in the same minds and at the same time. Yet, whether positive or negative, these experiences are all smoldering surges of feeling, affective-emotional—the mentality is communionlike and the associations are communionlike. Thus the yearning for the quiet community is a hope for the peaceful lot of country life; the idylls, which really mean community at one time and communion at another, do not eventually disappear. They are genuine and spurious at once.

In the end the external structures are thrown more and more into disorder. The barbarians break into exclusive masses. The communion character of the late period and the communion character of antiquity merge in a final syncretism within which the lifeblood of one is renewed; for the other, it is mixed. A vast schism, into which the world slowly settles, divides the two cultures—from which the new emerges out of the framework of the old, slowly growing into the "middle ages." Moreover, Christianity has arisen out of the syncretism of religion. And the most beautiful stones of its cathedral are borrowed from the treasures of antiquity and late antituity.

PROPERTY: OWNERSHIP, COALESCENCE, AND AFFECTION

Sociology considers itself only as the science of social relations between men. Besides this, there is a sociology of animals that has in general emerged separately from that of men. It also considers the social relations of animals among one another as its subject matter. On occasion it deals with the relations of animals to men, but not with those of men to animals. The latter are left out, although variations for whole cultures can be quite characteristic in that regard. More appropriately, however, the relations of men to objects of property and their variations find no place in sociology. Every now and then one might run into a thought about if and why mutual relations of objects of·property may or must be construed as "social." Yet this is never more than a particular instance, derived mostly from (systemic-constructive) inquiries, at times from speculative, and it is never pursued. The philosopher, of course, would know how to do something with it. Otherwise objects of property are, at best, interesting to the sociologist either as resultants or as conditions (assumptions) of social relations. As basic ties of social relations, objects of property are at times specifically ruled out. In this context, one is reminded of Simmel's statement that it would be senseless to consider the relationship of a cabinet-maker to his lathe as social.[1]

Nevertheless, the history of ideas includes whole decades characterized by their relation to, for example, nature. It was also the custom of our ancestors to inherit their household goods and even

From "Soziologie der Sachverhältnisse," *Jahrbuch für Soziologie* 3 (1927): 38–45.

parts of their clothing, perhaps even homemade dress, over generations. We behave quite differently today when we buy such things for short periods of time and throw the used ones away. The contrast was, of course, often thought of as important by economics, which, with due reason, has always been considered a science closely related to sociology. Sociology could have gathered much knowledge about possessions from economics, since they were already treated sociologically by economists. Yet economic sciences deal only with parts of these problems and from a point of view not precisely sociological. This is true even more for the science of law, which, like the economic sciences, develops an interest only insofar as ownership of property and connected problems are contested in civil and criminal litigation.

Yet a typology of property relations and through this its social quality may well be constructed by contrasting other property relations with those of ownership. For centuries, the inheritance of an old line of farmers was settled on the same estate. This changed when the offspring accumulated sufficient wealth to purchase other acreage, not only larger and nicer but also economically more profitable than that of the original estate. The new estate delivered everything that it promised, and satisfied the owner for much of his lifetime. Later on, with increasing age, he rediscovers the yearning for the old estate. Despite all its advantages, the new estate is not really the same as the one where the owner was born and raised, where his parents and forefathers lived and died. The attempt to repurchase the former estate fails. Economically and legally, there are hardly any problems. The inherited estate has been sold. The seller would simply like to buy it back even at an extraordinary price, because the estate, now a social object, has a sentimental value for him, but conceivably no affectional value for other people. The present owner may make an attempt to exploit this situation. He may also reject an outright sale for reasons irrelevant to our argument, i.e., he may, like the former owner, have developed a similar relationship to the estate and thus would not sell for any price. So everything is clear—the property is not for sale!

In terms of sociology, however, there is more to be said. The heir who disinherited himself knows very well: he sold the old estate; it "belongs to" or exists for the other. But it is "his" estate anyway; he calls it "my," "our" estate. The new one that he purchased is also "his," but only in the sense that he purchased it, and through this transaction was granted rights over it.

These two kinds of property relations may conflict with one another. It is more than theoretically known to the heir that he has no business anymore over at the old estate. He may be reluctant to go there or painstakingly careful not to touch anything at the "old homestead." Yet, the full realization (that much "over there" is not accessible to him) does not sink into his head or into his heart. He certainly cannot fully comprehend in any way that the other one has total access, while he once was, but no longer is, allowed to change this or to reestablish that. The "sociology of ownership," as the field might be called, dealing with the often cited historical origin or objective justification of ownership, has always treated the problem exclusively in legal or economic terms, or at best in political terms, as well as in sundry ethical categories. The real sociology of ownership would have to consider this as a special and independent form of social property relation, distinct from others, though possibly originating from them. The ownership relation is such a property relation, in addition to the fact and in the same connection and separateness, that it is also a legal and economic relation. That the ownership relation is also this distinguishes it from other kinds of social property relations, which take on at best an economic and legal meaning, while ownership relations are at once social, economic, and legal property relations.

So far, of the other kinds of social property relations that contrast with ownership relations, only one has been suggested—and vaguely. Furthermore, the example we gave does not provide a particularly clear case. It was our intention to establish social property relations (after they were distinguished from ownership relations) as conflicting with and yet connected to ownership relations. This blurred the clarity of the case. There is another example that stands more firmly by itself.

Consider one who left his parental home as a young man and established an independent domicile far away. After a long absence, he returns for a visit. He reenters the house in which he spent his childhood. The old rooms embrace him. There is the sewing table of his mother, her darning ball, as well as the many other little things that surrounded him in his early youth. All this appears strangely familiar to him, and hardly foreign even at this later time. He feels an attachment to these things that he never owned and presumably never will own. There may be a sister remaining in the house, and she is to inherit the household belongings. Mere ownership relation is not at all at stake. But the connection is present. It is a coalescence that grew out of long familiarity formed in the early period of his life. Metaphorically, this has grown into a big tree, in the crown of which are hardly any traces of the events that happened to the roots and lower trunk. The roots and the lower trunk show the traits of those early events anyway, and they will determine the whole further life since they permanently shape a later fate. The context provided by the things of childhood stays alive, also contextually, in the unconscious. Because these things reappear after a long separation, the consciousness of the context erupts. It is a consciousness of a real context, which the interpreting theorist should not falsely identify as mere, associatively-connected reminiscences. The context, formerly unconscious, now becomes conscious, and this happens without any need to consider some accessory consciousness built upon an existence in the unconscious.

It is clear that the coalescence has nothing to do with the other social property relation of ownership. At the same time, it also represents the potential of actual contact. This cannot be understood only in the way the first example suggests: that one wishes to connect or keep connected the coalescent relation with that of ownership; that their cleavage will be experienced as unpleasant, pushing for its repression. In this case, it may be just the opposite. One experiences coalescence as a burden together with all the other things inherited in the whole circumstance of early socialization; or one experiences it as a burden along with things to which one was perhaps never really attached, but which were, however, owned by forefathers and are reminiscent of their lives. One may call such things trash, wish them out of sight, wish to sell them or dispose of them—possibly in some distant place. Yet one has a certain reluctance to simply destroy them, for they may have some economic value, or some irrational value may be placed on their persistent "piety." The sale, however, does not mean only simple removal from the scene. This can, of course, make the coalescence seem less real, but it cannot dispose of it. It means most of all a dissolution of certain obligations toward those things. For ownership does not only constitute rights (right of disposal) but also obligations and responsibilities (e.g., for careful treatment). This holds also in economic and even legal terms; in particularly relevant cases, positive legal sanctions. To refine, to recognize the basic singularity, as well as the amiable and hostile contexts, of the social relation of coalescence with things and that of ownership, insofar as it is also a social relation, remains an important task. For the time being, however, we must demonstrate a third kind of social property relation, which is in turn special and independent. I "love" an object because of its beauty, its symbolic meaning, its moral character, etc. I love a vase, a landscape, the flag of my country, the ships crossing the ocean. In love one interacts with the object of love. And love constitutes further interaction. But this is obviously not the connection that was called coalescence.

With things that are related to me in an emotional sociality, I do not need familiarity in terms of inheritance or a long living together. The coalescence may even hinder the relation of affection. Things that are so close to our being, that we are so bound to by habit, result in disturbance and imbalance if they are taken away from us, and they hardly need to be consciously and emotionally present to us. Thus we do not spontaneously love them. In order to love these things, we must share some communality. . . . [There must be a coalescence.] . . . In contrast to this, somebody in love with an object may want to keep it explicitly distant from everyday life. He puts an adored picture not up in the living room but in a special room for appropriate rituals. He keeps a piece of jewelry in a box instead of wearing it. Only in rare and selected hours is interaction with it allowed.

On the other hand, the emotional connections with property and the coalescence with it certainly touch upon one another. While the ethos of the former may be hostile toward too much communality, habituation will lead necessarily to increasing coalescence; then the emotions, those vibrations and thrills flooding the consciousness, will disappear more and more, finally arriving at a stage of every-day communality. Wise insight may even welcome this, expecting from the repression to the unconscious a less obvious but a much deeper and lasting effect. Yet aversion toward this process is similarly understandable. He who wants to keep and constantly renew the emotional relation has to avoid its habituation.

As opposed to this, coalescence is a connection in and of itself, essentially in the unconscious—although perhaps known, but not in the sense of "knowledge" or omnipresent consciousness. Thus, feelings of coalescence need not always be felt, even though at times they do emerge as conscious feelings. In the above example (which again does not provide a pure case), the heir who had sold his inherited farm reacted to this with feelings of longing, tenderness, and sadness for it. So the estate had a sentimental value, an affective value, for him. But all of this emerged only after the sale. Originally, there was only coalescence, which was felt so slightly (barely even known) that the heir lightheartedly sold the estate. Only after the fact did he become conscious of the context. Here the context is not constituted by feelings, unlike the case of emotional relations. Instead, the feelings appear as one becomes conscious of the in-itself-unconscious context. It is also characteristic that feelings, while being in a positive coalescence, can be negative. This is the case of the other heir, who wanted to keep the belongings of his parents far away from himself. Positive feelings tend to emerge only on special occasions, particularly at times of disturbance or danger to the coalescence and at times of reunion.

It seems hardly necessary to distinguish further the emotional relation with property from that of the social relation of ownership, as we did for coalescence. The origin of ownership may of course be traced back as much to inheritance as to affective attachment. As a rule, an actual purchase occurs only because of its direct or indirect usefulness. The ownership relation as such is different from the relation of affective attachment. The desire to own a beloved object may even be experienced ambivalently. To purchase the charming birch tree, which someone may visit during lonely walks, might be seen as a profanation by the buyer. He would not even enjoy it as a gift; he would have to be wary of impinging on the tender relationship merely by fulfilling the obligation for its upkeep. Likewise, we are not utterly possessed by the desire to own a beloved work of art. Of course, impulses to that effect occur every now and then in each of us, and there are at times fanatics who may become thieves in museums. A short additional argument must be developed about the kind of social property relations represented by ownership. For ownership is paradigmatically quite representative for its class of relation, yet it does not completely fill all the requirement for such a classification. On the street, I am also in a social relationship with the car that I try to avoid. This relation stands in sharp contrast with the traditional and affectional relations of property. It obviously belongs to the ownership relation and yet is something different. The connection is constituted by the fact that in both cases these are rational relations, or, better, occur in the sphere of rationality. Within this whole sphere, the social relation of ownership is only a closely attended, particularly important, special case. The whole class, however, is quite different from traditional and affectional property relations, just as the traditional and affectional are categorically different from one another.

With these three kinds of social relations of property, I consider the modal categories of social relations of property fundamentally distinguished. As one can see, these are the basic modal categories which are the same for all sociology. The rational relationship represented by property is easily recognizable as society, defined in the narrower sense by Tönnies; the traditional relation is that of community; and the affectional, finally, is a relation which, beyond community and society, I have identified as communion. As with people, so one can stay with property—also, of course, with jobs, ideas, or whatever—in a community or society relationship, or in the relationship I have called communion.

At the end of this brief discourse, it may be appropriate to emphasize with a few additional words the direction a developed sociology of property relations must take. First of all, it will have to provide the historian with essential concepts for the comprehension, description, and distinction of whole cultures and historical periods. What is the relationship of men to their social or psychological circumstances, whether they comprise a *Gemeinschaft*-type context, a calculus of means and ends, or a more or less affectively intense love or hate? Toward what kinds of objects do the first, second, or third prevail? In which social strata is one or the other preferred? With all of this, the historical periods and times are also characterized just as much by the sociality of men among one another. The revolts and revulsion of craftsmen and manual workers against the first machines, of the townspeople against modern means of transportation, the conflicting orientations toward city and countryside, homeland and distant or foreign places, and status quo and change are pertinent examples drawn from modern history, which is in need of a sociology of property relations for its understanding. Particularly the meaning of historical crises can be clarified in this way, as can also the crisis of the present. What does the factory or the workshop mean for the employees, for the upper and lower white-collar and blue-collar workers? The mere categories of ownership, tools, usufruct, etc., are insufficient to the task. Most indispensable is the analytic dimension of inheritance or habitually determined coalescence. However, particularly for the coming decades and centuries, the communion constituted by emotions, by sympathy, or by antipathy becomes increasingly important. This tendency can be observed for all periods of unrest and transition. The consideration of this type of relationship is particularly important for the study of economic institutions. In the future, communion will become the dominant modal category for social reality and for its analysis, for sociology and the sociality of men among one another, and also for relations between men and property and for those of objects as such.

II. Human Experience and
Cultural History

ON LONESOMENESS

When we pay superficial attention to the term "lonesomeness," a merely negative connotation first comes to mind. To be alone reminds us of a more comfortable contrast—to be as one with another or with others. Lonesomeness implies that something is missing or lacking. Being alone seems unnatural.

NEGATIVE AND POSITIVE ASPECTS

The natural state of man is obviously to feel as one with all other men—indeed, even with the other animals, the plants, all the objects and items of everyday life. Such an ambience penetrates deeply into man's very soul. Certainly lonesomeness or the feeling of alienation from one's surroundings cannot abide in the innermost depths of the soul, for everything around us takes on a psychological significance as varied as the sounds of fluttering fern fronds or the rustlings of leaves on trees and bushes. They give

From "Die Genealogie der Einsamkeit," *Logos* 8 (1919): 62–96. *Einsamkeit* is perhaps best translated as "lonesomeness." When appropriate, we shall use that term. Two considerations dictate a freer rendering, first, cultural contrasts in the meaning of lonesomeness, e.g., Germans more often attach a positive quality to the term than do English-speaking Americans, while the latter more frequently conceive the condition negatively. See Peter R. Hofstätter, "Die amerikanische und die deutsche Einsamkeit," *Verhandlungen XIII. Deutscher Soziologentag* (Cologne, 1957). Second, Schmalenbach's treatment, as is the case with many other concepts, is extremely diffuse, encompassing the gamut of meanings from ebullient freedom to profound despair. In English, one can be "alone" to do "his own thing," or alone in the sense of being totally abandoned—utterly forlorn.

voice to breath or wind as they whisper the sounds of spring, transmit the joy emitted from the rising sun, or shake with the anger conveyed by rolling thunder. There is something almost primeval about this, reminiscent of attitudes possibly held by primitive man and the animism or totemism that tied men together with one another, with other animals, and with natural objects. Of course one is reminded of his separateness from the environment "out there" when he stumbles over or runs up against some concrete obstacle that is ordinarily viewed, if viewed at all, with indifference [Harry Stack Sullivan would say "selectively inattended." eds.] by others. Here, however, one discovers his separateness externally. At most, the discovery may erase momentarily such feelings as fright or lust which existed prior to the interruption. By no means does one become rapt in the mood of lonesomeness, nor does one feel forlorn by such an experience. Since one is basically identified with the significant psychic elements of his close community (which has even become a part of his biological life or being), any feeling of being utterly alone and by one's self as a consequence of such an external separation is completely unthinkable.

In contrast, "natural" man can also know the transcendent fear and desire that is imposed by being alone. It may even be conceived as a painful quality, often mixed with joy. Specific lonesomeness, on the other hand, is differentiated from this overriding mood. The latter may occur without any constellation of circumstance. It may even appear under favorable circumstances [where one would not expect it] and at times particularly under such conditions. Amongst close friends, the soul may be struck by the terrifying sense of being alone. This feeling is not determined by external conditions; it floods spontaneously out of one's very soul and, because of this, does not have, as does "accidental" lonesomeness, the character of the transitory. Lonesomeness is suddenly realized in its essence as an experience appearing in one's consciousness, at times briefly and at times for long periods. Where it is fundamental and, so to speak, essential, it lives permanently in the form of all the experiences coloring subconsciousness. It lies there always in wakeful slumber. This lonesomeness, even if it is not experientially permanent, has as part of its very character a trait of permanence—something that may consciously appear, disappear, and reappear—a fundamental condition which persists forever, and at best can be awakened by external circumstances though it can never be created from them.

With this, our first observation is called into question. There we viewed lonesomeness as a negative relational experience in correlation with multiplicity—negative in the sense of the false lonesomeness of natural man or as a circumstance of nature. There, only the conditions are turned back upon one and are consequently "unnatural" [not a part of the self]. True lonesomeness occurs despite such natural externalities and is realized only in one's soul. It is, however, positive, because it is more than merely a sense of something missing, mere deprivation. Yet most observers are impressed above all with the fact that lonesomeness implies something missing—a negative condition. Something lacking must be supplied. Something else is needed. This must be provided from without or through participation with absent others or objects. Still, this very impression betrays the positive quality of the "I." The negative tone of lonesomeness is aroused in the process of emergence into consciousness; it is not basic or fundamental. In contrast, the positive origin [in the subconscious] bespeaks the true and genuine character of lonesomeness. It may even manifest itself as independent of its origin in its sheer naked appearance.

We do not want to explore this positive character of lonesomeness any further. In all dimly experienced impressions strong and peculiar enough to mark its origin as positive, positive lonesomeness will appear in the consciousness as merely negative. Despite its positive origin, it will also seem negative in all other residual experience. This is even the case for that most common and frequent form of lonesomeness in the modern world, namely, where it is manifested by frenzy or endless striving. The soul is on a permanent search for social cohesion or sharing, although the failure of such a quest is foreordained by the fact that one soul can never totally assume the role of any other. So the feeling of lonesomeness deepens when it becomes clearly more positive in tone, despite the desire to share it with others everywhere. The possibility of sharing the feeling persists and does not abate, in spite of the painful awareness that the edge of the soul in its innermost being must always remain untouched by others. No bridge exists to cross from that border to the inner souls of others. States of mourning are also often defined as lonesomeness, as are other depressed states in which the soul is so much preoccupied with itself and flooded by moods that not even the burning desire by others to offer support to the depressed soul can help. Even art or music, and finally (as religious men must shamefully admit), trust in religion or faith cannot still the anguished cry of depression. Yet real lonesomeness is not even present in these phenomena (at least to the extent that the soul finds itself alone with its world), since the painful strain toward dialogue is not hindered only by the enduring core of the soul but also by an internal wall which is relatively accidental, and in particular, transitory. Of course lonesomeness as we have described it, as an individually encompassing form, is only possible where the cultural situation allows such an individual single-soul feeling to emerge so that, along with it, a real lonesomeness is established in principle. . . .

If we were to characterize in detail the positive aspect of lonesomeness, we would first of all have to acknowledge that a certain feeling of alienation is necessarily connected with lonesomeness, and this entails a certain distance from the environment together with the stark experience of that relationship which is expressed subjectively by the "I" in a very positive manner. One would perhaps have to further posit a differentiation of active from passive lonesomeness. Actively, extensive (perhaps deeper) searches are initiated for the joining of the external with one's own self, or conversely, the participation of one's own self with the external world. Beyond this, there is the question of the pain, and since it is also found today, the joy that lonesomeness generates. Most of all, however, the relation of lonesomeness to individuality and individualism,[1] and also to subjectivism would have to be investigated, and these are certainly interrelated though they are also completely different. We do not want to go into all this here. Instead, we intend only to respond to the historical and cultural-philosophical questions that probe the intellectual context and the situational causes of lonesomeness. Here, of course, psychology and psycho-phenomenology inevitably will shed some light on the problem of positive lonesomeness, which, taken together with the limitations set forth above, should resolve itself in short order.

PHILOSOPHICAL HISTORY

Even under such limitations, it is probably advisable to begin with the evidence indicating that the experience of lonesomeness seemingly takes on a concreteness as a dimension detached from mere life. This is particularly appropriate for philosophy construed as a metaphysical, conceptual scheme. Corresponding to the experience of lonesomeness is the dogma emphasizing the preponderance of internal perception, which transports unmediated reality into the consciousness of the individual so that, presumably, everything else can be inferred only from that consciousness. This is an idea taken from Descartes, and from which a great range of thought entirely dominating the new philosophy originates. Specifically, the Cartesian doubt, which was accepted as the methodological basis of philosophy, reached its limit in the "I"—but an "I" which was established precisely by doubt and thus persisted as the only self-certain reality.

This seems to be the thoroughly new idea with which modern philosophy begins, just as the experience of lonesomeness seems to be a completely modern phenomenon. Yet we already find in antiquity a special theory of value preference, as well as a metaphysics of the individual soul based on internal perception which is somewhat analogous to that of Leibniz or, in other ways, to that of Berkeley. We refer to the subjectivism of the sophists. Gorgias makes the extraordinary statement that there is no object of knowledge independent from the subject, and if there were one, it would definitely not be knowable. Even if it were knowable, then the knowledge possessed by one subject could not be communicated to another. This is probably the most extreme form that subjectivism can take—an absolute restriction of the experiencing "I" to its own self. The soul is abolutely closed to external things as well as to other individuals. It has, as in Leibniz, no windows and no exits or entrances—no doors.

It is the spirit of skepticism with which sophistic subjectivism resonates. It was skepticism or doubt that generated the Cartesian statement, but the direction was of course reversed, since the *Dubito* of Descartes was not what the sophists intended—an enduring purpose or a permanent self-appraisal—but a route and vehicle which positive knowledge could take, a mere "skeptical method," which has also been recommended by Kant and which is perhaps even necessary for philosophy in response to the demands of unconditionalism made by so many.

One could presume to discern in skepticism, be it absolute or be it mere methodology, the basis of a unified single-soul feeling, and thereby, the basis of lonesomeness. Actually, skepticism and also lonesomeness arise precisely from such a self-sentiment rather than from outside. In Gorgias, this is the argument; in Descartes, its limiting edge. . . . The joining of doubt and individual soul was very precisely and completely stated, not by the sophists nor by the skeptics of the sixteenth and seventeenth centuries, but first of all by their successor (missing in antiquity). Descartes was, in a preliminary sense, merely a follower, and therefore systematically narrower and more restricted. This might account for the fact that the development of a theory based on a narrowly circumscribed "I" was not so completely clear and tidy in the beginning. . . .

If we do not believe that individual soul feelings and particularly feelings of true lonesomeness emerged out of skepticism, then we are led to this by the general insight that the history of ideas never goes along such straight logical paths. Skepticism itself may be traced in this way through a mere history of philosophy. In the context of the whole cultural situation it has, however, connections and relations that call for broader and deeper explanations. To disregard this would plainly be to desert metaphysics because of its previous "anarchy." And the argument advanced by skepticism, that individual mental lonesomeness is so intertwined with such a multitude of life tendencies and life expressions that it must be treated in purely theoretical terms to understand it, is all too weak and wretched. Indeed, the obviously truncated nature of this genealogy may be recognized particularly by the fact that the sophists, first of all (the first that we have considered here), contended that every "I" is absolutely constricted and sealed off. But that means something completely different from what we are searching for. Certainly that statement of Gorgias bespeaks an extreme subjectivism, but it is a mere cognitive subjectivism, and nothing tells us that a real, individual self-sentiment was also included. On the contrary, the lively commerce of the sophists took them out of all political and social structures and placed them instead in permanent and open contact with numerous friends, companions, and disciples, establishing the custom of permanent, steady, lively talking and discussion. This by no means could be construed as a forceful overtone to an inner state of being alone. On the contrary, their very light and joyful activity must have completely suppressed the true existence of the individual soul. This could not allow inner lonesomeness and true, deep alienation from all externalities to emerge. What one must assume, however, is that the near-cognitive subjectivism of the sophist is really anchored in the deeper-lying layers of true affective subjectivism and may have originated from there, just as one must also assume the existence of such deep-seated subjectivism at the same time and even earlier. The sophists lived only after the original experience; experiencing it afterward, they used it for their own ends. Skepticism is not a wellspring. It is simply something one can turn around as an argument for the separateness of the soul. It follows subjectivism, but both are, first of all, completely independent of one another. They are autochthonous, although the repetitive historical conjuncture of both may signal the fact that they are in a common intellectual situation. Both are the expression of this situation.

ANTIQUITY

If we were now to analyze historically the deeper and genuine locations of true lonesomeness in its primary extensions, then we would least of all expect the appearance of this state of mind in antiquity. The Greeks lived in a completely original manner. Their religion emerged from and was reinforced by such behavior, so that they learned to view their environment not only in psychic terms, but as godlike. This feature of their human relations and associations is particularly important, because the state, in classic terms a comprehensive symbol of all-encompassing essence, wielded an emotionally coercive power. Even Themistocles, whose external fate, exile, seemed to cut all ties, never abandoned his devotion to this most secure center. . . .

In this old Hellenic structure of order, Alcibiades [acting] and the sophists [thinking] were the last passing witnesses of the whole period of this history of ideas, which had its origin in the seething periods of the seventh century B.C. Then in all areas—in that of ideas as well as in that of the state, in the societal as well as in the economic—the Homeric-aristocratic world burst with heavy disturbances, and a new period of history emerged. It has often been recognized and demonstrated in poetry and drama, how the consciousness of the "I" emerges during these important transitions. Lyric stands in sharp contrast to the realistic epic. Lyrics were not only songs of glory and mourning or ceremonial hymns of victory and worship, but they also established a gestalt that expressed the individual soul truly and exactly. Yet this individual soul—the soul, for example, of Sappho or Alkaios—does not rise from the wholeness of human relations. . . . Even the Prometheus of Aeschylus affirms, in his deepest aloneness, the passionate connection with other beings. . . .

Yet we sense, in the early period of the new conscience and spirit, secret areas disguised in hidden form, vaguely foreshadowing the first inklings of lonesomeness and alienation. The grieving of the wandering Demeter for her lost child (externally characterized by the image of traditional teaching), in sharp contrast with the anger and sorrow of Achilles, manifests the eternally directed, single voice that does not rise from the mere need for another, although seemingly motivated that way, but is positively and originally lonesome to the end. She could not be saved from this lonesomeness, even if her daughter were found. . . .

Considering Sophocles, one could perhaps think that drama as such and the spirit of the tragic were the cradle of lonesomeness. Also in the essence of the tragic, which cannot be further explored at this point, dwells the insulation of the individual from the surrounding cosmos, represented by any structure of order such as state or custom. The necessity of such individualization follows from the plan of the cosmos itself, which is developed only through individual orientation. . . . As a whole, the tragic spirit is very close to the experience of lonesomeness. All the pathos of the tragic poet, however, flows as much into the universal cosmos as into the lonesome soul. They were incorporated by Sophocles' specific style.

From still another form of art, namely, sculpture, and here particularly, one can perhaps see a fundamental affiliation with lonesomeness. Figures of sculpture, unless they are groups, stand essentially alone and unrelated in eternal space. However, the unrelatedness actually invalidates the predicate of lonesomeness, which in this case is not exhausted in the constitutive absence of any relationship, but expresses such absence explicitly. . . . One could of course imagine a sculptured piece of art which, regardless of the intensity behind it, also exposed that before it and demonstrated the merging of the past and the future where lonesomeness dwells. However, it seems as if history did not create such an artist as drama had created in Sophocles. . . .

Drama and sculpture as such are not documents of single-soul feeling in their mere form. It is the personal voice of Sophocles that expresses such tones. It is because of Socrates that these tones are not bound to a single figure at that same time. Socrates, much more than Sophocles, very early and in a very different way, like Plato, Aristotle, or the stoics, was claimed by Christianity not because of his teachings but because of his soul. . . .

His conduct and attitude are, however, not the subjectivism of a single soul. Yet from this emerges, and more radically than among the sophists, a new and completely original separation of the subject. Of course, the limits and standards [of this subjectivist conception] are not put to the test by the subject but by truth itself. Even so, it is the subject, separated from everything else, separated even from all ties of tradition, lonesome and alone with the truth in itself, that meets the test. Like Antigone's soul before the lowest and darkest power, Socrates stands before and in the empty, echo-filled space of truth. . . .

What appeared for the first time in Socrates and Sophocles did not disappear from the living period of antiquity, even if its documents were drowned in the noise of the Alexandrian centuries. We may not seek it in the heights of the mental life, nor in spiritual sociality—although traces may be found there, at best silent or vague. Plato's great soul was, first of all, oriented toward participation, if not in the state or in the realm of state, then in the objective and rich, enormously elaborated life of ideas. Aristotle was too much imbedded in the organically created, in the effects in and of the material. Thus there were no feelings left for lonesomeness and alienation. . . .

The religious yearnings of the time finally found their fulfillment in Christianity, where the feeling and consciousness of the single soul were bared. If one felt compelled to interpret the essence of Christianity as the first recognition of the eternal value of the human soul, then he would find himself mouthing mere empty talk. Christianity has, without doubt, other and more central ideas. . . . Nevertheless, if not in the teachings and preachings of Jesus, then from the tone of the evangelical accounts (particularly among the Synoptics) and also from Jesus' first historical impact, one can indeed recognize the peculiar, most puzzling emergence and blossoming of something unique—the reality of soul, that is, singular soul—which was never previously acknowledged. . . .

. . . While the rejection of the man who wanted to say goodbye to his loved ones before going with Christ may be reminiscent of the women sent away by Socrates before his hour of death, the startling, still terrifying order for the man, who before joining Christ wanted to bury his father ("let the dead bury their dead"), is indeed without precedent in its terrifying demands. . . .

Also in old Judaism, because of the remoteness of a bodiless monotheistic god, possibly more impressive than in paganism, one will find traces of single-soul feeling. In the midst of the exodus, one can at times, particularly from the psalms, sense something touching the soul. At any rate, particularly in Judaism, the new elements of lonesomeness and estrangement are fully expressed, become obvious, and contribute to a positive foundation. The older Judaism was, first of all and in its very essence, a communion. This was not only a communion, as usually understood, between the selected people and god, but also and particularly a communion among men who were united in their avowal of this one god. The separation of the leader, who is permitted to face or at least hear god on a mountain, apart from the others, does not mean intrinsic nearness to but distance from god. The terrible other-worldliness of the elevated god is forbidding—not all may see or hear him. Genuine nearness to god, however, is to be observed in the lonesome prayer of Christ ["My God! My God! Why hast thou forsaken me?" eds.] This, in turn, creates the lonesome prayer, hitherto unknown. . . . Lonesomeness in prayer and lonesomeness before death mean the same, because death is not only an obedient acceptance of a destiny fashioned by god, but also positive submergence in god, as in the death of Socrates, and Sophocles' Antigone, whose deaths were not only mere submission to the law. . . .

. . . The merger of the Christian stylization of the soul with Greek and Roman conceptions of god had already begun with Paul. Because religion and state were intimately connected in antiquity, this also led to a merger with ancient Greco-Roman conceptions of the state. Thus, early Christianity took on the form of a state-church and (after separation of both imperial groupings) was transformed in the West into papal Catholicism. The single soul merged ever more in the big roundelay of the faithful totality. The tight structures of the medieval church assign each single soul to an exact and predetermined position in the hierarchical system. And this position gives essence to the soul. It is basic to the soul as such.

Middle Ages

Yet some kinds of religiosity in the Middle Ages also preserved a vision of the naked and lonesome soul standing before its eternal god. Mysticism now and again continued to recognize that the individual "I" is completely and utterly alone. Mysticism accomplished this because it places itself beyond all the halfway, secular, mediating, and sequential steps of the church, and leads directly to god. This is also the case where the yearning for the adoration swiftly and fleetingly avoids any intercessor; mysticism carries on this way throughout the Catholic form of religion, to which it otherwise characteristically belongs. Adoration of god is the aim, and this makes the soul of the mystic lonesome and alien in Roman Christianity and makes his voice always so singular and clearly audible, despite his many companions in the great choir of the church.

Particularly in the destruction of the church, in the destruction of the mediating principle, lies the essence of the Reformation. "Sacredness of work," for Luther, is "idolatry of the flesh." For Calvin, it is the essence of Catholicism. For both, it is paganism. The constant contribution of antiquity to the construction of the Catholic church was quite correctly recognized as central. Moreover, the characterization of antiquity as depicting the interdependence of the divine and the secular was also seen quite correctly. In contrast to this, the Reformation was supposed, with some justification, to be a renewal of original Christianity. That the mysticism of the Middle Ages, which had a direct influence on Luther, was exempted from Catholicism is also of clarifying import.

Indeed here, as in primitive Christianity and mysticism, very intensively but in a more restricted manner, the theme and the consciousness of the single soul break through completely; this occurs, verifying what we recognized everywhere, through non-mediating lonesomeness before god. Both the Renaissance and the Reformation signified a negative—the destruction of the hierarchical status ladder. Yet it [the Renaissance] did not recognize the lonesomeness of the soul. Nowhere in the Renaissance does a lonesome soul stand miserably and silently before the dreadfulness or the sweetness of the infinity to which it would surrender itself. The present is its primary sphere, and it is here that it passionately enjoys life. A world always surrounds it, whether it be highly personalized or even a world of dreams and magic. This holds for Michelangelo, whose matchless mind was always filled with whole groups of moving bodies. . . . Leonardo was also incapable of experiencing lonesomeness. . . .

Luther was also really and totally lonesome, although only during those hours when he lived in his complete essentiality. In profane affairs this same man, the most lonesome in his religious ardor, was like Christ (at the marriage of Cana) or, like the believers of the early communities, very sociable—truly and sincerely sociable.

However, in the glut of religious experience, in the terrible dark night of the eternally sinful soul, in the sudden ecstasy of undeserved mercy, Luther is so very alone, like Christ on the cross or on the Mount of Olives—"alone with his god." The secular has been shed. No institution, not even of the most spiritual kind remains; no friends are left. Only the shivering, freezingly anxious, freezingly blessed, single soul is there before god. Toward the "daily bread," the symbol of earthly being, Luther and Lutheranism not only count "food, drinking, clothing, shoes, etc.," but also "pious spouse, pious children, pious servants, pious and faithful sovereigns," even "honor, good friends, and faithful neighbors." Even the piety of spouse and children is merely a material desire, a desire of earthly men who live together, not of the genuine and true man, who is "alone with his god."

In this all-encompassing formula, "with one's god alone," we have clarified in full measure, far beyond Luther, every development of the feeling of the single soul. Being free not only of this-worldliness, but also of all earthly godlike association, is not merely negative precondition. The positive nature of "being alone with one's god" creates the genuine lonesomeness of the really individual soul. And this had to be representative for each form of silent standing before something new and something shiveringly recognized as absolute. . . .

Unlike its interpretation in skepticism, and much deeper, the single-soul feeling is really based on lonesomeness before god. But the earlier explanations did not really lay bare the basis of lonesomeness. In the final analysis, the task embodied a further search for another, deeper basis, instead of for a basis with a fixed outcome. So we arrive at a juncture. Indeed, one had often seen the peculiar connection between skepticism and mysticism, the essence or import of which need not be dealt with here. . . . A statement of Nietzsche—"When skepticism and yearning are joined, mysticism appears"—deeply comprehends the mutual proximity of the three elements. Of course, yearning substitutes here for single-soul lonesomeness. Yet the original relationship is perverted here without doubt, since skepticism is assumed to be positive, mysticism to be negative, and yearning assumes impoverishment. The mystic view and the mystic union with god are certainly primary. Skepticism is the mediator. . . .

The aloneness with god is the only primary source of all feeling and consciousness. This is the result that our previous questions have produced. . . .

. . . [It follows] that the lonesomeness of the soul springs from aloneness with god, and only from this does all other loneliness of the soul arise, just as in Luther, after his return to earthly life, some hidden residue of the soul remained obviously separate. The complete union, the blessed self-sacrifice, self-devotion, harmony in god or death even up to the point where the soul is most alone, show that lonesomeness . . . is only a time span, whether of short or long duration, a time span where the soul, in which both eternity and this-worldliness reign, transcends the one through the other. Only in the worldly area is utter lonesomeness impossible, just as it is in any absolute sense. It goes its separate way alone, taking its departure with a blissfully painful glance.

With this we have found the determinants of experienced lonesomeness that contradict the earlier, although provisional, qualifications. Lonesomeness was conceived as a permanent condition and something essential to the case before, transitory, prior to the complete submergence in god, but this involved the soul. Now our fundamental thesis is that it is a basically transitory state. . . .

MODERN TIMES

Only in modern times do we really have genuine lonesomeness, consummated in the spirit of union and metaphysically concretized as an absolute. We find this absolutistic concretization stemming from broader religious grounds in Calvinism. Calvinism produces the strongest and most principled lonesomeness of the individual soul. And it produces this unutterable alienation and confinement not only as a transitory state, but as permanently maintained, as something methodically cultivated. The extraordinary practical talents of the Calvinists, which made his ethics the spiritual base of all the modern forms of economics, society, and polity, are, according to Max Weber, not founded in the openness toward the world of the Catholic and even the Lutheran, but in innerworldly asceticism. Calvinism prohibits, as evil, even the slightest contact of external things with the heart, not to mention the soul. Asceticism prescribes only for "proof," with no internal involvement in mere externalities, and thus it commends systematically methodical as well as rational care. This unutterable inner distance toward things is even generalized to human beings. Such a statement, appearing in many Calvinistic rules of life, so preposterous, almost ridiculous to natural or ancient man—forbidding friendship, any human closeness, any trust, and demanding instead reserve as an ethical ideal—is a document of a deep and ultimate lonesomeness, of a state of individuated soul, which is methodically enhanced and preserved. If we ask the reason for this peculiar state of mind, then the answer is here again and explicitly—standing before god. However, this is not, as was continuously, consciously, and intentionally maintained, the character of confrontation. . . .

Surrender to god is halted just before the moment of union. The change of the transitory, deeply fatal lonesomeness into a permanent and intentionally controlled state depends on the total disruption of the natural course of experience. In this quality of being essentially interrupted or cut off, which without doubt is a perversion of legitimate connections, we find, despite the religious reasons for the cutoff, also the critique that has been advanced by history. To bar any form of religiosity other than that which was ceremoniously conducted for the honor of god had necessarily to lead to the death of that religiosity as such. This is so even if the rituals, having become ends in themselves and because of such fundamental coagulation, have also clung even more tenaciously to enduring existence. This can still be observed in the puritanical-Calvinistic England of today, if it were carefully observed. The form did not die off together with its religious content, and neither did the ethos of innerworldly asceticism, which is still basic to broad areas of contemporary life styles. . . . And lonesomeness, the quality of the single individual soul, because of Calvinism has become a structuring factor in the whole modern texture of life, permanent and even expanding, although its religious basis has long been extinguished. . . .

Calvinism, with which we would also like to associate the Jesuit order, facilitated the emergence of the philosophy of Descartes, as well as that of Leibniz and Berkeley. Besides this, there was a curious amalgam of pantheistic tendencies drawn from other sources in Calvinism from the very beginning. . . . It is essentially because of this connection that the experience of lonesomeness, which would have had to disappear with the religious downfall of Calvinism, could survive at all. Even in mere restlessness and in the wandering quest of the soul for belonging, a yearning is exemplified in the mechanized modern world, which is in need of positive nourishment. Thus, in all weakened manifestations of lonesomeness, there is an impact attributable in part to the actual weakening of Calvinism. . . .

Lonesomeness was also cultivated in the arts through the benevolent patronage of the age. Rembrandt, especially in his later portraits, made an impact [on his time] similar to that of Descartes. The lonesomeness of that old woman in St. Petersburg who looks into another world where she imagines she is already at home, having been removed from the soil and yet being still part of the soil, is present and totally human. At the same time, a unique, genuine, and original lonesomeness is captured, as well as the realization and diffusion of this rare experience. It is hardly surprising that this painter of the deepest lonesomeness was, on the other hand, also the painter of the most tender and heartfelt outpourings of one soul into another—consider, among others, Rembrandt's "Jewish Bride." . . .

Rembrandt offers only one of the earliest and most impressive testimonials to the fact that the experience of lonesomeness was now abroad in the land. From that point on, we meet its expression much more often, although rarely in pure form and very rarely without experiencing its negative quality, which of course is part, but only part, of lonesomeness. This negativity, however, did lead (at the very end, and in a strange turnaround as well as confirmation of the original) to a new, but no less genuine, lonesomeness. . . .

The historical example is the lonesomeness of Frederic the Great, in whom the disregard for mankind showed only one side, while the other was the burning and insatiable desire for prayer.

A consideration of the lonesomeness of the older Frederic could call into question all our earlier speculations. A king, one could argue, has no friends, no companions. It is entirely the external momentum of his social position that produces lonesomeness in this case. The lonesomeness of the throne, then, is associated with the straightforward culmination of social structure, which is only apparently turned back on itself. In truth, only a socially and externally motivated lonesomeness is established for insignificant and impressionable men, and above all, it is a structural individuation [There is but one throne in a monarchy. eds.]. So does lonesomeness become possible. The result is that such an origin is always purely negative. This kind of lonesomeness is based purely on scarcity, a scarcity of the kind that we clearly distinguished in our introductory remarks, and it should not be confused with genuine and complete lonesomeness. At most, it is the quality of being left alone. To extend our remarks a bit, it is frequently one of the happy benefits that accrue to the occupation of the throne with the open and benign conduct and administration of authority, just as the sense of insignificance or inferiority may break out [among common men] in resentment or rebellion. At any rate, the exceptional instance of external position, whether it be disturbed from above or below, provides an extraordinarily fertile soil for the germination of true lonesomeness. The cultivation of the soil is a different matter.

However, the external position need not, under all circumstances, be understood as originating only from without. It can have an intrinsic origin in the existential quality of the personality, which, combined with the external position, would produce lonesomeness and would thus have to be regarded as its positive origin. Completely independent of all sociality (a parallel consequence) which the seed of lonesomeness selects, so to speak, as its most fertile ground, the final motive of lonesomeness may be found directly in the existential quality of personality. Thus, as in the case of Frederic the Great, the lonesomeness of human greatness can replace the lonesomeness of the throne. . . .

. . . Genuine lonesomeness is so severely limited to the most profound, and simultaneously most impoverished, nakedly vulnerable kernel of the soul, that a consciousness of one's difference from others can hardly prevail. It is even reinforced by a total consciousness that all other souls are, in their ultimate core, just as impoverished, in need of help, and hardly distinguishable from one's own soul. But those souls do not recognize the lonesomeness they share in the dissolution of each in the union of all, because it is silenced by the noise from without and by the trumpeting of individual self-importance from within. Where the lonesomeness of greatness is concerned, such greatness is built only on the fact that it confronts a newly recognized infinity without an intercessor, as the loftiness of the throne is experienced only as the solitude of the throne, where the crown assumes a priestly nature as the material representation of the deity. Insignificant, inferior men will also experience their insignificance and inferiority as lonesomeness only where it becomes for them a totally ideological symbol of all humanity, as is their insignificance before god or the universe.

"Lonesomeness before god" was also the lonesomeness of Frederic the Great, except that he did not believe in "god." But his nonbelief remained mixed with a passionate longing for belief. A crisis would surely erupt, were this unqualified lack of belief to permit transcendentally oriented lonesomeness to break out with no access to the resurrection of belief. This lonesomeness is also captured by the lonesomeness of Nietzsche. In line with popular modes of explanation, it is very easy for one to interpret such lonesomeness as mere profane aloneness deriving from the absence of friends and their accompanying, understanding companions, and the influence in action from without that could soothe the pain. The real basis of this lonesomeness is again an immediate and different "standing before god" and not the fact that others are confronting the same god. Yet this makes the lonesomeness of Nietzsche a totally unique and a solely negative, deeply frightening experience. God has been replaced by a complete deprivation of his divinity. The lonesomeness of Nietzsche is the lonesomeness of divine nihilism, a nothingness in which Faust also could no longer hope to find a universe.

SOUL—THE EMERGENCE OF THE CONCEPT

The modern German word *Seele* and the words referring to the soul in other modern European languages are being used in such a variety of meanings that it is difficult to recognize any common theme in them all. In addition to the soul that is accepted by the Christian religion as immortal, and the soul that represents an object of investigation for the science of psychology, there is the soul of a poem, a flower, a landscape, and finally, that of a people, a culture, and, on a lower level, of an enterprise. Among these one can recognize hardly any commonality at all. The soul presumably probed in such depth by poets or by such minds as those of Kierkegaard, Dostoevski, and Nietzsche, is possibly not even included in this range of meaning. If one takes note of the conceptions of soul held by the primitives, then the diffusion of meaning is obviously incomprehensible. There one learns first about the soul of blood and breath, shade or name; about souls that leave the body at the time of death, or earlier during life (if only for short periods); second, about souls that are inseparable from the body or from parts of it; third, about souls that assume a special body after departing this life; about souls that one can have in a multitude of different forms; finally, about human and animal souls, as well as those of plants, or about souls of such things as water, caves, and mountains.[1] In the light of the range of conceptual usage that is reported, one cannot avoid the judgment that, in translations, the term "soul" must serve to designate objects and events for which

Slightly abridged translation of "Die Entstehung des Seelenbegriffes," *Logos* 16 (1927): 311–55.

we do not have any terms at all and for which the concept of soul, itself quite obscure, must substitute without really facilitating any understanding. There may be considerable doubt that there is a unity at all. Perhaps we people of today mix up in the connotation of "soul" a diversity of items that are related in no context at all.

In order to bring more clarity into this mass, one is bound to confront two obstacles. First, in our use of the term "soul" we designate a phenomenon or a complex of phenomena that reaches back into the early history of mankind, long before there was any philosophy or science as such. These have either brought some clarification to the obscurity of the past, or have given an old name to a newly discovered phenomenon. Of course, they have been unable to avoid the slight, persistent traces or even the intensive representations incorporated in the old term—and they often are not distinguished from those areas dealt with exclusively by philosophy and science. Besides that established by philosophy and science, even the most concise conception of soul—provided by Christianity—remains rather indeterminate after 2,000 years. What is precisely meant by the object that the Christian believes to be immortal is never made explicit. Second, any method that can enlighten the whole concept of soul must raise the question of its emergence and development. Here one must anticipate the possibility that even in the beginning and in the early development of a concept, a diversity of different appearances is comprehended only in noumenal terms. The unity of the name should, however, be based on something generic, and that will have to be apprehended in the genesis of the phenomenon so named. Later changes and restructurings need not maintain the unifying bond in any optimal sense. They can well be radical new developments. Because we, quite properly, examine origins and transformations should not be construed to mean we employ the methods of evolutionary theory. Of course, the possibility of at least a persistent noumenal context must be there in the beginning and in subsequent transformations.

Here, however, there is a difficulty that all questions of development face, namely, they do not concern themselves with the development of something, but with something distinct that has presumably already developed. He who seeks knowledge about the emergence of soul must already know what soul is. On the other hand, the inquiry into origins is supposed to clarify this. Furthermore, one must be wary of the dangers of treating historical development in a specifically contemporary perspective.

In order to overcome the difficulties, one must vaguely account for the positive and negative import of the contemporary perspective and let it precede the analysis of emergence. This need not be exact, and thus it resembles our brief discussion of the diffuse range of observations which raised the issue of origins. It also is in line with our intention to provide only a general methodological orientation.

PSYCHOLOGICAL AND BIOLOGICAL APPROACHES

The clearest concept of soul is to be found in modern psychology as it has developed since Descartes. Soul is consciousness (*cogitatio*) and psychology, the science of consciousness. From that point of view, the concept of an unconscious dimension of soul must be dismissed as logically absurd. Even if one accepts an unconscious, he is constrained in this case to approach the concept from the standpoint of consciousness and must understand it as an "unconscious consciousness." The reasons for the emergence of a primary concept of soul as consciousness must be examined in the context of a theory of knowledge—specifically, an epistemology of imminent consciousness. Long before, Descartes's theories of knowledge had already produced and isolated the same result for the basic concept of soul; yet they were unable to break through to the major directions taken by subsequent routes of development. Conversely, the earlier meaning of soul persisted in modern times only here and there, unrelated to consciousness, and essentially without influence (even though there may have been whispers or mutterings to the effect that the meaning of the concept should deal with the unconscious aspects of the soul).

Historically, however, it is clear that the psychology of Aristotle and its subsequent great history started with observations on matters of the soul in the soul of plants. Thus the focus was not on consciousness but on life. This biological conception will then confront the conception of consciousness secondarily and only if it seems present in animals in the context of life and (as in men) penetrates life extensively. At any rate, consciousness never appears other than with the living. There is life without consciousness, but not consciousness without life. Consciousness as "real" consciousness can never be conceived of as bound to anything other than the living. This contention also rejects the notion that there is something like "transcendental" consciousness.

The biological concept of soul is considered by many to be held by primitives. Primeval man would have called soul that which living gives to the living, thereby certainly making the border between the living and the nonliving uncertain. Indeed, almost everything was conceived as living. This conception, implying a meaning like "animating," life-giving, or enlivening, does, upon close consideration, reveal that it is not based on either biology or consciousness as applied to the explanation of soul. One envisages by "enlivening" or "animating" that primitive man, either to explain the phenomena he experienced or (less rationally) empathizing with such phenomena, imputed a sort of will, analogous to his own, to these phenomena. The later biological concept of soul developed by Aristotle or the scholastics must, also be interpreted, if one strives for a deeper understanding beneath face validity, as primarily a conception of soul in consciousness.

Compared to the concept of soul among psychologists, either modern or Aristotelian, one will perceive the concepts developed by religious thinkers, predominantly those of Christianity, as being closer to the original phases of its development. Here one also recognizes the beginnings of longstanding and enduring philosophical and theological disputation. Historians have also investigated the religious conception of soul at different points in its development. Furthermore, many even start from the religious concept of soul in exploring its emergence and development. Yet it is exactly at that point that the conception is especially vague. The major characteristic seems to be immortality, which, however, is considered only one of the predicates—the belief or disbelief in immortality does not touch upon the necessity of whether or not to believe in the soul. Of course the concepts of soul held by psychology are of no help at this point. For the religionist gives great significance to immortality in the "process of consciousness," even if one may doubt that that line of thought considers consciousness as erased in immortality. Moreover, the primary biological concept does not penetrate this far. In the psychology of religion it is ridiculous to consider the soul of plants at the outset, if one is basically interested in the immortal soul. In the "definition" of the soul in Aristotle, even in Plato[2] if not before, we already find the discrepancy: "that through which we live" is weakened as soon as the soul is conceived to be immortal and thus to enliven no more anything in this world, not to speak of giving life to the body.

What can be derived in any case from these introductory considerations about the explanation of origins and emergence is the obvious original location of the concept of soul in the realm of religions. The specific biological conception and, even more, the consciousness dimension of the concept of soul can only have split off from religion. Their connection with the primitive world and their development are, of course, a persisting problem. The other initially mentioned concepts of soul, surviving even today, appear to be later transformations, at times only metaphors. Of course their potential influence has remained ever since. If, on the other hand, the religious concept of soul is still vague, one may even consider this an advantage because it would not permit an approach to origins with rigorous but misleading modern terminology. Thus, in exploring the earliest concept of soul, one must first proceed methodologically to an interpretation of early religion. Only then and from the perspectives of religion can one explore the concepts of soul and subsequently the soul itself. Thus a generality of method will be reached as the only means to transcend the dilemma inherent in the twin study of origin and emergence.

PRIMITIVES, CHILDREN, AND THE NOUMENON

It is counterproductive to this aim, however, if one interprets religion itself in terms of some concept of soul that it is presumably based on. The theory of animism, of which E. B. Tylor was the classic proponent and which W. Wundt tried to incorporate into his system, has been abandoned, in more recent research. Yet it was not abandoned as a consequence of any critical analysis of the assumed and highly questionable concept of soul, but because of the fact that the early stages of mankind did not manifest any kind of belief in the soul—at least, there was no need for it at that primordial time. Such judgment, of course, could not be accomplished in exact terms without critical analysis. Thus, the real reason for rejection of animism was not a negative attack on it but rather the positive formulation of a new and more thorough conception of original religion.

The theories of "preanimism" comprise a number of diverse approaches. Under this term, first and in a narrow sense, appeared a group named the "magistic" or "pedantic," with which the name of Frazer is included if one overlooks the pedantic points of disagreement with his writing. They maintained that there was an original unity of religion and magic, as well as a basic duality of both. They still owe us some insight into the exact emergence of specific beliefs in gods as well as specific beliefs in souls. The turnabout which Andrew Land and Pater W. Schmidt[3] are trying to accomplish these days is nevertheless characterized by a systematic bias. The most penetrating involvement and the deepest layer of religious experience have been disclosed by R. R. Marrett.[4] It was Rudolf Otto's well known analysis of the holy[5] that took his study even further.

No belief in soul or spirit and also no belief in many gods or one god in any specific sense are to be found in the most primitive thought. Even less did early men derive religious concepts as "explanations." The experience that is the characteristic of their whole being, often daily if not several times a day, is the experience of the "noumenal shudder."

Conceptions of the childhood of mankind as a state of paradise, innocence, and unclouded fortune, which were specifically established after Rousseau and, in a different way, after Herder, have long been discarded, although they were actually in existence in antiquity, the Middle Ages, and the Renaissance.[6] Of course, they were not abandoned in favor of the earlier teaching of Thomas Hobbes, which posited a "war of each against all" and lupine antagonisms among men in a state of original nature. More mature insight comes to recognize this, in the phrase of Jakob Burckhardt, as a "prey to endless anxiety."[7] Also in the lives of children—with which the development of primitives and of mankind has been compared since the eighteenth century in the fashion of the historians of religion, De Brosses and Johann Nicolaus Tetens—a major phase of shuddering, horror, and fear (a "being afraid") may be found. This occurs, regardless of their good fortune or innocence, just as the moment of "paradise" is evidenced to a certain degree to the primitives.[8]

Of course one should not overlook the shuddering and horror, even among children, found in the character of a specific noumenon, as demonstrated particularly by Otto. One must also recognize in the noumenon not only the noumenal fear and anxiety as well as the *tremendum* [a compulsion to be afraid], but also a moment of fascination. Only this permits one to understand the positive meaning of such original experiences in the life of primitives. In both respects, the all-too-negative interpretation of Burckhardt is amiss.

Objects of the noumenal experience can be anything, although some objects are particularly appropriate. Since such an experience is a removal from the ordinary, having the character of an altogether different event, it tends to seek its focal points outside of daily life—in the pouring, coagulating, rushing, stinking blood; heartbeats and breathing of sleepers; shadows of the sun at noon, in the evening, during night; the dead, the stiff, lying corpses; furthermore, the phallus and phallic atmosphere; pictures of dreams and names. Also they may be the metallic bodies of lizards and snakes, or the primeval eyes of cattle; night animals, like owls and bats. At any rate, they tend to focus on the animal before the human, on death before life. The orb and sickle of the moon and its gloomy light also belong here. Stumps of trees gleaming with sulfur; erratic small flames over the swamps; certain noises, in particular the humming of quaking trees, which do not lose their ominous power even if one is able methodically to reproduce the noises. Drums, percussion, and pipes need to be mentioned. From here there are transitions to the reeling of dance and also to the state of mind that one may realize when possessed by drugs. Beyond the area of noumenal "objects" and the "objective" noumenal experience, we confront the more intransitively based noumenal sensations of *Gemüt* here. They are important for the emergence of ritual. Of course ritual can be established in a more objective way, e.g., if someone, by his own act, initiates and accidentally produces the picture of falling raindrops into a pond may experience a shudder from that; even more so, if the pond were noumenal to begin with. From there each individual may arrive at a state where, through conscious repetition, he believes he has gained some mysterious power. Only after the fact will he then interpret it in line with a specific aim. For example, in such a way rain magic is discovered. Thus magic customs emerge.[9]

At this point, however, our topic does require special attention to the noumenal objects as such. Again one should stress that, on close observation, anything can become an object of noumenal experience—not only something out of the ordinary or a qualitatively appropriate element. This includes elements of everyday life and those serving the most elementary needs, such as the stone in front of the door, upon which I step at each entrance and exit and which, with long experience, has become a part of me and seems to have no other meaning than that it is a slab facilitating the way to and from my threshold. One day, in the noon sun, is there a secret motion in it? Does it glimpse at me in a curious manner, dangerous and enticing at the same time? A shudder touches me, and perhaps I will be chased away with my hair standing on end. If I am ambivalent, and the other impulse (the fascination for the stone) does overtake me, and I return without wholly losing my aversion, I may well reconsider the stone, believing that I now own a valuable treasure which has incorporated a magic power in which I can partake as its owner. Thus, a "fetish" is born.[10]

First of all, according to Otto, the essence of the noumenon is to be found in its specific noumenal mystery. This elementary and basic dimension must be kept in mind for all further interpretations. Beyond this, the history of religion has long since observed that the most important dimension of the noumenon is power—something dynamic which may be latent, but is a potential for enormous force or can be actuated in more or less wild eruptions

As concerns the two major symbolic or representative concepts of the modern history of primitive religions, namely, taboo and mana, the former refers to a noumenon as such; the latter, to its more dynamic character. Within mana, Otto distinguishes moments of "majesty" and "energy." He does not recognize, incidentally, that the distinctions must be treated the same. The dynamic character of the noumenon makes it especially important for the construction of the primitive world view.

Levy-Bruhl[11] elaborated extensively on the indifference of primitive men toward secondary causes. Illness and death, above all, are thought to result from mystic causes, even if the sick can tell where he became infected and even if it is obvious to everybody that he fell from the spearthrust of an enemy in a fight. The same is true if one should die gradually of old age. Also, the deadly result of one's own action, e.g., to kill an animal on a hunt, is never construed as the result of direct action but always as the effect of "magic."

One understands how these opinions developed. The great impression of the often, daily and several times daily, renewed experience of the noumenon did overwhelm primitive mankind with such a shower of material for all kinds of superstition that it finally could not conceive that anything happened without the intervention of these elements. Moreover, the frequent repetitions of such deep tremors of conscience do sensitize one to the likelihood of their recurrence for a long time.

It may also be of importance that the real causal context, clarified and explicated by advanced knowledge, is quite insufficiently understood. Of course its character as an obstacle accounts for the fact that the noumenal shudder impresses men so much more easily that they take it most seriously, and finally build the whole framework of their thinking and world view on noumenal bases. Even though such a condition is plainly negative, one should not overestimate the significance of missing a "better" insight. "Education," for that matter, does not eliminate the most abhorrent primitive hallucinations, even in late cultures and among contemporary schizophrenics.

Only the noumenal experiences have positive meaning. This is directly traceable to the weight of each single experience—its massiveness and its inescapable seriousness. The meaning extends beyond its primary quality, so that an ever-more-encompassing framework is built. The latter emerges with the already developed capabilities of the mind in often surprising ways. Such a framework is constructed from the initial conditions in a relatively rational way, and consequently with a relatively rational plausibility. As childish as the forms of thought may seem, and as much as the absence of conceptual rigor, the preeminence of sensual response, the freedom of fantasy, and not least the obviously enormous egocentrism may allow for peculiar ways, the impervious backbone always remains the noumenal experience in all its manifold forms. These include the magically effective forms that are observed in such an experience. Free fantasy and finite framework build from this imperturbable base. Thus they can entertain as their goal a final proclamation of the general dominance of mystic powers. In this way they are seen, particularly in the context of efficacy, as the sole truly operative influence.

It is also important to note how, from the framework built on the noumenon, noumenal subjects are assigned different functions. The noumenal experiences are primary. They are many and they are initiated from a diversity of events. The emerging framework must respect noumenal experiences, and it must respect the diversity of their materials. Thus the fantastic perspective, interpreting magic powers as the real originators of all efficacious outcomes, will assign different magic powers to different tasks, each to a special kind. One will be assigned to establish life for the body. At times this may be subdivided into nutrition, growth, health, strength, or sex. Others will be assigned to bring good luck on the hunt, in war, or in male councils, or to bring glory among people, or prestige among friends and foes. It would be easy to add to these, and also to refer to much further removed examples from the early history of religion. Many of them still survive. Most "saints" have special tasks which they are asked in prayer to perform, such as growth of a good harvest, help in danger, etc. In particular, we can refer to the specialties of gods in antiquity. Of course, one may take these functions too much at their face value. The "substance" of god is the noumenon, although uniquely configured so that different functions will then be derived in corresponding meanings. Among the gods of antiquity, as well as among the saints, specializations can also be assigned to particular men or groups of men. Communities or status groups may be protected specifically by this saint or that god, or they may assemble for such protection. Such is also the origin of the—at times exclusive, at times inclusive—totemic clans. Selective inclusion often reaches as far as the individual person. Even in modern times the individual "guardian angel" may be found. At the same time, one learns that it is not only gods, or those coming close to them, who can have special magic powers. Blood, breath, shade, or name, though far from being gods, may, like guardian angels, be close to individuals and can perform different tasks for different individuals. At this point, one must also understand why some of these powers are effective for one person's lifetime, but disappear at the moment of his death; why others exert their full power at the moment of death; third, why they accompany the living only for a while, disappear, but come back; why, furthermore, a great number of such powers may act upon a single person at the same time—even when they conflict with one another. We may now enlarge our view of the concept of soul.

LIFE-SOUL AND DEATH-SOUL

At the outset we asserted: If the shadowy concept of soul must be taken into account as it appeared in its primitive form, then there is no doubt that the shadowy concept that persists today originated in that same prehistoric complex and survived as a distinctive element. This means that the word "soul" did originally describe a noumenon that grew to general recognition and importance. It was, of course, a noumenon within a special configuration or perspective. At best, linguistics[12] can tell which specific noumenon was originally called soul. Its original function may be understood in part from there—from myths and fairy tales—but it will in large part remain undisclosed. More important is the course of development that the concept of soul took.

There are several lines of development for primary noumenal terms. They take different directions—to gods and God, to demigods, to demons, to mere elements of cults, and to the later concept of soul. The courses of these developments are little known, although adequate knowledge about them can be gained rather easily. Moreover, insight into the development of the later concept of soul is still difficult to establish. Even preanimism leads us in the wrong direction at this point, particularly when it takes us to animism so that we come to conceive of the origin of the concept of soul as appearing at least in parallel with the origin of the relevant noumenon, which, after all, is not really soul.[13] Developments mean simplifications at the same time. Different elements are pieced together. Others are totally ignored.

As for the soul, we can basically assert: In its origin, it is a noumenon. It has nothing fundamentally to do with the elements that later on become so prominent for its conceptualization, such as life (in its profane form) or knowledge. But the soul is one form of noumenon. There are many other forms, all with different functions.

In the process of clarification, a specific group of noumena is comprehended with the ever-more-embracing name of soul. The next most important problem, therefore, is to investigate the principle of this increasing comprehension. Of course, one must emphasize that this is a post hoc comprehension. This necessarily means an incompletely unified form, and even more, a form not at all sharply delimited on its borders. It has also resulted in some differing comprehensions, appearing under different names, which have been unified only at a later stage. The comprehensiveness of the final connection is, of course, hindered by the diversity of the preceding ones. Thus, the final form is often only a Procrustean fit.

In parts of previous research, a great duality of the original concepts of soul had already emerged. This must be explained in such a way that, to begin with, two great groups of noumenal essences are comprehended without any consideration of their later connection. These are the death-soul and the life-soul. One is important after death; the other, during the life of man. Both exist side by side among contemporary primitives. This is still the case, because in some primitive communities the comprehension of either concept has not yet occurred. Man in some tribes still accepts a whole set of different souls—life-souls and at times even death-souls.

Among other peoples, the unity of death- and life-souls has occurred nominally without actual realization. At still other times, people may be on the road to such a conceptual accomplishment, but we will immediately show how the duality of life- and death-souls persists in the concept of soul even into modern times.

For individual primitive peoples, this has often been recognized. Ellis observed this for the Malagassic people;[14] Codrington, in the concept of "tarunga" and "tindalo" for the Melanesians; and Preuss, for the Cora Indians. Most explicitly and most generally, A. C. Kruyt elaborated on the duality as it was found among the East Indians.[15] Among the secondary authors, N. Söderblom in particular arrived at the same distinction[16] without, however, paying much attention to that important insight. Where the Homeric Greeks are concerned, E. Rohde has already exposed the implicit duality of life-soul and death-soul in psyche, even if it was not particularly emphasized and the nominal connection was not gone into. Of course this was not his major interest, since he was hardly concerned with the life-soul but instead with that of death. In an exaggerated polemic against Rohde, W. Otto[17] gave the duality so much importance that he did not pay any attention at all to the nominal unification implied by the single term "psyche;" it presumably meant "soul" in general only as a death-soul, and "life" only in the profane sense. Even though this is obviously misleading in that it dwells on the death-soul in total neglect of its other potential forms, the emphasis on the original duality is still an important insight.

First of all, life-soul and death-soul are fundamentally different. The experience of life-soul, of course in noumenal form, proceeds from the experience of breath, heartbeat, and blood. It is recognized in the living, and much more specifically (to be discussed later) in sleeping, in unconsciousness, in being wounded, and also in dying. The experience of the death-soul, in the noumenal form, proceeds from the dead, from the stiff, cold corpse; from its re-emergence in a dream, in a memory, or in a name; when it is heard, dreamed, or hallucinated.

Consequently, the soul as life-soul and its immortality have primarily nothing to do with one another. Immortality is not for the soul but for the dead, his picture, or his name. Of course all these are experienced as noumena. Perhaps it is a noumenon of the dead as such, if we can, in a manner of speaking, absolve it from its "bearer."[18] At any rate, this concept of soul, which is at first only important in life, can only subsequently unite with that essentially immortal noumenon of the dead. Now the seeming immortality can be affirmed or disputed without necessarily making an argument for or rejecting the soul itself. Nominally, this happened in Homer, although the unitary conceptualizations, termed psyches, of the living and the dead, still had completely different appearances, different forms, and consequently, different tasks and abilities. Elsewhere the connection is much more intense. This is particularly the case in the widely accepted belief in the wandering of the soul,[19] because one experiences the noumenon of the dead as such, yet at the same time ascribes to it a perpetuity imposed by the sanctions of the life-soul.

One understands how the connection of the life- with the death-soul could occur. This is most obvious in the experience of the act of dying, in the transfer from the just previously breathing and kicking life to rigor mortis with a now noumenal face. In this, the same soul lost its movement and, at that moment, the always noumenal power of life; but at the same time it gained a smaller, yet also higher and more advanced, noumenal power of death.[20]

The fusion of life- and death-souls, on the other hand, considering their widely different abilities and tasks, is certainly impeded. Thus, either the fusion was never really and finally reached, or it parted again and again, following momentary unifications. The introductory remarks did discuss the difficulty for Aristotle and the scholastics in unifying the life-soul concept, already applicable to plants and biologically defined, with immortality, on which Christianity put all emphasis. The discrepancy begins in Plato and still earlier, and it has not been overcome even in modern times. When, in the introduction, we confronted the religious and psychological concepts of soul, it was a result of this original duality. That it [the duality] remains in this case seems almost absurd. Imagine a theologist and an experimental psychologist discussing the soul and arriving at a belief in immortality, assuming that neither knows anything about the position of the other to begin with!

A further consequence of the never complete or lasting fusion of life- and death-souls is revealed by the fact that the problem of the emergence of the concept of soul and the concepts of soul among primitives can be raised in different ways. This depends on whether the researcher approaches the question more from one side or from the other, leading to patently different, at times even discrepant, results. Most times, determined heavily by the interest of religious history, the question is approached so vigorously from the conception of a death-soul that the alternative is completely overlooked. Indeed, the death-soul still poses rich problems, insofar as differences in the noumenal death experience, either directly derived from an experience with the corpse, or indirectly from a dream, a memory picture, or a name, may result in quite a diversity of concepts. In this article, the emergence of the concept of life-soul is to be followed more closely from here on. It leads to the basic concept of soul held by psychology, though at first to the biological concept of soul.

One must always be aware of the fact that the biological concept of soul, with regard to the death-soul as well as to a great number of other concepts of soul, has a historically selective meaning developed from an earlier conceptual mass. One may also claim that the biological concept was, besides the death-soul, the most important. After all, it had to survive in the process of extraction from an originally much broader field. . . .

. . . Of course, the concept of soul from its inception had possibilities of expansion. It had such a potentiality only because it was never conceived as only biological, but first of all as something noumenal or experienced. Insofar as the biological concept of soul was, from the beginning, a comprehension, it was at the same time combined with many other possibilities, which surrounded the biological fit as a ring of noumenal meanings and always provided the germs of further growth. Finally the noumenal aura thinned out in the surrounding ring, allowing a pale shine to penetrate even the innermost depths of comprehension.

VITALITY

The original concepts of soul were never as generally understood as was the mere principle of vitality. They were rather a selection from the great vastness of the noumenon. It would be easy to defend this thesis, if the discovery of the concept of life occurred simultaneously with such a selection. The primitives would then not have known the difference between the living and nonliving. Only the category of the noumenon, a part of which seemed to be concerned with life, would then have comprehended life as such. In that case, it would appear that the concepts of soul were primarily principles of vitality anyway, with a noumenal character only in the beginning. The latter would only be an accident, a coloring that would not be missed and that could not constitute the concept of soul.

Quite to the contrary, it must be demonstrated that the distinction between living and nonliving has actually nothing to do with the experience of the noumenon. Something like a concept of soul never emerged from such a distinction—not even in the sense of mere vitality principles.

The distinction between living and nonliving was thus already obvious to the primitives before any experience of noumenon. This "before" has to be construed as a logical priority, since there was never a stage of mankind without noumenal experience in concrete historical terms. Of course, the primitives had neither developed concepts apprehending the principles of life, nor had they any general concepts to distinguish living from nonliving. Better, they did not have any words for such matters. When such words develop, the concept of vitality mixes with the distinctly different one of noumenon. In practice, the primitive does distinguish between the living and the nonliving, at once and without the detour through the noumenon. Men and animals may stand for one and stones for the other. . . .

How the distinction of living and nonliving developed from their original unity is a problem still awaiting a solution by research. It was approached too clumsily, e.g., in asking the question of the animation of the lifeless instead of starting with the indistinguishable unity of both. . . . Moreover, the common criteria used to determine whether something is living or nonliving are too imprecise. . . .

The area where such problems can be studied best, besides the study of primitives, is that of child development. Important insights have been gained there. Yet one may be fooled by the fact that the child plays at living, even if, in "serious attitude," he has long developed the distinction between the living and the nonliving. Growing up, especially, is sustained by playing together and by stories about such play. That the child treats something living as lifeless during a game, or another child uses a poodle as a pillow, or anything rollable for that matter, seldom confounds (most of all, but not exclusively) fundamental humanitarian and historical principles. Above all, we find here the network of an original unity rooted in play.

The present emphasis is upon the fact that the difference between the living and the nonliving was already suspended in principle at an early time. As it is with children, so it is with primitives and even with the higher animals. In any case, what is seemingly playful can establish a basic original unity. Furthermore, this difference is not arrived at initially in a circuitous path about and around the noumenon.

Concepts of the principles of life will never be developed in this way, nor will those of the soul as a principle of life, not even (as many have contended) in contrast to death or the process of dying. To be sure, when breath stops, it is understandable to conceive of that breath as something that animates the living. Yet such theoretically conceived, rational thought is lost to all primitives by necessity. The noumenal experience, first of all, destroys all such rational thought completely. . . .

Following Levy-Bruhl, the importance of noumena for the construction of a total world view among primitives was discussed. The noumenon proved to be the basis of world view, and all efficacious perspectives as such, besides those of life itself, can be interpreted from there. . . . Life is, indeed, particularly puzzling even for modern science. He who has a conception of noumena will use it readily, and thus glimpse at least a possible solution to that problem. But there is also another special reason for the noumenal interpretation of life. Just as the first conception of life could not be developed solely with the positing of a life principle, a life-soul, or the noumenon, . . . so the conception of the noumenon can never be traced back to that of life. Yet there is an affinity between the noumenon and life.

There is a form of life which is not necessarily noumenal. Moreover, noumena also animate the nonliving. The stone which appears noumenal to me also seems to be something that contains a secret life. As a consequence of this, every object, even those which appear to be without life, can be transformed by the primitive into something living. First it becomes a noumenon and then, as a necessary consequence, it is transformed into something alive. Furthermore, because of this the noumenon proves not to be identical with the vital, since the conception of the latter is crisscrossed by the former, and the distinction already achieved between living and nonliving is lost again. This means that living as such is not noumenal. We have already mentioned that noumenal experience occurs in the face of death rather than in immediate contact with life, and with animals rather than with men. . . .

In a certain way, life—the "inner life"—is closer to the noumenon than simple and plain nonliving. In order for the stone to appear noumenal, an "inner life" must appear in it, or it must appear simultaneously with a noumenal object. . . . In order for it to appear noumenal, life cannot be construed as clear, customary, open, or mundane. More removed, the staring eyes of cattle look at us more intensely than the bright eye of man. We shudder much more quickly when we observe life in the metallic, shiny skin of the lizard or the snake than in the clothing more appropriate to human life. . . . The pulse and breath of the sleeping tinge our view of life much more than those of the awakened person. What is dead is almost life as such. Thus, one must understand the meaning of life's relics, e.g., hair or nails, before which all primitives experienced a frightening, holy aversion. An animal that appears to be dead, even though it lives, can thus become something absolute. Here the myth of the turtle may have originated. Also, an egg is

like an optical illusion, the more so if it is seen as it is being laid—
a mysterious miracle long before it is unquestionably established
as a source of life.[21] . . .

The questions then arise how the noumenon has an affinity for
the living so that the living can appear noumenal; how the nonliving gives evidence of internal life so that it can appear noumenal,
even though living as such is not necessarily noumenal and one can
recognize only secondarily the force of the noumenon in the fully
living.

A concept of soul is used in Greek philosophy which is not devoid of its original religious meaning, though it has a deeper religious essence and functions, so to speak, in the biology of the
body. This soul is described more precisely as "autokinesis"—self-
generated movement. This is contrary to the notion that a soul is
moved. One finds this in Plato, who in this respect has objectively
incorporated as predecessors all earlier philosophers, such as the
Pythagoreans and Alkmaion, in his terminology; also in Aristotle,
despite his polemic against autokinesis, we find the soul as life-soul
construed as life power. The idea is understandable. Unlike all material which moves only when pushed or dragged, living is something that moves by itself under its own power. . . . Whether modern science can still make use of the idea of intrinsic movement for
theorizing about the concept of life is, of course, not the point of
this discussion.

Spontaneous dynamics, as the latent capability for extraordinary
force or as an actualization in more or less wild eruptions, also
appeared as the first qualification of the noumenon. Here obviously
lies the reason for the affinity between the noumenal and the vital.
This does not mean that the vital is noumenal or that noumena can
even be traced back to the vital. The vital also appears as profane
vitality. Noumena begin with nothing but noumena. But the noumenon is a spontaneous dynamic and also unified with vitality. Of
course only a noumenal dynamic is vital as such. First of all, the
dynamic does not include all vitality, but only that of a noumenal
character, which preferably is attached to certain vital forms. The
nonvital, as it evidences a noumenal character, also appears to be

vital. Consequently, all noumena are vital. Gods "live," and thereafter vitality is gradually understood to be in itself vital. Thus vitality is understood as noumenal.

It is the originally noumenal conception of soul that includes the
specifically vital (even that which appears profanely so) more than
the merely vital functions. In this, the concept of soul can strip off
the original noumenal meaning, although it happens seldom and
never completely. The essence of soul is the spontaneous dynamic.

KNOWLEDGE, CONSCIOUSNESS, AND SPIRIT

In all of this, the conception of soul as consciousness has been
ignored almost artificially. Consciousness too, is a familiar concept
for the primitive—first as knowledge, or at least as knowing something special, distinguished especially from not-knowing. Again, we
need not detour around the noumenon to establish the foundations
of consciousness.

It is often contended that the concept of knowing emerged rather
late in the history of mankind. The importance of the concept for
explaining how man proceeded from knowing to knowledge was
stressed. Even the first attempts at philosophy did not apprehend
such a turn. However, it was apprehended rather soon and became
quite problematic for philosophy, preeminently concerned with the
problem of being. At any rate, philosophy did not discover knowing. Long before philosophy, there were words for ways of knowing—seeing and hearing. Why such terms emerged need not be
discussed here.

At this point, we do not have to ask at all about the actual discovery of knowing. Something is considered to be knowing, and it
is distinguished from not-knowing, even if there are no formalized
concepts to accomplish this. In this way, knowing and not-knowing
were categories developed early and were in use for ages. This is
particularly obviously important when we consider that living is
only assumed to be knowing. The stone that I step on is not living
and thus not knowing. . . . , however it is perceived.

If only living directly or living is assumed to be knowing, the
concepts of being alive and knowing do not completely match.

While only living can be knowing, there can be living which is not knowing.

The primitive knows sleep and unconsciousness, where knowledge is absent but life continues. These characterize living without knowledge. More dubious is whether the life of plants can also be drawn into this argument. Of course it is different from true non-living, such as the existence of stones. This can be conceived without detouring the noumenon. The delimitations are everywhere diffuse, even among us. Yet the life of plants has not merged with the animal-human into the unity of the realm of life, although this may happen soon. Consequently, knowing can be conceived as occurring only in living, but not in all living, nor does it have to be known under all circumstances.

Despite the many doubts of philosophy, this is the way it is among us. Only in the living do we recognize the knowing. We cannot imagine knowing without the act of living. Yet there is living without knowing at that moment or perhaps ever. Living is a prerequisite of knowing.

Also, knowing is qualitatively entangled in life in many ways. Unconsciousness and fainting spells are known by different terms, but point to the same fact. Sleep is something that refers to life; it is also known. Illness may first be a condition of life, but that condition similarly alters knowing. Conversely, there are examples of the impact of knowing on life.

The concepts of knowledge and knowing obviously are not of noumenal origin. As one recognizes profane living, so one recognizes profane knowing. The still unconceptualized but already distinguished recognition of knowing as compared to not-knowing and the explicit discovery of the difference do not require a noumenal experience. If the discovery occurs at the inception of unconsciousness, as in the case of a swoon, noumenal experiences are close. But it is characteristic that it is the unconscious person, not the conscious bystander, who appears noumenal.

Despite all this, the noumenon itself is consciously experienced in a hidden and still deeper sense. This does not happen by bestowing one's own consciousness on the noumenon, as is held by animism. . . . Neither can one contend that the noumenon is conscious because it is of the living. Living, as such, is not necessarily conscious. Of course, only the living are conscious, but not all living is conscious nor is everyone conscious all the time.

Later on all living does indeed appear, and in a certain sense it appears to be conscious. Important documents of this have survived up to the present without the living appearing noumenal at the same time. At least, the noumenal character of living faded out in its special mode of consciousness, although there are traces of it still to be observed. At the same time, knowledge of living as something conscious in a special way came into existence only out of the experience of living as noumenal. Living did not provide consciousness for the noumenon, but the noumenon did provide consciousness for the living, and gradually for all living. Consequently, the noumenon itself is primarily the consciousness experienced in its own way. . . .

The specific meaning of living has been related above to the capacity for original movement. Biology conceived of living in a different way, particularly when it claimed it was impossible to understand vital phenomena by merely mechanical principles. Not the mere capacity of power, but rather functionality is unique to the organic, in contrast to the inorganic. . . . In the theory of science, functionalism came to mean that of biology, although after Kant it was considered to be a problematic concept.

Incidentally, functionalism is perhaps a one-sided and inappropriate term. What is meant is that there are interdependent relations in the organism that work consistently as an internal unity and actually shape behavior. . . . Such thoughts are not alien to modern biology, particularly where one finds nature, after extreme disruptions, acting very "sensibly" and "reasonably." This happens in phases or spheres where there is no real consciousness. It was even thought possible to discover a functionalism of unconscious behavior that transcended individual welfare or the purpose of the species.[22] In a period of clearly dominant mechanistic ideas, Eduard von Hartmann held that there is a vitalism, in the sense of the influence of "unconscious mind," in the life of organic nature. Today, in a related way, Driesch uses the word "psychoid."

It was charged that these statements were senseless to begin with, because they claimed an unconscious consciousness! . . . Whether this can be called senseless must still be investigated. The assertion is still defended by well-known philosophers and biologists. And they are doing more than just defending it. This can be helpful for answering the question about the consciousness of the noumenon.

. . . Wherever there is noumenal shudder in man, he is aware of something. The primary character of this is the noumenon; the second, noumenal power; the third, that the something has "intentions." Maybe they are for me; maybe they pass me by. These intentions are often not understandable. It is not plain force, which is curiously threatening and seductive. It is a force that "knows," but not in a human sense. Its intentions can be devastating. All the time there is something threatening about the noumenon. Something of the evil eye, of cunning and artifice—because of this, the "envy of the gods" is taught. If one exposes oneself without harkening to those warning signals, which after all are only the result of fantasy, the grace and goodness of the primarily threatening becomes obvious. Yet all the time what is experienced has a veiled "eye."

Here we are at the point where the noumenon gives rise to gods. In their case, consciousness is clearer, more wide awake than is that of men. This holds even if (in its further differentiation) it approaches human consciousness. On the other hand, the consciousness of the noumenon is experienced in a much gloomier way, when the particular noumenal subject is somewhat sleepy. But even there it is far superior, in deepness, wisdom, and in device, to human [intention]. . . .

Besides the word for soul [*Seele*], the German language has a word whose meaning is partially similar to that which has been discussed here, mind or spirit [*Geist*].[23] There are similar pairs in other European languages—psyche and pneuma, anima and spiritus. For a long time, the relationship between both concepts received considerable attention. After Wilhelm von Humboldt's statements in the postscript to the fragment "*Über den Geist der Menschheit*" ["Concerning the human spirit"], "*Geist*," the article

by Rudolf Hildebrand in Grimm's dictionary, became highly regarded. Like Humboldt, he pursued the relationship of spirit
(mind) to soul. Unfortunately, his interpretation suffers from the
fact that it does not rigorously treat the obvious major dimensions
of the relationship.

In their origin, both spirit and soul are closely related. At that
stage, spirit means—like most of those words in European languages—breath, whiff, or wind. In their development, they move
apart. Spirit then becomes less human, less close to body and life.
It is more "objective," and the soul is then called "subjective
mind." At times, it will even be construed as something abstract,
while the word "soul" even in its most diffuse meaning, retains a
close tie with concrete reality. It is not that spirit is distinct from
body and life to begin with. The name *Lebensgeister* [spirits of life]
still maintains the relationship. Originally, spirit is not powerless
either. It is, rather, the real power in this relationship, even within
the soul, for spirit often appears as part of the soul, either as its
surface area or as its deeper layer. This can be observed in the
terminology employed by quite a few approaches of modern psychology. There the spirit may also be perceived as unreal and powerless, while the soul is considered real. Otherwise, the spirit extends far beyond the soul, and (quite differently) from extensions
of the soul. The "spirit" of the Roman law, capitalism, or the
Gothic spirit are obviously different from what might be comprehended as their souls. . . .

The relationship between spirit and soul cannot be analyzed here
in every direction it has taken, or from every standpoint. Each is
of noumenal origin. And the meaning of both can be made profane,
perhaps more the fate of the spirit than that of the soul. . . . Spirit
is, of course, abstract, unreal, powerless, and much more so than
is the case for the soul. But we are reminded that the spirit was
never regarded only as life in the biological sense, and never at all
only as consciousness in the psychological sense. Spirit has also
been construed as consciousness, but it goes beyond it. This was
particularly the case whenever it was lost in discussions of the soul.
It has even been comprehended as included specifically in the soul
—and then, unconsciously, as the realm of consciousness. But even

there and beyond, the spirit could survive as the higher range or the deeper essence of consciousness.

It is remarkable that god and gods are spirits. Noumenal essences are such in general. For the most part they can also be souls, but they are always spirits, or at least always spiritual. In general, noumena are spiritual in a unique, hard-to-conceptualize form, an approach to which may be attempted by imaginative, empathic understanding.

An attempt has been made here to describe spirit so that it could be clearly differentiated from consciousness. Yet to characterize spirit, one had to acknowledge at the same time a unique, special kind of consciousness. Doubtless both are akin to one another on the surface, although the fundamental difference between the two lies in the fact that spirit is primarily noumenal, while consciousness is primarily not. Their kinship is comparable to that found between noumenon and vitality, which we discussed earlier. A basic difference existed there also, since vitality too can appear profane. Nevertheless, a commonality could also be observed, since the essence of both is a spontaneous dynamic. This is the reason why the noumenon is preferably to be found with the living and makes the nonliving appear alive. In an analogous way, noumenon as spirit is akin to consciousness.

One could argue that the differences between the two proved to be something very specific, and a very particular emphasis has been given to such proof. The spirit is also unconscious. It appears at other times as a merely objective spirit. Subjectively, the spirit also seems purely suggestive, interpretive, or guiding. Finally, in a weaker way, in a strictly and purely objective sense like a footprint, one may take it as he sees it.

As opposed to all this, the spirit as unconscious must be more precisely understood as a form of unconscious consciousness (whether or not one seems to depart ever further from true understanding by such word play). "As" reality, not only "in" reality, spirit is always subjective. "As" and "in" reality may even be identical. The suggesting, interpreting, guiding spirit, if it is real and subjective (not objective) in reality, moves obviously then into unconscious consciousness. For the primitive, the footprint not only has an objective meaning but also a dynamically charged one which subjectively confronts him. With but little intensification, something "personal" looks out. With this, not only unconscious consciousness but conscious consciousness is soon reached.

There are transitions between the objective and subjective spirit just as there are transitions between the unconscious and the conscious, though the first may seem absurd. At this time, philosophy has not arrived at the necessary distinctions which must precede the knowledge of sequences in such transition. But at any rate, it is clear how the consciousness of the spirit emerges for the primitive. From the existential form of noumena, which is total unconscious consciousness bordering on clarity, a personal thing develops with ultimately clear thought.

It should be mentioned that, like primeval power, in a puzzling way the spirit is not made out of the noumenon. Its primary essence is always precisely that it is a noumenon. That is its "mystery." Primeval power and also spirit are only the existential attributes of the noumenon. Like original power, spirit, even as something puzzling, is also known later on to profane thought. At least in some of the forms that we suggested comprised the completely objective spirit, "as" or "in" reality, we find the unconscious consciousness. At least in this case, the spirit is also dynamic. Thus the connection of spirit and dynamism does not comprise the noumenon. It is impossible to analyze or synthesize a noumenon.

Of course it may be that the condensed conception of spirit, at least in its puzzling form, necessarily carries the quest for knowledge into metaphysical depths that always have a slightly noumenal coloring. One may also have reached the disordered concepts of those puzzling forms of spirit only from the experience of the noumenon. Historically, this was definitely the case for some of these concepts, particularly those of the unconscious life of spirit in organic nature, which even today retain traces of their origin. Primeval power also carries the quest for knowledge into metaphysical depths, although neither the discovery of this concept nor its nonconceptual treatment may proceed from a noumenal basis.

The change of the noumenal spirit in its stages of development toward closer approximation to consciousness and finally to consciousness itself shows the way in which consciousness itself is realized as noumenal spirit or as an emanation from it. This proceeds, not from consciousness to spirit, as animism thought, but from spirit to consciousness. At best, this route is connected with that discussed earlier, which began with the noumenon as power and not as spirit. Even if the primary noumenon, on its higher levels, were understood as consciousness, it would not mean that the profanely perceived consciousness is noumenal. Here it may be added that the generalization of the noumenon to the sole moving force in all being so surely blanketed the profane consciousness that the noumenon as spirit was now close to consciousness itself, or was consciousness itself.

CONCLUSIONS

The concept of soul is now defined as knowing, as consciousness, or at least as unconscious consciousness. The concept of soul that had been bypassed in the previous contexts must now be reintroduced. Its treatment was not recommended when we raised the question of the soul as consciousness, inasmuch as the subsequently developed concept of the soul as profane consciousness obstructed investigation, since the exploration of the nearly-noumenal soul dynamism took precedence over the establishment of the spiritual quality of all noumena. Thus the soul first led us to the spirit and then to an eventually unconscious consciousness. In the first place, the soul is nothing but noumenon, noumenal dynamism; in the second place, spirit; and only after that point, consciousness.

Of course the concept of soul is narrower than that of noumena in general. This narrowing of conceptual focus developed from the dynamism in which soul becomes the noumenon that, in a rudimentary view, should stand behind the vital functions of living beings. The focus also shifts from noumenon as spirit and beyond to the place which the soul occupies, where the development of the spirit as (eventually unconscious) consciousness is consummated. . . .

We discussed how quite different souls could lead to the formation of concepts designating different functions that can set in motion a conflict with each other by their very existence in the same individual. The classics formed a picture of this from Homer. . . .

The exposition of different concepts of soul began with their common essence as power, which lent itself to different configurations with still different outcomes. It is perfectly obvious how the outcome as consciousness had to be a peculiar task of a unique, peculiar form of soul. Although these are all matters of the spirit, the foundation of the specific consciousness is something special. The unification of the concepts of soul occurred only gradually. The principles for this were discussed earlier. Only one remains and must be specified at this time. This is the capacity for transformation of the noumenal form.

Noumena are met only in some kind of context. Certainly among primitives, this will be a sensual one, as a rule. But in this the primitive has the terrifying experience that contexts can change. The stone which glared at him one day both dangerously and seductively may have appeared for a long time before only as a dead thing. It is also frightening afterward that it can appear to be dead again. At times it will reawaken. At times it looks evil; at times, seductive. Then one day the primitive finds something else which looks at him in the same way. Sometimes it is a completely different incarnation. This is the basis for all the many myths of metamorphosis (and their relics in fairy tale) in all elementary religions—but not only in the elementary ones.

It is also the basis for the differentiation of souls from their bodies, and for the recognition that the souls will possibly enter into other bodies and not necessarily those of specific living beings. This noumenon is also the basis for the belief in the wandering of the soul. At least ideally, in all of this the soul is a separate thing, the noumenon separated from its bearer. This last notion of ultimately bodiless souls is certainly not original, though it may be something artificial and possibly unrealizable. At least souls do not cast a recognizable shadow or have a "light body," either permanently or during their transformations. Perhaps they wander forlorn and long for the blood of life, or in the liberation such ephemeral insubstantiality permits, they are the more blessed.

The metamorphosis of souls (of all noumena, and thus of all souls) is what made the unification of the concepts of soul possible. Above all, this occurred in such a way that the vital functions and (unconscious and conscious) consciousness were the productions and manifestations of the soul. Both remained noumenal for some time; even today, despite its weakening, the soul still retains a noumenal glow which is seldom fully disclosed. This, the most elemental, could easily cease to exist. While the duality of the soul persisted, the soul might have lost each part of the duality, as well as its noumenal glow. This duality really created the soul. Beyond the kernel remained, above all else, a broad rim. It was an aura around each single soul, a loose area of thin and independent conceptions of soul. Perhaps the rim itself retained the noumenal character or at least a trace of it (ultimately, only an echo). Perhaps only its pieces were profane. The rim may as well have been formed from relics of the more comprehensive conceptions of the original soul as from the beginnings of new approaches toward permanence; or it may have been formed from analogous metaphors, individually or together. All of this, discussed earlier in the apprehension of the soul as power and as life, could now be repeated for the soul as spirit and consciousness.

Also, the kernel of the concept of soul surviving from prehistory, the connection of soul and life as consciousness, is a unity that was conceptualized only later. It did prove itself, and its base is located in the quintessential depths of both links. Yet an attempt to break up the two has been made with great success, following the efforts of centuries.

What could not be broken away is soul as power, not yet understood in its specifically vital meaning and as (eventually unconscious) consciousness. The unity of that duality endured, although there were low-key, but indecisive attempts to break it up also, even after the noumenal origin of the concept of soul had long been forgotten and after the concept of life-soul had been destroyed or become dubious. In this, the relationship of dynamism and spirit, unconscious and conscious consciousness, is actually the terminal problem posed by the soul for systematic philosophy.

While nothing shall be said here about further developments of the concept of soul, one single point is to be noted, at least perfunctorily. One of the most important turns that the conceptualization of soul took in the first period of European philosophy occurred when Socrates expressed the opinion: Man should not have to care so much for his body, but rather for his soul. The soul referred to is obviously not the basic biological one, nor is it consciousness. Neither is it primarily the death-soul. What man is supposed to be so much concerned about is something that can possibly be designated by the phrase "ethical personality." Plato's metaphysic of soul was originally founded on such an ethical conception. That created internal difficulties for the ethical conception of soul in itself, but it also led at once to unresolvable conflicts with the biological life-soul conception, with the consciousness concept of soul, and with the still-persisting unity of the two. The central ethical concept of soul in Plato is connected to all these concepts. The biological conception is the definitive basis to start on, consciousness increasingly gains philosophical interest, and the ethical conception has Plato's enthusiasm. They are all interconnected, and the ethical one is particularly connected to the concept of death-soul. Even there conflicts arose, because the ethical concept of soul had nothing originally to do with the biological concept of consciousness, nor was it, to begin with, related to the death-soul at all. Only secondarily can it be removed from all of these. The joint root in this case is again the noumenon. While Socrates posed new tasks for philosophy because of his ethical emphasis on the concept of soul, he certainly did not create it by himself. He also inherited this from religion, from an era where the "ethicalization" of fundamental religion was of general importance for the history of mankind. It would be a task of the first order to investigate this matter—with it, the foundation of the ethical conception of soul, and ultimately its substantive determination. Today more and more the ethical conception of soul commands great interest when taken together with other conceptions, which nowadays are even more separated from still others, specifically, the modern conception of soul as consciousness. Contemporary efforts concerning the relationship of explanatory psychology and *Verstehen*, of psychology and characterology, are directed toward what is called the "person," although at times with different or vaguely defined intentions. They would find a most fertile seedbed in the insight probing the essence and the related emergence of the ethical conception of soul.

III. Phenomenological Analysis

ON HUMAN EXISTENCE: REALITY, PLAY,
AND SERIOUSNESS

THE REALITY OF MEN

First of all, with regard to the philosophy of human existence, it is important that man can escape neither from apprehending[1] truth, being, and existence, nor from any apprehension of reality. Even the conception of pure logos carries with it at least the apprehension of itself as reality. No less important is the fact that man apprehends reality itself in object-oriented apprehension only as vaguely real and specifically real, only in the implicit nonobject-oriented self-apprehension of apprehension. . . .

All apprehension apprehends itself as the apprehension of an "I." We have not talked about the I, and there is no reason to, since the most important discussion of the I can be found in Kant. Perceptual psychology attempted to conceive of experience as primarily not related to the I. It asserted instead that the I creates itself from a multiplicity of experiences. Such a conception is post hoc and views the I, in its unity and in its consciousness of its unity, as something merely added on to experience.

Contrary to this, Kant held: (1) Each individual experience is necessarily I-related and any concept of experience not related to the I is meaningless; (2) in a sequence of experiences, any given experience is apprehended in the I assumed in that singular experience. Thus, the unity of any sequence of experiences and the consciousness of that unity is neither something added on later nor

From *Geist und Sein* (Basel: Haus zum Falken, 1939) pp. 286–289; 291; 293; 299–328.

is it identical with the I. It follows from the assumptions made in the apprehension of each experience and the sequence of experiences found in the I.

Yet there are problems with the Kantian perspective. To begin with, and according to Kant's basic constructions, the perspective is restricted to the thinking I. As such, the I can be interpreted as an epiphenomenon, so to speak—an abstract, insubstantial, attenuated I. The I-quality of feeling and conscious conduct is different. Here the objectively experienced body that belongs to the I is also added on. Furthermore, there are layers of the I. Finally, the persistence of the I must come to terms with change, which, incorporated in the same I, is apprehended from experience. . . .

It follows that the conscious memory does not reach back to its beginnings. It is lost in the darkness of strange, raveled remnants, though it knows it has been there from the stories and related experiences of others. . . . In touching, feeling, willing, and conscious conduct, conscious experience "knows" itself as reality (but not only "as" reality). It knows itself with minor emphasis, just as in seeing or thinking. That the emphasis in seeing or thinking is minor rests on the fact that the stress is placed upon seeing or thinking as such. As in willing and conscious conduct, so it is that in much touching and feeling a stronger emphasis is placed on the objective dimension.

General experience tends toward objective orientation. Yet there is also a type of person who focuses his interest on himself and his experience. . . . Still, such a direction of interest is object-oriented. He who typically turns toward himself and his experience with no special reason is considered sick. The coordinating distinction between introverted and extroverted types [The reference is to the work of C. G. Jung, Schmalenbach's colleague in Basel, eds.] is wrong. However, much has been subsumed in psychology under the term "introvert" that is only falsely labeled.

THE REALITY OF THE WORLD

That will and conscious conduct are object-oriented, sometimes emphatically, with the result that the activities themselves are often totally ignored, is strange in a way. After all, the I acts and wills actively and with an active consciousness. Yet precisely here the emphasis is placed on the willing and the doing—on the "objective" side. But willing conduct and conscious conduct are only somewhat self-conscious. So minor is this that it is not known how they will and act, nor is it noticed that for the most part what is willed into action is only indirectly willed and carried on. With the turn toward the object, experience places its emphasis where a specific reality is no longer given to it. . . .

Only a small part of apprehension is the apprehension of something real. Even in apprehending something "as" real, one must stress that apprehension, as a rule, is accomplished just by occurring and is not conceived as something real but as something different. Yet this is done with the assurance that in being there—occurring—something of the reality that is the basis for it is captured.

LIFE AS THE APPREHENSION OF SYMBOLS

. . . Man is surrounded by symbols. On the one hand, man cannot escape the apprehension of reality. In another respect, he lives in the apprehension of symbols and their meaning. On the one hand, he apprehends the necessary reality—indeed, reality itself—as well as the supporting hypothesis of real objects as apprehensible. On the other hand, the emphasis of apprehension is placed on symbols (and often primarily interwoven with them), upon reality in the distance, or at any rate upon some reality. Even conscious conduct relies on the fact that it is in contact with some kind of reality through the apprehension of symbols. This is the case only if, from the start, one is truly concerned with meeting reality.

FANTASY

When the practical man senses indications and addresses[2] from the symbols he confronts in his conduct, then everywhere in his behavior there are episodic sprinklings of thought and reflection. Perception already is by necessity meaningful apprehension, and actions and reactions are the same. But the episodes of intertwining thought have turned off the perception (at least in part). Actions and reactions hark back to it again. Episodes of thinking sprinkled into practical behavior line up at first with the perceptual act and are in the service of acting and reacting. But they can, at least methodologically, stray far away from perception and from all practical direction, even to the extent that there is no longer any phenomenological relationship.

Yet this aloofness from the practical and at the same time from the perceptual and the phenomenological may also be viewed differently. Animals dream. One can notice the dreams of a hunting dog that must spend boring hours sleeping in the sun. Children "dream" when they are awake. To listen to fairy tales or read them later on is a delight. One can also "think out" stories. This is not thinking, although it is understandably interlaced with thought. (It is meaningful apprehension, at any rate.) Basically, one will ascribe the pictures of fantasy, on which that fascination with colorful events is placed, to the area of perception in contrast to that of thinking. But the devotion to pictures of fantasy is not actual perception and also does not blend with it. The preoccupation with pictures of fantasy is completely distant from all practical conduct. Yet such distance is only one possibility. In other cases, fantasy—like thinking—can serve practical purposes, e.g., by laying the ground for the preparation of "correct" practical conduct through the prior imagination of future situations.

Certain theories, like any comprehensive thinking, will also justify the talent of men with fantasies and their devotion to them by appealing to praxis. Such men would be familiar with a vast range of alternatives which they might at one time or another confront in practice. Indeed, daydreams tend to incorporate dreams in action and with relation to the aspirations of the dreamer. The real position of praxis, however, tends to disregard fantasy and dreamers. Daydreams will at times flow from the reality of dreams and will illuminate dominant situations whose resolution is unlikely and rarely to be justified as a practical possibility. Much more likely, the daydreamer is transported from his immediate reality into a far-distant world.

Finally, stories work their magic without any relationship to the one who indulges in them. To a degree which is difficult to justify from praxis, or indeed from any conceivable praxis, children and youth live in fantasy. Old men live in reminiscences. In childhood, only the dimensions of play and games compete with the dimensions of fantasy.

PLAY, GAMES, AND SERIOUSNESS

Play is something quite different from devotion to the images of fantasy. Play is again praxis. It is conscious conduct. Here again we find indications and addresses, and they are real indications and addresses, whereas in fantasy they are symbols in the flow of imagery. Yet play is play. Language counterposes seriousness and play, but the seriousness of many games seems to contradict this. It is at any rate a phenomenon; and while in a way it is seemingly contradictory, giving proof to the counterposition of play and seriousness, it is a phenomenon and thus at least a problem.

Play often seems to merge, so to speak, into "real" seriousness. But then someone is sure to remark: "This is no longer play. The play has gone too far." Here we should find the place where the difference between play and seriousness becomes obvious. Play is conscious conduct. One may try to differentiate play from serious conscious conduct by stating that the latter is directed toward ulterior purposes while play is purposive in itself. However, if the first were true (which appears to be debatable), there are purposes —at least playful purposes—in play. It is important for the players to realize these purposes.

Especially by referring to the idea of purpose, theories of play have tried to comprehend play overall as a means for realizing serious purposes, e.g., the play and games of children as training for later serious endeavor; the play and games of adults as recreation, and thus preparation for renewed serious conduct. With this, such theories not only destroy what they had conceived of as play, but they contradict the very meaning of play. Of course, there is "playing" which is construed as a means to accomplish future (or renewed) serious behavior not only in retrospect, but is undertaken with such an intention to begin with. Programmed recreational play is not real play. And retrospective justification is not the problem at all, because the meaning of human life must be investigated first, and play must be grasped as a fact, above all. It is important to note, however, that the purposes within a game are playful in themselves. If one wants to investigate how play is distinguished from seriousness, then inquiry is best directed toward playful and serious purposes. Indeed, one must ask whether all playful and all serious action is directed toward purposes. When play is criticized for "being no longer play" or "having gone too far," no light is shed by raising questions about purpose.

It has also been claimed as essential to play that the expenditure of effort be not too extreme. At first glance, that seems not to be true. Sport games and tournaments in all historical periods are and were such that effort was often extended to the utmost. Yet it is precisely for this reason that play is criticized. Play is conscious conduct. There is also suffering in play. However, if the pain is too great, play seems to be discontinued, although the degrees of suffering that will discontinue the play can be different. At any rate, the limit of play is reached when the very edge of life is touched. Of course such things happen. In some games it is demanded that the willingness for engagement be carried to the utmost. Here again, such play and games are also criticized. One could opine that such totally committed players would not call the play of others play—that the difference between play and seriousness is differentially dependent upon evaluated importance.

However, play can be more important than any mundane, serious event. That is play; this is seriousness. This happens with the child who is called home from his play to the dinner table or to his bed. Yet he who throws dice for his wife, his child, or his own life may believe he is only playing with them. Yet he plays desperately and considers his play contrary to all good sense, even if at the same time he prides himself on it. Moreover, when the very basis of life is touched, it seems to be a different matter. The ethos of play may demand that one gamble on one's life. Honor, in particular, has its specific place here [cf., the duel. eds.]. Basically, however, the risk to one's life is the place where seriousness starts. Only an ethos, sometimes with a change of name, can transfer serious motivation into the spheres of play that will remain primarily play.

PLAY AND REALITY

Language contrasts the concept of play with the concept of reality. In most games, playful goals are pursued. Such goals are not "real" goals for the players, but only goals in the game. Because of these goals, games are contexts of meaning. At the same time, contexts of meaning are more clearly etched because of the goals in the game. Games may also be contexts of meaning even with no goals for the game. The players situate themselves in contexts of meaning. The players take on "roles." Play markers are symbols. The rules of the game are a formulation of logos that must abide by the other laws of logos (otherwise the game would not be played). In the context of these meanings there are also the meanings of indication and address. Through meanings, indication and address are perceived. He who does not perceive them "isn't really with it;" does not play cooperatively or else plays badly, contrary to the logos of play. This annoys the other players. The indications and addresses are those of the game within its contextual meaning. Of course the indication is not only indicative meaning; through it, something factual is indicated. This factual [indication] also has a factual meaning, and a factual [indication] of this meaning is established only within the contextual meaning of a particular game which, as a whole, has a contextual meaning of something special. Even so, indication is not only indicative meaning, but also (through it) a real indication—only, however, for the player insofar as he is playing. This is possible because playing is conscious conduct, although playful conduct only within the contextual meaning of a particular game.

The contextual meaning, or even more, the peculiarity of the contextual meaning in the game, is what makes the game a game and places it in contrast to reality. Man always lives in contexts of meanings. Explicitly, he lives only in contexts of meaning. But he does so with the sure knowledge of relations to reality, in which he apprehends the objective as well as the subjective side of reality itself (not only something like reality). From this relationship between meanings and reality, man delivers himself to games. Even more, in play and games man cannot avoid apprehending all being as supported by reality, while apprehending reality through being. Yet, while his real and serious behavior is conducted in contextual meanings with the sure confidence that the relationship of meaning to reality will square with that reality through meanings somewhere in his apprehensive conduct, in play and games this relationship to reality becomes irrelevant—a trifle. The relationship to reality is erased. Even the relationship to reality on the subjective side is erased. However, even here apprehension of reality in the act of apprehension is certainly a dimension of all apprehension typified as serious, whereas in play and games, the apprehension of reality in the act of apprehension becomes a trifle. The player consciously takes a role to conceal the relation to his own reality, and this renders him elusive and acts as a disguise. He attempts in a way to make himself clearly and plainly meaningful—in principle, impossible—or at best, a being (although unreal) with meaning. The latter is, above all, impossible in principle. Even in play, in a roundabout and, most of all, opaque manner, there is only slight confidence that whatever reality, whether objectively apprehended in a very indirect way or subjectively apprehended in the background, is actually there and present in some distant background.

In such a way, the justification of play as exercise or recreation is established at the expense of and by downgrading reality. Conversely, the basic conception of play is totally destroyed. Not only is reality unknown, though so much about it is known, that it also supports play as play. Because of the formal trifling of reality in play, it is established in a profound way that play will discontinue when it touches the basis of life. The basis of life is precisely real, the point at which reality is most surely apprehended; on the subjective side, it lies in the very existence of the subject. At the same time it is indicated that play and serious conduct overlap curiously. . . .

Making a Trifle of Reality

The apprehension of pure logos, at least where reality is not even suggested, though certainly where reality can be indicated, is methodically restrained from the turn toward reality. Thus, the apprehension of symbols, not only an apprehension of their meanings but also some apprehension of both symbols and their meanings, is constituted as a unity; so are fantasizing that serves no practical purpose and, finally, playing. All of these—apprehension of logos, symbols and meanings, fantasy, and play—are necessarily tied to reality, but trivialize the connection with reality. So the apprehension of pure symbols, purposeless fantasizing, and playing constitute existence, even though they are not apprehended as real, or at any rate they trivialize reality. . . .

Purposeless fantasizing and playing are two different things. Playing is action; fantasy is, at least, unnecessary, and at best, internal action. Whenever one wills fantasy, *Gestalten* must come in as responses to that will. Yet one can say that those who fantasize are "playing." On the other hand, fantasy is involved in much play.

The apprehension of pure symbols and their inseparable meanings can be termed aesthetic experience, although it is found not only in artistic experience, nor does it comprehend artistic experience. It necessarily belongs to artistic experience. The creation of art is also the creation of pure symbols. But creative art is not only this; artistic creation is also the creation of pure symbols. Schiller conceptualized artistic creation as a kind of play. He will hardly be charged with not being serious. Apprehending logos, which methodologically fulfills no practical purpose, could also be called play, and this, despite foreseeable objections, could appeal to Schiller. There are other reciprocal overlappings between play and serious conduct.

True Seriousness

As the first examples of serious conduct, one may list the immediate satisfaction of animalistic needs. They can be trivialized, and other things can be considered more important. Furthermore, the satisfaction of animalistic needs can be thoroughly suppressed. Yet they always make a claim, and as a rule they finally establish their priority. When they are not taken into account and do harm to man in his capacity as an animal—indeed, destroy him—there is no doubt that there is a seriousness to the experiencing and satisfaction of animalistic needs, even if the experience is eventually treated as serious in an unimportant way. (It is always treated as an example of what could happen to anyone.) The complications of human life, however, have necessitated preparations for the unmediated satisfaction of animalistic needs. In this way, man takes care to live in a condition of seriousness. At the same time, he "lifts himself above" [the requirements of the animal] and can detach himself, in his purposive relations, from the future satisfaction of animalistic needs. [He takes them in stride, so to speak. eds.]

The greatly lessening dependence of human existence on the satisfaction of animalistic needs brought money to mankind. It makes possible conduct that is not at all tied to the satisfaction of animalistic needs, nor merely a detour around money. At the same time, it frees human conduct from other burdens by providing alternative means for the pursuit of goals. On the other hand, money opens up a new world of playful conduct. In its own realm it is no longer oriented toward the satisfaction of needs. It intensifies the release of the total residual economy from purposes that are related merely to the satisfaction of needs.

At any rate, money is the point where great parts of human action, released from other considerations for satisfying animalistic needs, remain indirectly bound to those needs. Money is thus the serious locus of such action. A serious locus of that action, by virtue of its own autarchy, enables trivializing, indeed, sequestering; in any case, it can exclude from any influence on the style of playful conduct whatever has a place in seriousness (which can then be shoved to one side). In contrast, economic behavior as play is keyed in principle toward the satisfaction of needs. Besides this, there is conduct which is playful to begin with.

One never speaks of the areas that proceed only from animalistic needs. Even animals participate in unmediated serious conduct that is not to their own advantage but to the advantage of their nearest relation. Mothers will give their lives for their offspring. Should a mother not do this, she will be taken to task.

LOGOS AND ETHOS: ETHICAL SERIOUSNESS

For a long time, play has been conceptualized as a release of "surplus energy." If one also perceives it as serving serious conduct, then this is a contradiction: mere superfluity constitutes play (whatever the supposed meaning of the play is). But this superfluity is such that, through it, man "elevated himself above mere nature." We have long recognized "leisure" as the expression of *Kultur*. It is dangerous, however, because it appears to be non-serious or playful. That danger should not be exaggerated.

When man plays, he lives in the apprehension of logos. In serious conduct, he also lives in the apprehension of logos. At the same time, reality is close to serious behavior. Reality is also somehow present in play, though the relationship there is more distant. And thus it is more exclusively oriented toward logos.

The world of logos is a world of rules, and the orientation toward logos is an orientation toward rules. The player as player subordinates himself to the rules of each specific game. The rules of logos are not forces at all. Logos does not cause or operate. Rules never command or give orders. They never govern or enforce. Nothing obeys them. They "are," in the sense of being, just as logos "is."

Whoever apprehends logos "knows" the rules of logos. He does not have to acknowledge them, and he cannot acknowledge them. Thus, whoever recognizes logos must therefore recognize its rules (although this is not a sine qua non). The player need only interact with certain areas of logos, while ignoring others. By ignoring those other areas, it is implied that he subordinates himself to the rules of a specific game and recognizes them. Yet this concerns only specific assumptions. Playing is a conducting of oneself in the apprehension of logos, which, after the recognition of the specific assumptions, is no longer subordination but instead a more differentiated apprehension of logos. Logos captures, without force and without command. . . .

Secondarily, there are escapes from the narrowed areas of logos
. . . in whatever way. . . . Here ethos assists. Ethos itself is the
recognition of or a seizure by logos, because ethical orders are in
themselves a kind of logos.[3] . . . Ethos at least reduces the danger
of the nonserious and playful in the trivialization of reality. Real
seriousness is replaced by ethical seriousness. This can be more
powerful than reality or mere mundane seriousness. If ethos and
ethical seriousness do not have that power, then they increase their
importance by linking the honor of the devoted to ethically underscored areas of logos.

HONOR

Honor commands the first rank quite early. In the games of children, the spoilsport is "morally" rejected, and the "honor" of the
child spoilsport is somewhat diminished. Honor appears, first of
all, as a social phenomenon. Yet not all respect culminates in
honor. One can also be respected because of one's wealth, physical power, talent and knowledge, ancestors, or because of one's
achievements. One can find his honor respected on any of these
grounds, but then one situates his honor in them.

Becoming respected can be expressed by being honored. This
points at least in the vicinity of sociality. That honor is not basically social, however, is clear from the fact that one can know his
honor is neither damaged nor lost even when all others think so.
Honor is also rank or dignity, and has the tendency to demand respect. External disrespect can translate easily into a loss of honor,
even if others have the opportunity not to deny one's honor. And
honor is a rank requiring moral qualities. Whoever places his
honor in them and seeks to transform other qualities does so because he sees those other qualities as also morally valuable. Whoever both respects and honors another lets honor fall on him because of those other qualities. Such a person considers those other
qualities as being simultaneously of moral value. Although there
need not be excessive respect, there is at least a fiction of unity
between such qualities and moral value.

Because of moral qualities, something contains corresponding moral rank. It is not necessary to refer to those related qualities.[4] But one can apprehend them and realize them in the act of apprehension (whether that is successful is beside the point). In this way, one attains the related honor without further ado. In spite of this, it is not necessary for honor to be situated in every quality on which it is based. Although pertinent honor is tied to every moral quality and to every ethos, and consequently to the attainment of the moral quality accruing to the related honor, there is, on the other hand, a special ethos of honor. Honor, then, is not primarily connected to esteemed ethical qualities or to their realization in itself, but above all to this act of realization. In this, one certainly respects those ethical qualities, but one must not know and must not have a binding respect for them, because honor does not reside in the emphasis upon those qualities. Rather, it is tied to the honor established by their realization. Without this special ethos of honor, when one gives emphasis to ethical qualities and their realization, . . . one finds the achievement of certain ethical qualities, which one esteems tacitly, much less understandable. A claim on the honor tied to the attainment of such qualities goes with most of them, as anyone knows who has questioned or attacked them. . . .

. . . That one holds fast to established ethical demands,[5] that one is never released from those demands, that one sees the borders of conduct—at times widened, at times narrowed—as established by respect for esteemed moral qualities and the obligation to realize them should not be passed over or dismissed. It is a matter of honor. And the "point of honor" is affected by the menacing danger of avoiding it.

A matter of honor can be established through the faithfulness[6] that is maintained, even if the original motives which founded some inchoate union are suppressed. A paradox is certainly disclosed here, namely, that there is an ethos of infidelity, or in any case of newly emerging, deep emotion, coupled with dutiful obedience on the part of the person in the grip of that new emotion. Then one can remain faithful to this ethos and can find his honor in such faithfulness. The differentiation of so-called primary ethical existence from the dignity of the foundations connected with it is situated in the ethos of honor (or the latent ethos of honor), which also encourages social respect, or at least causes its undisputed existence.

Even children are exceptionally sensitive to damages inflicted upon honor (even if it is presumed). . . . It is tied, though not directly, to reality. Honor also belongs fundamentally to the world of meaning. Grounded in reality, one can always attempt to trivialize honor. But the function of honor is precisely to maintain its position in the world of meaning or, even more, to assign a practical importance to its rank. This is expressed in the odd, dual relationship of honor to money—that most telling representative of practical reality. On the one hand, through money, honor permits one precisely to disguise his position in reality, if one is devoted to the world of meaning. On the other hand, honor makes one especially finicky—sometimes reticent, cautious, even fearful, and at other times firm and exacting.

Games with money have long been construed ambivalently as dangerously seductive enticements and abominations. This is the case in "playing the stock market," whereby the private interest of the player, as in all higher economies, tends to become trivialized, along with his own thinking and real state of mind. This is so for anyone who surrenders to other delimited areas of logos. Noteworthy is the fact that the debt of play is also a debt of honor. In exceptional cases, honor is an instrument that is used to give the world of meaning the importance of reality. One may respond to the retention of honor with the question, "What can I buy with it?" Then not only has the ethos been disgustingly repudiated, but also the revelation has occurred that one is without honor and on his way to the menacing, irresponsible freedom of (not only "moral") death.

ETHICAL SERIOUSNESS AND REALITY

Neither ethos as such nor its accentuation through honor connects immediately with existence. Without ethos, though, reality demands a much higher priority. Its demands can be subdued or negated, and this can happen even without ethos. . . .

Reality is, first of all, animalistic reality. In animals it implies something basically social. . . . There are strata of differing degrees of importance in reality. . . . Even areas of logos can be considered more important than reality, but they can be so bound to reality by ethos that they acquire the practical rank of reality. . . . At this juncture, logos and the devotion to it remain playful, although they will eventually emerge from an ethical seriousness that has priority over a real seriousness.

The ethos cannot emphasize real seriousness; it can stress only ethical seriousness, although the latter will proceed from this to a practical coexistence with real seriousness and at the same time will be given greater importance. In any single case, it is difficult to know whether a sentiment of real seriousness or ethical seriousness is predominant. Basically, there is a difference. Specific reality, in this case, has a simultaneously brutal and banal character. At least it stays that way as long as ethos does not comprehend reality as being simultaneously logos: when life is risked for logos. There is only one other way in which man encounters reality. . . .

THE CONFRONTATION WITH DEATH AND THE NOUMENAL POWERS

Risking one's life for logos, when the specific logos is not assigned the value of ultimate surrender by a different ethos, is either condemned as an outrage or praised as heroism. Both may occur at the same time. The glory of heroism is itself a glorification of a form of logos, though accomplished with a thrilling shudder.

Man also trembles when he confronts the death of others. Death meets man only as the death of others. No living person has experienced his own dying. The death of others appears to man as existentially there. Like other existential events, this confronts humanity on its own terms. So existence confronts man either as a reality in itself or as sustained by reality. Such a reality, itself lying behind existence, appears only as a very uncertain reality. The confrontation with death is a confrontation with reality itself. To be sure, this is fraught with mystery. Therefore, an uncertain reality is met up with here, albeit immediately. Consequently, reality itself is not apprehended directly as lying behind existence, nor on the other hand, as an unproblematic constitution of existence with reality. Rather, reality itself is present in its totality. Therefore, it is "as" reality, though as reality in its totality, that it is present—on the foundation of reality itself.

Before death, man stands in total seriousness, not merely ethical seriousness. One meets his own death only at a place where no living being has traveled. But closeness to death or its impending danger can be experienced. This is the danger of death itself in the sense of death "as" death. This is almost apprehensible as reality itself, in the sense of total reality. And death grows closer as life increases.

Man cannot escape from the apprehension of reality and especially from reality itself, both subjectively and objectively. Reality, as the totality of reality, squarely confronts man in death. All life rests on the certain apprehension of reality. To be sure, reality itself—to the extent that reality meets life in its totality just at the point where reality is not dominant, though human reality is at least threatened—raises deserving questions. There it impinges upon the death of the other, and indirectly and at least imminently, on the death of one's self. This is where the game of life as well as the ethically serious game, the game in areas of logos, is threatened and poses questions. Yet death is not the only place of such confrontation. At least, it has not always been.

Forces such as the power of death confront humanity where it meets up with what is called godly. There are certain exceptions, but even in these exceptions names are preferred here, such as God or a god. Here again the addition of reality itself, in the total sense of reality, is necessary. Religious life is life with reality in its totality. Modern humanity has preserved something of this in the confrontation with death. Humanity cannot escape at all from the apprehension of reality nor from the apprehension of reality as such. Specifically tied to reality, man lives in the banal reality of his simple, animalistic existence. There is, of course, another serious reality in his religious life. In between, the game of life is played out, ultimately in high ethical seriousness but not in real seriousness. In its totality, reality is experienced only in the religious life.

METAPHYSICAL PERSPECTIVES

Even in religious life, the fullness of reality is confronted only in such a way that the totality of reality itself is not encountered, but rather reality itself "as" in the totality of reality. . . . The question, then, is: how is reality confronted "in" its totality? Above all, reality is "fuller" ["more" total] than sheer existence, if one considers this "fuller" as only ideal being. Suffering the apprehension of reality is itself fuller than that which is not suffered, since apprehended reality that is suffered is also apprehended "as" more total. . . . Moreover, confronting that which is met as the most complete totality of reality [the "fullest totality"] is suffering apprehension. Indeed, in the sustained fullest totality out of which an object emerges from that total reality—as is the case for all suffering observed—it emerges only "as" an experienced apprehension in that totality.

Here the comparative discussion of "fuller" and "fullest" existence is misleading because, since one does not progress from ideal being to existence and finally to reality through a sheer (or even gradual) culminating grasp of totality, it is much more necessary in principle to make qualitative distinctions. Noumenal experience and the experience of noumenal powers—the noumenal experience of powers as noumena—are differentiated from vigorous suffering, not by their main force, but qualitatively and in principle from still other suffering. In addition, it is very necessary to note that the experience of death, as an experience of the noumenon, is an outstanding representative example (at least for later humanity). This reality itself is not experienced as total reality (and simultaneously a manifestation of total reality) nor as a reality insofar as it is part of logos (however mysterious), but as the logos of this reality instead of a proxy in the realm of logos. . . . In spite of everything, there is a surrender to a logos in which death itself is present in the indication of the imminence of death. In such a moment, this sentiment will apprehend even heroism as insignificant. Instead of exalted ethics, or merely ethical seriousness. This is expressed in a mood which can be a sullen obligation to the logos. . . .

All religions are so constituted that, on the one hand, they need images and icons even if they are hostile to such images and icons; on the other hand, each religion always suffers from iconoclasm. Perhaps most noteworthy is the possibility that not so much reality as the totality of reality itself must be experienced. Also, not the pure logos of total reality or symbols which indicate this total reality from a distance, but rather symbols of total reality are to be experienced. At the same time, only symbols of total reality take such a form that the totality of reality itself will be experienced as present only in a symbolic manner: if the best part of humanity is tied to total reality and its seriousness not only through the practical introduction of heroism and every authentic religion, but also when the two are encountered in literature, as in tragedy and the poetic demise of heroes, and in religious art (with the exception of the cults). . . .

The real attitude of seriousness will (or must, insofar as its path can be traced) revolt against play on the side of the "most holy," as has often happened in history. Philosophy, which is often affected by such revolt, recognizes that there are a nonserious apprehension and a suffering apprehension of logos and the symbols contained in the logos at such peaks. Philosophy does not have to correct such events so much as it must investigate them. Philosophy may furthermore recall that it also knows that humanity can never escape from the apprehension of reality or from any reference to reality. Nor, incidentally, can it ever escape the apprehending of logos. It may be added that culture is the interaction with logos, while barbarism even though at times it may be a necessity—even a logical one—will still remain nothing but barbarism.

The secret—although it must be revealed as much as possible by metaphysics—of reality will have to struggle with the problem by itself and from its own depth in order to find out how the fantastic apprehensions of logos and symbol can exist along with their often loose connections to reality. For metaphysics this will be a key to unlock the mysteries of reality.

SUMMARY

The last [sections] have been neither metaphysics nor philosophical anthropology. They have only pointed to the places where paths toward metaphysics can be located. They have shown anthropology the peculiar dualism in which man is entangled. Only from a distance did it appear that this duality would be metaphysically strange. The knowledge of this "duplicity" is no assertion of dualism. A polarity was, of course, observable in that man may never escape from his relations to reality and from his apprehension of logos. . . . Polarity appeared particularly in the opposing principles of the interdependence of persistence and apprehension, in the enduring apprehension of logos, and finally in conduct in the interaction with logos. . . .

PHENOMENOLOGY OF THE SIGN

SIGNIFICATION, NOTIFICATION, AND APPREHENSION

A roadsign is an example of a sign [*Zeichen*] having a signification [*Bedeutung*] through which it is also the indication [*Anzeige*] of something. In former times, when one distinguished only the physical and the psychic, one tried to explain things as follows: what is given to me first is the physical sign; added to this, by virtue of an inference or an association, is the idea of something psychic, to wit, the psyche of someone other than myself. I reach it by leaving my own psychic state, which is only "given to me for the moment," but which is associated for me with certain manifestations of my body that resemble current physically given conditions.

Half a century ago Husserl showed, in his *Logische Untersuchungen*, that meanings are not at all something psychic, nor are they physical, but rather something quite specifically different. Their mode of being, unlike the physical and the psychic, is not at all something that can be called real. Actually, the analyses of Husserl are still marred by certain inexactitudes, to which his successors have added still others. For my part, I will limit myself to the presentation of conclusions I have reached on my own.[1]

"Phénoménologie du Signe," translated from the German by P. Godet, in Pierre Thévenaz (ed.), *Être et Penser*: *Cahiers de Philosophie*, "Signe et Symbole," vol. 15 (Editions de la Baconnière, Neuchâtel, Switzerland: April, 1946), pp. 49–103. We have been unable to locate the original German manuscript and wish to express our appreciation to Professor Sandra Soares, Department of Modern Languages, University of Wisconsin at River Falls, for providing a literal draft of the French translation. Of course, we accept full responsibility for errors that may have derived from our editing. [eds.]

The roadsign is thus originally experienced as the carrier of a meaning which as such has nothing psychic about it; through this meaning, it is also understood as something which indicates a real road as well as the place to which the road leads. This indication should not be confused with the originally given signification. Let us suppose that some rascals had amused themselves by turning the arrows of the sign in the wrong direction. The signification of the arms of the sign remains, as much for themselves as for those who have played this prank, but it has ceased to indicate. Naturally, it still seems to indicate, and indeed, the rascals have counted on this to misdirect the traveler. Thus, as a rule, the pure and simple signification contains at the same time the indicating signification. Yet the latter can be suppressed, as we have just seen. But it can also be lacking from the start, if, for example, the sign in question is reproduced for study, because of its particular form, in a graphic array of the various sorts of roadsigns. Here it no longer indicates to anyone a real road (which would not generally be reproduced, and hardly could be). Even in this case, it is true that the general signification of the object "roadsign" continues to imply that of the indication of real roads, although the sign cannot indicate correctly unless the conditions are appropriate. In that case, it will be promptly understood in this way, though there is a possibility of error even here. In other cases, the significations have no connection to any sort of indication. They can then be understood as "pure" significations, without there being any occasion to wonder if they also indicate something else (although this could happen by chance, even when the general signification does not imply anything similar). It is also important to note here that a general signification that is already in itself a general signification of indication cannot be understood as a "concrete" indicating signification except under certain specific conditions, in which case it also happens that it may be misunderstood.

Faced with the roadsign which presents itself to him in the country, the hiker can also say to himself that it has been put there by someone (a tourism association, for example), because that also is contained in the signification of a roadsign. But that is a completely secondary dimension of the signification. In most cases, that does not prevent a direction from being located. We usually become irritated when, in a discussion, our arguments are taken by the interlocutor not in their objective [*sachlich*] sense, but in a personal sense. This is, however, a common thing in polemics between political parties; it is the legitimate attitude of the psychiatrist toward his patient, and we can scarcely avoid it when someone tells us obviously incredible things or things which, on the contrary, are only too obvious. These examples confirm the both clearly distinct and normally secondary character of what one might call, in cases of this type, the "psychological" comprehension of a signification.

The apprehension of a sign as a notifying manifestation [*manifestation notificatrice*][2] coming from a subject (*Kundgabe*, as Husserl—who was still not able to perceive all the problems posed therein—has named it) is also grounded in an aspect of the signification which is secondary in relation to the objective signification and which is in addition—except that it is all the more secondary—an indicating signification. The grasp of a sign as a notifying manifestation of a subject is also that of a sign as indicative, but precisely indicative in a particular fashion, a dimension subordinate to the objective indication. As a rule, the apprehension of a sign as a notification is not always possible. When one sees black clouds coming over the horizon and interprets them as the signs of a threatening storm, those clouds are always taken as signs having a signification that includes the indication of approaching rain, but not (or only under particular conditions where many human beings, particularly at certain times, find themselves) as a threat coming from a psychic subject.

This example teaches us something more: it is that, as a rule, the sign-signification category is not made up starting with that which one could call the "sending" subject [*Sender*], but rather starting with the "receiving" subject [*Empfänger*]. From this results, of course, a second and quite important stage of the same process: it is the moment when a sender—once the sign-signification category has taken shape in him as in the receiver which he himself was in the first case—addresses to some other receiver a sign, which can be simply signifying, or can ultimately imply in itself a sign of indication, and eventually also a sign of notification. That can be done even when he addresses himself to indeterminate receivers (like a call for help by a tourist lost in the mountains); or when the receivers do not understand the signs addressed to them; or still more, do not even recognize them as meaning anything; or finally, when the sender does not personally direct them to any receiver, unless to his own self, as he envisages that self in some future. This last case is that of the man who formulates his thoughts in words, orally or in writing, for the sole purpose of clarifying them. All of this seems to be possible in principle only after the sign-signification category has been formed in a subject, starting, as we have seen, with the reception, or to put it more clearly, the apprehension of a sign precisely as a signification. (That can, however, lead to singular complications.)

Conversely, a great number of things, and ultimately everything, can be grasped as a signifying sign without being thus understood by the sender and even without the necessity for a sender. Let us add in passing that in the case of the black clouds taken as an example above, the primary signification is not indicative, and if it is matched with a general indicating signification (approaching rain), it is not necessary for this indication to correspond to anything concrete, as when the black clouds are represented in a painting.

The objective indication thus may not be accompanied by the personal indication which we have called notifying. In other cases, however, indication and notification can coincide. It suffices, for example, for a person to speak to you of himself for there to be produced in your direction some signs having a signification through which that person indicates to you something, while at the same time he notifies you, since it is of himself that he speaks to you. By doing this, the person can naturally be mistaken, and he may also be lying, and in lying betraying himself through his facial expression and the tone of his voice. But this tone and this expression are still, for the receiving subject, signs whose signification includes among others an indicating signification, which in this case is united with the one that we have called notifying. (Besides, instead of betraying himself, the sender can also successfully simulate sincerity.)

Husserl and those who have chosen to follow him have insisted above all on the general signification of the sign, on the objective indication that it contains, as well as on the difference that one must make between the latter and notification. These points are doubtless very important, as it is also very important to establish what sort of "acts" permit the sending subject to symbolize a general signification by signs and to indicate, through this signification, something objective. But apart from the fact that the sign-signification category is formed starting with the receiving subject and that, from this point of view, the problem is differently posed, it is no less important to see that the apprehension of something as a notification presupposes also that the sign has a signification, in which is contained, among other things, an indication that, in such a case, is identical with that of the notification.

It seems that our interpretation is approaching the traditional theory. But there is an essential difference. It is that, as we have just seen, the primary given is a sign having a signification which is, among other things, that of an indication comprehensible— either additionally or only—as a notification. (Is it now the case, by analogy, that the subject is established between one's self and another person? This we must ask ourselves.)

Once we have abstracted it from other difficulties that it presents (errors of a phenomenological order), the traditional theory can still run up against a problem which will greatly disturb it, since the theory is particularly unsuited for resolving it because the problem touches upon real life. The relations which the human individual maintains with the psyches of others—the earliest being that of the baby with his mother, then that of the schoolboy with his playmates, and finally that of the adult with all the humans who are involved with him in the realities of life—are in appearance so direct that the thesis according to which these psyches would be given to him only indirectly (through the intermediary of a given physical state, which would be itself inferred through an analogy with one's own experience) seems from the start to be inadmissible. But is it not necessary to say the same thing, with even more reason, about the new thesis, according to which what is given me is not the psyche of an other, but at first is only a sign having a signification, through such signs certain indications, and among these some notification? This last is of a more secondary order, even when it is accompanied by objective indications. An individual is quite angry with me and, trembling with fury, he threatens me sharply. If in this situation I am concerned immediately only with signs carrying the ideal signification "fury;" next, among them, with the indicating signification of a real fury; finally, through this but not before, with the real indication of fury which only then will appear to me as a (notifying) manifestation of the man who attacks me furiously, will one not think that such a complicated process runs a great risk, in the interim, of putting my life in danger? For a soldier at war, engaged in hand-to-hand combat, the theory would appear difficult to sustain.

Perhaps one could answer first of all by invoking the indirect nature of the many givens tied to our behavior in practical life. What happens, for example, when I light a fire? I scratch a match on a rough surface and, as I have learned from experience, the flame "appears;" it appears, in fact, to speak correctly, more than I can say that I "make" it. In the same way, the pianist strikes the keys of the piano, which in turn put in motion little hammers that make the strings vibrate, while the tones resound. Whatever the intermediary operations may be here, from the psychological point of view the consciousness of the person who lights a fire, like that of the pianist, is directed much less toward what he is "doing"[3] (and can only "do" in the literal sense of the word) than toward the flame or the sounds that, in this indirect fashion, are to appear or resound. Certainly, when faced with an anger that endangers us, it is advisable to be able to recognize rapidly the indication of a danger. But to identify this last, as one is easily tempted to do, with its apprehension as another person's anger, is already a construction. In war, for the soldier involved in combat—we know this from numerous narratives—the indication of danger never gets confused with the adversary's will to kill. This is quite another thing, to which one must reconstruct his attitude (with the risk of doubling the danger he runs).

It happens also that an individual feels himself to be strong enough to see in the signs of another person's anger only their pure and simple signification, disdainfully neglecting both what they indicate and what they notify (a disdain that serves only to heighten the anger of the other). Schoolboys often behave in this way toward their teacher. In his words and his gestures, they see only the signs of a certain signification and make fun of them, perfectly inattentive to the indication and notification that they imply. This irritates the teacher, and he falsely interprets the response as an intention to irritate him, though most often it is only a notification of a playful attitude. From then on, the teacher is reduced to imposing "forcefully" on the class a serious attitude, namely, the attitude that takes into account what he claims to indicate and ultimately indicates.

That the apprehension of something as notification is, first of all, only that of the sign as simple signifier, and (through it only) as indicative, then ultimately (either also or only) as "notifier," we have already the proof in the fact that the signifying signs can be given in the form of simple images (for example, the illustrations in any work on physiognomy) by which nothing is indicated (or is indicated only in a very indirect fashion) and even less is anything notified (in any case, not in the sense with which we are dealing here). One can thus imitate artificially by simply signifying signs. This is what happens in the theater, and it is a misunderstanding of the actor's technique to believe too completely in his reputation of playing the role of a particular character so completely that "he almost loses himself." Besides, the question is all the more complicated because in the theater there are also indication and notification, but at the heart of the play itself.

To return to the schoolteacher, it is certain that he can "forcefully" substitute a serious attitude for the playful attitude of the class; but this force itself is only given to the class by signs. Yet if it is not to be recognized only as signified, but rather as something to be taken seriously, it requires something else in addition. In order for an indication to be given, starting from a general signification, it is necessary that, through the latter, an indicating signification, which is contained in it (but only in a secondary fashion), be understood. However, it is not enough for it to be understood merely as an indicating signification. The perception of a "real" indication must be added as well. To accomplish that, the consciousness must turn its attention away from the domain of pure significations and direct it toward reality (or at least toward a state of fact). This requires the intervention of other organs than those needed to grasp significations.

The oldest theories, insofar as they were not unaware of significations as such, attributed the power to grasp them to a "thinking" whose particular nature, they maintained, was to surpass "tangible perception." Thus we will have to show soon that perception, taken simply as such, not only perceives signs but is also capable in itself of grasping them as signifiers, of comprehending significations just by the act of "perceiving." But there is more. It concerns the most fundamental consciousness, which is neither thinking nor perceiving—these are, above all, dynamic modes of consciousness, that is, conscious modes of acting and reacting. All these, precisely as modes of consciousness, are already necessarily able to comprehend the signification of signs. But this is not all. Through this signification (by itself and, secondarily, as an indicator), they can comprehend real indications. Such comprehension demands organs other than those of comprehension alone, which come into play by themselves where comprehension is already established through the mode of dynamic consciousness.

It is thus necessary to insist on the double power of the modes of dynamic consciousness: they are, on the one hand, able to understand signifying signs (including their secondary indicatory signification), and on the other hand, they are also capable of grasping through them real indications. That, however, does not prevent the comprehension of pure signification (and secondary indicatory signification) from remaining always "logically" anterior. We mean that former psychological doctrines have been able—if not in principle and perhaps not in an explicit fashion, but in fact—to distinguish in some substantial way between theoretical modes of consciousness and "practical" modes of consciousness. Between the modes of consciousness taken as such there doubtless exists no such demarcation, or at least not always; but logically, in any case, it is indeed appropriate to distinguish in them a theoretical element and a practical element. And the traditional doctrine was also right to attribute to the first a logical priority—only logical, it is true—over the other. In order for something to be perceived as an indica-

tion, it is first necessary that its signification (including the indi
cating signification) be understood. It is only then that the rea
indication can also be perceived through it. It is important to ad
only that it can be perceived, like the understood signification, b
the same modes of dynamic consciousness which function here a
organs both of understanding and of perception.

What we have just said about the perception of indications—
and that is true also for notifications, which are only a particula
type of them—is even more true in cases where the receiving sub
ject must not only simply understand significations (ultimately in
dicative) or even also perceive indications of reality. It is particu
larly true in cases where he is awakened and, in a way, suddenl
roused and shaken by the necessity of reacting practically to
situation in which he is personally involved.

Here it is necessary first of all that significations be understood
that an indication be understood as well, and that it also be per
ceived as real. But all of that will not suffice to "rouse" the receiv
ing subject. Besides this, being roused presupposes in itself, in
logically secondary dimension of the signification, something tha
presents the characteristic of rousing, and it is necessary that thi
element of signification be understood first. But even this is no
enough. One can clearly see here that this comprehension, althoug
it is logically primary, of a signification (logically secondary) "a
a rouser" will be in itself insufficient. There is still a necessity tha
the receiving subject be really "roused," and this demands tha
there be put in motion some organs which are no longer those o
purely theoretical import.

It is important here to add an appropriate observation. The dif
ference between the theoretical and the practical does not neces
sarily correspond to that of the modes of consciousness. A mod
of consciousness which is essentially practical, an experiential dy
namism, can also "understand" significations as theoretical at firs
(logically speaking), including in them their secondary dimen
sions, but it will draw from them the practical consequences b
itself. This is doubtless its principal operation; but to do this it doe
not need a previous experience [*Erlebnis*][4] that would be purel
theoretical, because it is capable of understanding theoretically b

itself. In fact, considering the matter in its psychological aspect, it could happen quite easily that, upon hearing a cry, I might jump instantly to my feet and run to help someone or to flee, without yet knowing exactly what is happening. In such a case, it is necessary in principle that I have already understood the general signification of the cry, through its indicatory aspects and ultimately its notifying ones, and then perceived through them the real indication and perhaps the real notification. Necessarily added to the signification here is a logically secondary element, but one of vital importance nonetheless, which comes as an appeal—an appeal to me—and which must not only be understood, but must also be perceived as a real appeal. This perception has already acted. There remain only the particulars of the signification (and of what it indicates and notifies) of which I am unaware and about which I must still find out.

The indirect character of all practical behaviors, or at least of a great number of them, and also of the manner in which the psyches of others are given to me, although incontestable in itself, is attenuated nonetheless by the fact that practical, conscious modes exist. They are essentially there, but are at the same time capable of theoretical comprehension without the intervention of any other mode of consciousness. This is quite important, but it is just as important a fact that in practical behavior, which, psychologically speaking, is produced as an immediate reaction, it is no less necessary to attribute logical priority to comprehension. This is always the comprehension of signs. Even indications and notifications, like any appeal which reaches me, always presuppose the perception of these significations (however logically secondary) as "indicating," as "notifying," and as "calling."

EXPERIENCE, EMPATHY, AND ADDRESSING ONE'S SELF

That the psyches of others are given to me through signs having a signification in which is also implied a secondary dimension, that of an indication, and, still more secondarily, that of a notification; that, on the other hand, indication and notification not only must be understood, but also really perceived: this thesis which we propose still seems to run up against certain difficulties—in particular, that the category "psyches of others" seems presupposed by the subject which understands and perceives. In speaking above of signs and their signification, we have omitted a consideration either of the categories which govern them or of their origin.

All that is lived or experienced, even in the most rudimentary experiences, is done so with a signification. Even if one holds fast to the traditional conception (itself erroneous), which maintains that the primitive experience is a perception, it is certainly necessary that that which is perceived be perceived "as something." It is impossible, in fact, to perceive a red something-or-other without perceiving it precisely "as" this red. According to more recent views, however, one has been able to establish with good reason that primary perception is not only of a theoretical character. On the contrary, what it encounters in its most elementary mode is grasped right away by the tendencies which govern our practical behavior. That is, this perception is already a perception with the significations "agreeable" or "repugnant," "frightening," "painful," or "welcome," "benevolent," and the like. It is similarly so with the characteristic of "making an appeal," and this characteristic is not only understood but also grasped right away, so that the subject draws the practical consequences. Nevertheless, it is perception which precedes, in the sense that there is in it the logical priority of understanding, so that this comprehension of that which "makes an appeal" relates to a logically secondary dimension of the signification. In reality, the most elementary perception—for example, the simple vision of red—already implies that I "understand," that I apprehend [*meinen*] this red insofar as it is precisely this red. That is a logically more central signification, even though at first it can be neglected as less vitally important and can limit itself, insofar as my apprehension [*Meinen*] is concerned, to the essential. (All that is ordinarily put into relief by old psychological theories of perception and willingly left aside by contemporary theories—such as the origin of depth perception and other similar facts—remains important, although the points which are emphasized today are no less important.)

The significations, insofar as they are of the order "this as that" or "what is perceived is always that which is perceived," are narrowly specified. This specification depends on conditions that are as subjective as they are objective. Thus, objectively, nothing can be given where no corresponding organs of apprehension exist, nor can anything be given to existing organs if, in principle, it is not able to be grasped by them. As for subjective conditions, they are in part "innate"—as such, they can only appear at a relatively late stage of development (at puberty, for example)—and in part acquired by "experience," but even here, always based on capacities, dispositions, or innate tendencies. The new psychology of animals, notably the study of what has always been called their instincts, has brought to light a host of phenomena which show that on the basis of their instinctive modes of behavior, animals grasp some significations in what they perceive, which may appear to them as only responding to their own tendencies. The bird that builds its nest at a certain period of the year—it is doubtful that the bird does it because it has seen others do it, without knowing what the nest is for—gathers the necessary materials, finding, and even seeking what is suitable to its construction. On the basis of what it perceives, a category of signification is formed: that which is "useful for the nest." Given its instinctive mode of behavior, this defines precisely the special group of things it perceives. The female butterfly, when she lays her eggs on plants that will furnish the appropriate nourishment to the larvae, doubtless does not know why she does so. (There is no need that she herself have anything to do with these plants; perhaps she will draw no nectar from their flowers or not even find any of that type of flower. She knows nothing of the caterpillars that will come out of her eggs, nor anything of their future nourishment. Nonetheless, it would obviously be false to say that she is provoked, as by a pure reflex, to lay eggs on plants of this exact type. The fact is that she seeks them, nor is this by a simple tropism, because in the butterfly there is "consciousness" (the essential mode of "perceiving"), and thereby the perception of something "as something."

These remarks are meant to lay the groundwork for treating the problem which is posed by given "psyches of others." There are different degrees to distinguish here. The first is the grasp of the "other" as simply leading to an end. In order for something to be experienced as favorable or adverse, as frightening or dangerous, as exciting desire or disgust, as providing pleasure or displeasure, it is not necessary that it be experienced as implying the "intention" of affecting the subject for ill or for good. That, however, can come about quite quickly. For the infant, a bright light that is suddenly projected on him or the outburst of an angry voice can be something disagreeable, upsetting, or frightening without being something that intends to produce these effects on him. But if the stream of light persists or if the brutal tone of voice is repeated, a category will soon form in him which will attribute to these givens the character of a bad intention directed toward him. It is the same for many adults, of whom it is known, for example, that all misfortune which strikes them is taken by them, not as pure bad luck or a simple, unfortunate event, but as concealing a malevolent intention directed against them. Education often takes it upon itself to teach people to get rid of such ideas, but the tendency to form them still appears quite distinctly.

When there really is a malevolent intention, the infant does not grasp it as something that would be hidden behind the phenomenon whence he feels hostility nor does he seem to suspect the presence of a subject that would be the source of it. It is directly in this phenomenon that he places the intention, and places it as personally directed toward him. It is grasped not only as harmful or adverse to his well-being, but also as hostile and as "wishing" him harm. For the infant at this stage, it is the phenomenon as such that is malevolent and evil. It can be seen that the first stage occurs when the blinding light or the violent outburst of a voice is experienced by the infant as a pure event, and (as such) as disagreeable or irritating, but not yet as bearing bad intentions with respect to him. However, the category which provides the second interpretation seems to be constituted only a few weeks after birth.

In concrete cases, it is true, it is often difficult to distinguish the two degrees. Even an adult who has personally experienced it would often have difficulty in saying if, in today's type of warfare [*Blitzkrieg*], the buzzing arrival of a group of airplanes that sow destruction and death is experienced by its witnesses as intentionally aimed at them, or only as a formidable and dangerous phenomenon, but not directed by a will. (Besides, if it were purely mechanical, it could appear more terrifying than a human will, no matter how evil.) The difference still exists in principle. One can ascertain clearly that the infant is capable, not from birth but very early, of grasping an event or a phenomenon not only as adverse to his well-being but also as evil and having, as it were, evil intentions directed toward him.

This difference between the two types of experience, depending on whether or not the first has added to it the second, is certainly also a result—and this helps in distinguishing them—of objective factors. If, for example, the too-bright light shines suddenly but is quickly extinguished, if the brutal vocal outburst is not repeated, they are experienced as disagreeable. If, on the other hand, the light persists in shining on the infant, who is disturbed in his sleep, if the noise of the voice returns ceaselessly to strike his ears, the half-awake child will have more and more the impression that an evil intention is hidden there. Even a grown adult will sometimes be very close to entertaining such a suspicion in the presence of certain phenomena. For example, seeing a chunk of rock detached from a mountainside rolling down the slope in his direction, threatening to crush him, he will often have difficulty escaping the impression—which, in any case, is that of the primitive man—that the stone signifies for him not only an objective danger, but that it is also pursuing him itself, as if it wished to do him harm.

Here again it is necessary to take objective factors into consideration, for certain phenomena are in themselves more likely than others to provoke such an impression. Also, from this point of view, its rectification in the subject will take place little by little. This rectification will consist either of abandoning all suspicion of this type henceforth, of categorically banning it as inadmissible, or on the contrary, increasing it to the point of transforming it into certainty, with the final result that one will distinguish, in objective phenomena, between those which can never imply an intention or which do not imply one in the particular case, and those which in fact are directed toward an end and are actually, so directed in the present circumstances. (The previous impression can appear briefly from time to time, but without being given any credence afterward.) The differentiation, which is implicitly given from the start but which becomes more specific by degrees and can thus be radically transformed, is thus of an objective type. But it appears no less clearly that the point of departure of this objective distinction is itself of a subjective type: it is in the primordial makeup of the human being to experience everything that happens to him, either as a pure event and, as such, already favorable or hostile but not intentional, or as bearing an intention directed toward him.

As for this last point—the capacity of grasping the intention—we can presume that man would not have it if he were not endowed with the very special faculty of behaving intentionally, of pursuing his ends, and in pursuing them, to experience himself as doing so. There is no doubt that he was made this way from the very beginning. Also incontestably, starting from these simply-lived modes of behavior, all the fundamental categories are built up in him. To these the adaptation of the means to the ends that he pursues is soon added. It is not necessary, however, that the object in view be already experienced by the subject as leading on its own account to an end. Is it necessary for this, as we might suppose, that there first be a projection from the subject upon the object in the manner of an "empathy"? Phenomena, such as are given to us, show us nothing similar. Man feels or experiences the other immediately as leading to an end, even though certain conditions must be induced to account for the object, so that the category can be applied there by starting with one's own nature.

More precisely, it is in the subject and in the experience of an appeal that the apprehension of someone else as being directed toward an end is founded. The stimulation of the subject by something which is experienced as an appeal coming from somewhere else causes it to be such that the encountered object is not encountered simply as a stimulus, but also as something which implies a direction toward . . . , an aim toward an end. It is thus by virtue of his own stimulation that the child receives what happens to him as "wanting to do something to him." Nevertheless, this stimulation of a subject is only the general form of his participation in the object, of which the experience of an alien intention is a specification. The experienced stimulus—and thus, in this sense, the experience of the appeal—does not necessarily imply that the stimulus be experienced as exerting an intention with regard to the one who experiences. But this specification alone can still be added to the particular stimulation of the subject.

At a later stage, there can also be an experience of something which is given as directed toward a goal, but without aiming precisely at the person of the subject. In this case also, the latter often has no consciousness of the fact that, objectively, the direction toward a goal can be given to him only by signs having this signification, or even only by signs that are interpreted exclusively in this sense. The signs are immediately experienced as directed toward a goal. In this case also, one cannot say that the category in question is only applied to them by the immediate experience, after having been incorporated by the subject in his own behavior directed toward an end. In any case, one cannot say that the subject projects onto others his own directed behavior, by means of some empathy. What one could perhaps call empathy, in the sense of "putting oneself in the place of" the one who is aimed at by the intention of another (in such a case, not the subject himself), is a certain personal emotion favoring a third person whom one considers to be threatened. This is really the subjective basis of the experience (always logically anterior) of others as directed toward an end, but as directed here also toward others. All the more proof that the original apprehension of the other as headed toward a goal is the application of a category based on an experience which is certainly of a subjective nature, but which is not to be interpreted as a projection of one's own ego on that of the other by an analogical inference. It is thus that I am affected, and not stemming from my own act that I experience others as directed toward an end. I experience this especially where I am touched myself (and not only by substitution), and in such a way that it is I personally who am aimed at.

Logically, what is "direction toward a goal" is only one type of that which is "direction toward . . . ," where it is not necessary that the object be seen precisely as a goal, but only as that which shows itself to me as an object in general; this is a specification of the intentionality common to almost all the experiences. In fact, except for the pure psychic states, every experience is intentional, both in principle and of itself—"tending toward . . . ," in the sense that something "meets" it. It is already this way in the infant, even when there is in him the preponderance of the subjective element of a simple state. But there is no need for objects thus grasped to be grasped as being themselves, and on their part, directed toward something. On the contrary, in this first essential form, the experience of the subject is not at all directly related to what it faces; objects are not grasped as aimed toward an end. When they are, it is first of all in the manner of this more general specification of "directed toward . . ." which we have just discussed, that is, as directed toward a goal and a goal that is me myself, insofar as I am the target of an exterior intention. It is in this form that I am at first affected. Something other than myself makes an appeal to me (without that, it would neither interest me nor would I even notice it). This is the primary given of the "other" in general. Starting from this experience of the appeal, the other becomes specified in something which affects me not only as an appeal, but as something which "wishes" to be so and has me personally in view. It is only then that the category can be enlarged by becoming that of "directed toward . . ." in general, which nevertheless remains logically anterior. All this becomes still clearer when one passes to an experience of a more elevated order than those with which we have already dealt, which in relation to the first of them is not only new but is also independent of them, and starting from which the concept of the psyches of others is made. But it is appropriate to insert here a few remarks on the history of these doctrines.

Traditional theory proposes that the human individual acquires the idea of a psyche other than his own by first perceiving in himself the bodily expression of his own psyche, which is immediately given to him, and then perceiving in others similar bodily manifestations from which he can infer, by association and by analogy with himself, the existence of this other psyche—(thus allowing him to pass on to the psychological interpretation of "signs" and of their "significations" (while these are, in reality, objective). This theory has been questioned for the first time by Theodor Lipps. According to Lipps, the passage through the experience of one's own bodily expression is a useful detour, and also usually impossible. The child already interprets as the psychic expression of others something which is principally given to him by sight. Yet at that early time he cannot know his own bodily expression by sight. The sense of the other, Lipps infers (with perfect justification), is given right away to the senses (feelings) of an infant as part of all that he perceives. The author tries, nonetheless, to finish the explanation of this phenomenon by referring to an empathy, through which the infant projects his own feelings onto others. Following Lipps, Max Scheler tried to make the psyche itself an "immediate given," with no need to distinguish one's own psyche from the psyches of others. As is always the case with him, he has brought to bear on this point a mass of interesting indications, suggestive of new problems, but they fail to demonstrate what they are meant to demonstrate. His positive thesis maintains that all psychic life, including that of others, is given immediately in "internal perception." He intends these terms to designate precisely the immediate character of "given," but this is all the less satisfying because the terms are only substitutes for true comprehension. They constitute a way of speaking that is traditional, and consequently misunderstood. They are only valid semantically as a definition, except for two further developments which were added on: first, the "double direction of the act," through which the distinction was to be established between one's own psyche and the psyches of others; second, the notion of a "bodily scheme" [*Leib-Schema*] where all that is derived is already known. Otherwise, Scheler seems not to have enlightened us at all. Ludwig Klages, who seemed to base himself on Scheler while also returning more or less to the views of Lipps, next spoke of an "immediate" comprehension of the "expression" of others. In his work, it is the use of this word "expression" which stimulates thought and demands further precision.

The category of expression cannot be grasped any more easily than can others by means of purely mechanistic concepts, i.e., by the simple notion of cause and effect. That was recognized by the very person (Darwin) to whom, most of all, it was important to draw upon the principles of pure mechanism in the explanation of the phenomena of life. When he turned to the problem of expression, he certainly saw that things would not go so simply. He attempted to understand them by employing the only category that he knew outside of causality, namely, teleology [*finalité*], a concept that has been abandoned today. Moreover, he tried to interpret teleology as a result of mechanical principles. Actually, this teleological category (neither Charles Darwin nor Wilhelm Wundt went beyond it) did not lend itself on its own terms to the explanation of expression. In whatever way it may be necessary to understand it—the term "discharge" used by Spencer may have put us on the right track—it is certain, in any case, that one cannot speak of expression without first considering the subject who is expressing himself. It is this which one must take as a point of departure, and it is only then that the category can be enlarged and applied to interpreting the expression of others. This holds even for cases where there is no need for the expression to be experienced as such, or even in any way, by the one who is expressing himself. It also holds for cases where an expression is not experienced directly as an expression either by the one who produces it or by the one who interprets it. In any case, it is not necessarily interpreted as mere expression, but insofar as it "expressed" it must be grasped, above all, as "directed toward . . . ," as "addressing itself to . . . ," or as "indicating" something (thus not only as an expression, per se). It can be seen that this is not a question of a simple problem with words; we are dealing instead with a designation (the term "expression") whose inappropriateness risks obscuring the phenomenon to be explained.

Before saying more on this subject, it is fitting to look into the very phrase "psyches of others," and, even more generally, psychic phenomena. Recent authors have often observed that merely using such terms presumes a mind-body dualism. Yet the first idea that occurs to us about this phenomenon, as we are considering it here, does not imply such a dualism. Rather, what is grasped, as far as we know, is a "psycho-organic unity" [*leibseelische Einheit*], although we must caution that such a way of speaking is basically defective because it does not succeed in expressing the unity other than as a duality. The formula, in our opinion, certainly represents an accurate insight. The dualism remains, however, in the idea of an action directed toward an end, the direction of intention, the sight, the "will" that presupposes something good, doubtless in the "directed one," but also behind the behavior thus described. This is even more the case when we deal with the fact of "addressing one's self to . . . ," of indicating, and, finally of "speaking to. . . ." In this sense, the idea that one has of such phenomena quite directly implies a certain dualism, but not yet involving a "soul," or more specifically, a soul that conserves its "identity" even when it does not behave as if directed toward an end and is consequently capable of other things, etc. . . . But we do not have to consider here the genesis of the specific concept of the soul. It is not our subject.[5]

Unlike the experience of which we spoke at first, where the subject grasped the other as directed toward himself—which is doubtless possible for him only on the basis of his own intentionality, but even so, cannot be derived from it—one finds at a higher level a mode of experience of greater significance, which is not only new in relation to the first, but is also independent of it and leads to the constitution of the category "psyches of others." It concerns at first an attitude or a behavior that is simply "experienced in itself" [*sich selbst erlebend*] and that implies logically the signification "other" without there being any need in this case that the other be given as such to the subject—although certain objective elements can and even must be given to him in order to trigger the experience in him. I call this behavior, experienced in itself, the original *s'adresser* [addressing one's self], and I affirm the existence in man —and not only in him—of a primary tendency to "address himself" without anterior experience of an object to which he addresses himself.

The first reaction of the human being to what happens to him or presents itself to him is pleasure or displeasure, and also repugnance or fright or, on the other hand, a welcome reception. Since the most precocious feelings of pleasure or displeasure are experienced, at least very often, as pleasure or displeasure "with" something, one can scarcely speak of pleasure and displeasure as simple states which are situated at the lowest level [of experience]. On the other hand, there is no essential difference between being afraid of something and getting away from something; the same is true for the passive reception of similar impressions and the principally passive reaction that results (fleeing, hiding), in addition to the active defense that this reaction can become. Even the fact of putting oneself on guard much less fighting furiously against . . . , does not yet constitute "addressing one's self to. . . ."

These first reactions of man to phenomena or events are also expressions. They are so for the one who expresses himself and they are experienced by him as such (this is "discharging oneself"), unaffected by the fact that they are also actions. (That expression and action can be one is what gives to the Darwinian theory of expression its appearance of truth.) But expression can also be such that one will hesitate to call it action, for example, a simple cry of pain or a smile of well-being. Here we still see that man can either simply express his well-being or his discomfort, or at the same time make present to himself their object (get irritated or be delighted "by" something, as well as take pleasure "from" it in advance, which is something other than depicting to himself the cause of his pleasure or his pain, as can also happen).

As soon as the human being is capable of speaking—and this is a new problem with which we will have to concern ourselves—he can also give expression through words to his pleasure or his displeasure, often in the presence of its object. He can thus rail at the thing which irritates him or rejoice at the welcome event, without the verbal formation being anything more than a subjective expression of his mood and without it [the thing] being exactly addressed.

But we must examine this behavior of "addressing one's self." For the baby in his cradle, its muslin curtains are not only soft (to the touch), they are also "kind," and a tenderness can be born in him for the curtains. In the same way, children love to caress the silk of their mother's dress or the fur of her coat. It is possible that, in the caress, there is only the quite subjective need to procure a pleasant sensation; but this caress can also be aimed at the object as such, can address itself to it or in some way speak to it, even if this is done without words. Later the words will come. However, the important point here is the "addressing one's self" as such, which can in principle be done without words—just as, conversely, all words are not necessarily addressed. The primitive tendency to address one's self does not presuppose in the other the corresponding ability to understand, but is directed also to objects which—as experience teaches the subject only later—are incapable of understanding.

This phenomenon does not disappear even with age. There are, we know, adults capable not only of raging at inert objects which irritate them, but even of actually abusing the objects, under the impact of a violent attack of anger that makes them ridiculous to possible spectators and also to themselves as soon as reflection permits them to get hold of themselves. To abuse is, in principle, to use words; but we understand we could say that words here are only a surrogate means, that what is primary is a movement of anger which is already in itself "addressed to . . ." and which needs to abuse the object so long as words are lacking. The mother whose child has bumped his head on the back of a chair and who beats it for him acts exactly in the direction of the need of the child, which here is to take revenge on the chair and even to punish it, not only by blows but also by words addressed to it, without yet knowing whether this object is or is not capable of receiving and feeling punishment. For it is the original tendency to address one's self that is the basic foundation on which alone experience of what is capable of taking it in and responding to it can later be formed and progressively revised.

Ludwig Feuerbach has claimed to find the origin of the belief in God—or in gods—in the need for help which is characteristic of the human being, who, from the depths of his misery, would call upon a helping being (without yet knowing if such a being can exist) by inventing it himself in response to the original tendency of which we are speaking. Let us set aside the thesis itself as a genetic explanation of the belief in the divine. It remains that Feuerbach has really discovered the primitive addressing one's self in such a way that presupposes in the particular case no knowledge of a helping being, nor even any previous experience of any help actually received. This is the same addressing one's self that one also finds in the fact of recognition, in a primordial need to thank, about which it is always necessary to wonder, as in the case of tenderness for . . . , if it is really addressed to someone [who actually exists].

The "addressing one's self" can also have an indeterminate significance by being directed toward a wide field of possibilities; for example, the stranded traveler who knows only that there do exist human beings other than himself who may be capable, should the occasion arise, of putting him back on the right road. But the same phenomenon also presents itself in animals, without a similar case necessarily existing.

That animals are capable of addressing themselves is ascertained by the cries of appeal and alarm that females direct to their young. One can doubtless presume that in these cases the mothers already know their young as such. Nonetheless, one must also admit that in principle, knowledge of representatives of their species, or more generally of other living beings, is constituted in animals in a way analogous to that which is natural to man. In the animal, there is not only experience of the other as simply existing, nor only of what happens to him insofar as he is directed toward a goal (which he is from the start); one also finds in him, independent of these phenomena, the original "addressing himself" without the previous experience of a capacity of comprehension on the part of the object to which he does address himself. On the contrary, this experience is constituted from the beginning by the primitive tendency to address one's self. It is in this sense that the dog "barks at the moon" (literally, according to appearances, he addresses himself to the moon). And if this same dog howls, alone in the night for a companion of whom he knows nothing, his cry is not only an expression of his solitude or of a still vague desire, but a very precise appeal to a partner to whom he wishes to address himself.

Despite all, the original tendency to address one's self implies logically, if it can be said thus, the presupposition of a corresponding comprehension on the part of the object. To put it more clearly, it is not the same thing to admit that in addressing one's self one is understood; rather, it is simply that the object is capable of experiencing pleasure or pain. This is so because the first addressing one's self is not at all just a phrase addressed [*Ansprache*]. It is purely a wish to give pleasure or do harm, but, as such, "addressed." As for doing harm concretely, it is perhaps difficult to tell whether it consists simply of tearing to pieces, of destroying beings or any objects, even inanimate ones (or those thought of as such), or whether it already addresses itself to the object in such a way that it logically presupposes in that object a sensitivity to pain. Perhaps one can discover on the face of the cat that plays with a living mouse an expression of cruelty that would not be found there if this same cat played with a ball of yarn. It is true that, for the cat, the fact that the ball rolls is perhaps a sign that it is living, or else is simply what attracts the attention of the animal, since it might not notice the yarn immobile in a corner. In any case, there is, both in animals and in human beings during their period of growth, besides the pleasure of destroying, a primordial tendency to cause suffering, and this assumes that the victim has some sensitivity to pain. It is not necessary to introduce here the capacity to understand, for the act of inflicting suffering does not imply that the victim knows that he is aimed at; only the capacity to suffer, not that of grasping the "addressing one's self," is supposed in the victim. Still, in the one who addresses himself—it is not the same for the one to whom he addresses himself, with which we will deal soon—there is a passage from the first supposition (capacity to suffer) to that, still purely logical, of a properly so-called comprehension. So long as he stays at this first point (he will go further), it hardly matters in principle that his behavior brings out in the other sensitivity to pain, or similarly, receptivity to tenderness, capacity to recognize, etc., or the specific ability to understand. It is also possible that he has, or thinks he has, the experience that the being to which he addresses himself is really capable of understanding, that he reacts to the torment inflicted on him not only by manifestations or suffering, but, in the true sense of the word that he responds to it, or more simply, that he speaks. Here for the subject there may be a new and very important experience. But this concerns not only the ability to understand what is supposed in the other; it also concerns the other insofar as he himself addresses himself and insofar as he speaks.

As we said above, concerning the grasp of another as directed toward an end, it seems true that this category could not be formed in man if he were not himself capable of behaving intentionally. But it is not made up through the projection or transfer from the subject onto the object. It is directly apprehended, just as in certain cases the other is grasped as directed toward an end, especially toward the subject who comprehends it. It is the natural tendency of the subject to experience a similar impression, which is preponderant although it is passive, with the object bringing to it only progressive revisions. In the experience of addressing one's self, it is the primitive addressing himself on the subject as action experienced in itself which is primary, by virtue of an original tendency to act thus and not to undergo something. This action implicitly contains an apprehension of certain objects that is not derived from these objects themselves, for these objects have their basis in the tendency of the subject toward this action. At the same time, these encountered objects (insofar as there is an encounter) cannot be completely indifferent to the act of addressing one's self, because this can be either positive or negative, i.e., sometimes benevolent, sometimes hostile, etc. . . .

We still must ask whether there is not also an original experience of "addressing one's self" in others (and not only of their direction toward a goal) about which one can suppose that it is given only by nature to beings who are themselves capable of addressing themselves without there being a need either to cause some transference or projection or to intervene by empathy. Indeed, it is so in fact. Here too, one must speak of a disposition, of an original tendency of the subject, which does not presuppose on the part of the object the real "addressing one's self" that he will experience later, although he will need some objective data in order to be able to grasp it precisely as "addressing one's self."

Just as in the grasp of another as tending toward an end, the organ (if we can call it that) through which the subject grasps "the other" as addressing itself to him (and not only as directed toward an end), is the experience of appeal, of a "called being" [a being appealed to] by some "appealer." Taken in itself, this appeal signifies only something that concerns me; it calls out to me in some way: "Attention!" It tells me that something is happening that is important to me, without necessarily addressing itself to me. But if it is understandable that this appeal implies the idea not only of a more or less indeterminate warning that would signify, for example, danger, but also of something that is directed toward me or against me, by the same token one can also see that the same experience of the appeal can be a more definite basis of this other idea, i.e., that what is happening to me is not only directed toward me but is aimed at me in the exact sense of addressing itself to me. The difference is this: something or someone can be grasped as directed toward a goal without one attributing or imputing to this other the possibility on its part of counting on the comprehension of the goal that it pursues. On the contrary, it is this imputation which is the nature of addressing one's self. The tendency of the subject to address itself doubtless does not imply the experience of the ability of the other to understand, but this ability makes up the "logical sense" of it. The logical sense of addressing one's self is to count on the possibility of being understood, a possibility to which experience will bring the necessary rectifications. As for the complementary tendency to grasp the other as addressing himself to me, that implies that I consider the other as aiming at me in such a way that he also counts on my capacity to understand him. I repeat: The direction toward a goal cannot be apprehended in the other except by a subject who is himself capable of it without projecting or transferring his own capacity on the other, because it is the appeal, according to its particular mode, that is specified for him in just this way. Likewise, the addressing one's self of others can be grasped only by a subject capable himself of this behavior, which he does not attribute to the other by some empathy, because it is the very experience of the appeal that is the organ through which an appealer identifies himself this time as one who addresses himself—who counts, then, upon the possibility of being understood.

It is not senseless on the part of a mother to address to her baby words of tenderness which she knows he cannot yet understand, or to murmur in some way tender things without even using words. She implicitly counts on the fact that the infant feels or experiences this way of addressing herself to him, or that this appeal which is made to him will soon become clear to him, first in a behavior that is directed toward him as an end, and then in an "addressing one's self to him" (a combination of the two categories).

The addressing one's self of others is not grasped by the subject only as directed toward himself. He can also grasp it as directed toward a third person. But in this case also—as in that of the "directed toward . . ." perceived in another—it seems that the phenomenon is grasped first of all insofar as it is aimed toward the subject himself (or concerns him). For it is only there that the subject first of all is touched. One must start with the appeal which is directed to himself to understand the experience of addressing one's self by others as a specification of a more general appeal, a more indefinite appeal. By the same token but of secondary importance, the addressing of another to third parties can also be explained. It is not only that eventually one comes to understand the signs that signify "addressing one's self to . . ." It is in the way—in some more immediate way—that the same organ of appeal can function here as perceiving this appeal, and as perceiving it by substitution, by inserting itself into it. In this case, the "putting-oneself-in-the-place-of" can be located on the side of the actor as well as on the side of the person to whom it is directed.

Man addresses himself in general through words. That he can also do so without them is witnessed by the act of smiling at . . . or of caressing without saying anything. One can understand fairly well how the passage is made from a mute addressing one's self to one that uses the language of words if one considers the signification which the area of the mouth can have for the human being, particularly in acts of tenderness. The mouth is capable of emitting sounds which are bearers of tenderness as much for the subject as for his object; they take on the signification of an addressed act and can thus become the first "words" of tenderness, a tenderness which is also addressed to someone. It is more doubtful that the experience of addressing one's self of others also has, as some people have thought to observe, its first point of departure in sounds and noises (murmurs or various mouth noises). There is something else here. When the mother holds out her arms to her infant to embrace him, these open arms at first are for him a place where he can nestle. Then they are experienced more as something which leads to an end: to welcome him, to receive him, and then as an invitation—"Come here!"—which is addressed to him. All of this comes from the appeal signified by those open arms which he saw at first as an indeterminate appeal, and which later became specific, in turn as an act directed toward him and as a gesture addressed to him. In addition, it is possible that certain proffered sounds also play their role here.

To return to the point of view of the subject and to the possibility of addressing one's self by sounds, great importance has been attached, as far as the origins of "addressing one's self" are concerned, to the period referred to as babbling [*Lall-Periode*], where the infant coos, that is to say, tries out sonorous formations to which he simultaneously listens—preliminary exercises, it seems, for the future action of speaking, particularly when he begins to repeat them, and (according to all appearances) recognizes them and tries intentionally to reproduce them. In such a case, he obviously discerns the connection between certain movements of the mouth and certain sounds heard, which he thus practices producing. These sounds certainly do not yet have any verbal signification, as they have no relation to the part of his surroundings where the conversation of adults can be heard. (Deaf-mute infants also have their period of babbling, but that does not last long.) One passes to a second stage when the mother herself—and this clearly is of great importance—imitates the sounds proffered by the infant, and he, recognizing them, tries in his turn to emit them as she does, [an effort] for which his own exercises have already prepared him. Yet these sounds do not in any way have the signification of words, even when the mother deliberately pronounces words of her adult language for the infant, which he strives also to say after her. Sounds to him are still only sounds, foreign to the significations of the spoken language.

Given these conditions, one could not consider what is produced during the period of babbling—any more than the addressing one's self that is developed in the emission of certain sounds—as what has been called "the root of the language." But perhaps it is per-

236 PHENOMENOLOGICAL ANALYSIS

missible to say that in the temporary pleasure that the infant takes, through "natural disposition," in babbling sounds still bereft of meaning, the future language of the word—by virtue of this natural disposition—is at least prefigured. From the very beginning, sounds always have a signification in their own way: high or low, strong or weak, affectionate or hostile, eventually directed toward an end or signifying this or that direction. In the end, they can be addressed—addressed to the infant or addressed by him.

In fact, spoken language evidently has a double root. On the one hand, it proceeds from the formation of sounds, which, prepared and practiced during the babbling period, has nothing as such to do with addressing one's self. It is independent of it, even though it is an original and spontaneous tendency of the human being. On the other hand, it proceeds from the tendency, no less original and spontaneous, to address one's self and to grasp the addressing one's self of others. But then the two tendencies are rejoined. The addressing one's self already has its own inclination to use (among other means of approach) the region of the mouth and the sounds that it is able to produce, while at the same time the natural disposition to receive appeals as being addressed to one leads to perceiving them particularly in the form of sounds, and thus to grasp these sounds as addressed. To put it differently, the production of more or less signifying signs, more or less comprehensible and understood, starting from the period of babbling where they are prepared and practiced, is in a sense an end in itself. Yet this [production of signs], in joining the tendency to address one's self, which it does not imply in itself but which accompanies it, or rather, precedes it, puts itself somehow at its disposal as a means which is welcome to it. We could conclude from this that the true root of spoken language, lived as an end in itself, is this production and comprehension of sonorities pregnant with significations with which babies, and later, men as poets, love to intoxicate themselves. (Here is an idea that could be fruitful for the understanding of the language of poetry.) In this sense, the word is not at first a social phenomenon. It becomes so through its union with the need of addressing one's self and finally of addressing one's self in speaking, at the same time that one receives in words what is addressed to him. The tendency to address one's self remains anterior to the word itself. It is only through their liaison that the act of speaking becomes "speaking to . . ." [*Ansprache*].[6]

One sees right away what this liaison means for "addressing one's self" as such. The living being is already capable of producing it himself and of grasping it in the other at the moment when he can grasp it as a response (although without words) which is made to him. This must be an important event for him. Even when, by addressing himself to others he must "logically" presuppose in them the ability to understand him, the real experience that he has of it—not only does one understand him, one responds to him!—can fill him with amazement. But the impression will be stronger yet if, in addressing himself to the other by using words, he perceives in return, perhaps addressed to him, words which are this time, in the proper sense of the term, a "response." At the same time, one also sees what language, insofar as it is "objective," gains in being used as a means of addressing one's self. From the fact that it has now become social, it develops numerous new categories of signification. I speak to someone and someone speaks to me. A conversation, a dialogue, is born. To this one must add that, in this exchange of words, the word can remain above all a means of addressing one's self, but that, conversely, this same means can also fall into the rank of an accessory element, from which language as such is increasingly enriched.

Yet spoken language does not serve only to address one's self and thereby to notify. It serves also to indicate. (If there is added to it a notification, it is of secondary importance, insofar as the notification is only a type of indication.) It is thus appropriate to inquire into the origin of indicative behavior.

We have already inferred that animals are not limited to "being there," that they are in one way or another "living," and that they are endowed with consciousness and thus with a consciousness which is necessarily consciousness "of" something "as" something. They too are capable of reacting to an appeal, which could be specified in them as an intention directed toward them and which is sometimes contradicted by a later experience to which they are also susceptible. Similarly, they have the original tendency to address one's self and to grasp what is addressed to them with the capacity to take into account the contradictions of experience. Finally animals are capable of showing [*zeigen*] and indicating [*anzeigen*]. Their cries of appeal (seduction) and alarm, as much for themselves as for those who perceive them, are not only expressions, nor even only addressed expressions. Even if the cry signifies nothing more than "Come!" it also says "I desire you;" this is already an objective invitation, and it is understood as such. Even if it only signified "I desire you," it would indicate (and thereby notify) to the other something that the other would certainly understand right away as an indication. The cry of alarm, in addition to the fact that it is the objective indication of a state in itself subjective—the anxiety of the one who emits it—obviously indicates an objective danger.

It has been disputed whether the act of showing, the first form of objective indication, can exist in animals. People have especially invoked the fact that a dog does not understand the signification of your pointed finger, because he looks at the finger itself and not at the direction shown, unless he has been trained to do otherwise. But the very fact that one can train him to do this proves that the category "show" is not inaccessible to him, although the gesture of extending a finger naturally remains foreign to him, since he does not have such a finger himself. Animals, too, "show;" for example, they show their young how to get food. The hen who has scratched up some seeds shows them to her chicks, drawing back herself, but not without repeatedly looking first toward them and then toward the uncovered food. Besides, this way of "looking toward . . ." while oneself abstaining from an act is a common manner of showing, in man as in an animal.

It is time to clarify definitively the structure of the phenomena examined in the preceding pages. We have established the basis of the categories of signification, and more particularly of the category "psyches of others." It was necessary to formulate the problem by beginning with the comprehension of signs and their signification. This seemed to be contradicted by the fact of an immediate given, which the psyches of others present and which emerged from the following considerations:

1) The bases of experience are, in the subject, original tendencies, to which the objective given (insofar as there is one) doubtless cannot be entirely indifferent. They are brought into play sometimes in one way and sometimes in another, but are not founded primitively on experiences, since they often contradict subsequent experiences. Consequently, these tendencies, on the one hand are the primary basis of subsequent experiences, and on the other hand, can be modified by them;

2) Insofar as in principle "the other" is given to the subject, it is given to him in the experience of the appeal, which, on the basis of his own tendencies and according to each mode of this appeal, becomes defined for him at once as one or another way of "being called," i.e., not only through the appeal of the other as such, but also through his relative capacity to comprehend and through his way of "addressing himself" (or what the subject believes it to be).

None of this in any way contradicts the thesis from which we began. We can even say that this thesis has been confirmed by it. On the part of the object there are only signs having a signification, but the subject does not notice that, because the categories of signification (those, in any case, which involve the meaning to be conferred on the psyches of others) are made up in his original mode of experience and in the experience of the appeal coming from the ultimately given object.

It seems apparent from what we have said that we must bring certain modifications to our thesis (which in no way abolish it), concerning the "logical" structure of the primary experience of signification. It is characteristic of this structure that it is only through signification, and even through its secondary directions—which must be understood first—that the real indication can be grasped, whether or not it is complemented by a notification or by the appeal itself. Insofar as these are present, they must also be understood so as to comprehend fully what is signified. Here we have doubtless previously answered that the organs of apprehension were already in themselves capable of being "touched" and of "understanding," and that the subjective phenomenon could normally be primary without weakening the order of reverse succession in the logical structure. Still, there is a possible objection here, which obliges us to modify what has been said of the logical structure, without rejecting the principle.

In particular, it seemed that our logical analysis of signs permitted us to affirm that their comprehension was formed in the "receiver" and that from then on, he alone could "emit" signifying signs in which the category "sign-signification" was previously formed by their "reception." This was a mistake. In fact, the original "addressing one's self" already logically supposes that the subject who addresses himself presumes in the one to whom he addresses himself the ability to understand him. But this logical condition is not a real condition. Psychologically, one addresses one's self to others in whom the category by which they are able to comprehend is formed on the basis of their original tendency to address themselves, which can always be rectified subsequently. Just the same, logically, there is in the original addressing one's self the presupposition of an understanding by another, even though only an analysis made after the fact can make this clear. There is more. Addressing one's self itself is possible only if the sender addresses to the object some signs having a signification. It is thus necessary, one will say, that the one who addresses himself already knows the sign- signification category and that he presumes the comprehension of signs by the object. Whoever addresses himself wants to make himself understood, and no one can make himself understood except by signs which signify something. Nevertheless, the one who addresses himself by signs does not do it by virtue of the knowledge that he has of the sign-signification category. No doubt one can certainly admit that this category is already formed in his own experience, since there is no experience that is not experience of something "as" something, and thereby a bearer of a signification. So addressing one's self can only follow the experience taken simply as such.

But the original addressing one's self does not presuppose an experience in the sense that it has already learned something from it; more particularly, the one who addresses himself does not use signifying signs because he already knows this category from his own experience. Similarly, in addressing himself, he presupposes logically—only logically—some objects capable of understanding him, the corresponding category being formed psychologically only in the very fact of addressing one's self. By the same token, he already uses signifying signs as the only means available for addressing one's self, without forming in his own experience an understanding of the category which governs them. Man—and not only man—possesses by nature a knowledge of signs as signifying and of the possibilities that they offer for addressing one's self by using them, but this knowledge, sui generis, is not yet true knowledge. It has required philosophical analysis (and even this has come late) to elucidate the conditions, on the one hand logical, on the other hand psychological, of the phenomenon. In such a way, it has been established that the messages emitted through signifying signs are not originally notifications, that they do not at all have that meaning, and that they are not at first anything but purely signifying signs. Secondarily, they are objective indications—such as the cry that the female animal addresses to her young, both warning them and putting them on guard. Only thirdly, should the occasion arise, are they notifications. It is possible that the prime motive of the female who emits a cry of danger is only the fear that she feels for her young, and her cry is only the expression of this fear. Nevertheless, for herself, what is thus addressed to them is already essentially the communication [*Mitteilung*] of an objective danger as well as an effort to put them on their guard against this danger. It is understood that she does not know that the message thus emitted can exist only through signs having a signification. Besides, it can happen (to her despair) that these signs are not understood.

We feel that it is useless to push the analysis any further, although one could still get some other interesting results from it. Let us note in this connection that the "messages" made by means of the word give evidence of a singular, complicated structure of various natural dispositions toward the pursuit of certain ends which seem foreign to these dispositions when taken separately; or to put it differently, toward the "cooperation" of natural aptitudes that were originally separate. When carefully considering, as we have done, the true origin of language, one establishes that it is in itself a system of forms made solely to signify, and which the speaking subject uses only to indicate, to notify, and even to address himself, with the exception that this last behavior inclines more toward using the signs of the spoken language. One can also observe that our knowledge of the psyches of others is based, on the one hand, on certain vital modes of behavior (the natural tendency to address one's self). On the other hand, certain ways of grasping the appeal (experience of the other as directed toward a goal and as addressing himself) become, as soon as the category "psyches of others" is constructed and eventually rectified, a simple accessory element which is taken as autonomous. In animals, when the mother addresses to her young a cry of warning that is principally the communication [*Mitteilung*] of an objective danger, and at the same time a warning to be on guard against this danger, it is as a communication to be on guard that the young grasp it above all, and only in an accessory fashion as the mother's own manifestation of her will to warn them and of the fear for them that she feels.

On the part of the object, we have seen that nothing but signs bearing a signification can make the subject grasp the existence of the psyches of others. One can find here more evidence to support what has been called "physiognomical vision." As all elementary teachers know, the letters of the alphabet and the numerals, which have generally already been seen but must now be learned, do not yet appear to the beginning schoolchild as having the signification which is the very thing he must learn. These signs already have a signification for him, but it is simply of another type. To his eyes, these are not at all simple, geometric figures (which as such would also be grasped as signifying). The significations that the child sees in the letters and the numerals are rather the sort of things he would call them; for example, thin, fat, etc. . . . These figures will also appear to him as having arms and legs, sometimes heads, and they will often even be insolent or modest in his eyes, scolding or jolly, gloomy or joyous, etc. . . . If we have been able to call this sort of vision "physiognomic," it is because it has been recognized that letters and numerals appear to the children with a "psychic expression." It would seem that this might be doubted, if it were only a question of fat, thin, ungainly, etc. . . . But it is also necessary to note that the characters so designated are *leiblich*, that is, those of organized and living bodies, and are grasped as human or analogous to those of men or animals. Insofar as living organisms [*Leiber*] are something other and more than simple physical bodies, they are given as phenomena in which something "is expressed." In this sense, the word *Leib* is only another way of designating a phenomenon of expressive character. One can readily understand from this that one easily passes from these "organic" categories to those of the arrogant, the amiable, the malicious, the modest, etc. Still, the category "expression" from which these notions come relates, it seems, to something that is expressed which is different from the expression itself. In fact, when characters of printed type are called insolent or malicious, it implies that one sees these qualities "on" them. However, their being as such [*Sosein*] is not exhausted by their appearance. Behind that appearance there is something else that could provide some surprises. Now the child knows quite well that this is not true of letters and figures. He takes them as presenting a psychic expression without supporting the existence behind them of a psyche that would be expressed through them. Their expression is for him pure quality, pure character, pure signification.

Such letters and numerals (one could add to this, among other things, wallpaper motifs) are not the only examples of physiognomic vision. Everyone knows that children see everywhere—in objects, eyes, noses, mouths—things that have a comic effect on them. They laugh innocently at them, and one can easily see that for them, in these cases also, physiognomy only signifies. It is not the true expression of a reality that might be found behind it. On the other hand, however, children are never completely sure about this, because the same physiognomical appearances can, in other cases, make them anxious or afraid—as if they made them grasp, beyond a simply expressive signification, an indicative signification.

Here there is a logical distinction which is manifested early for the child in a psychological difference. What leads him to make that difference may be, for example, that the same "mama" is sometimes "nice" and sometimes "angry," but can also pretend to be angry. (The child is not sure of the difference, insofar as the identity of a real psyche which also transforms itself is not yet formed in him as a category.) Yet the child amuses himself by pretending, and most of his games, starting with "hide-and-seek," "tag," etc., consist of simulating, by adopting a role. But we cannot here approach the problem of imitation. We will limit ourselves to recalling that other things in turn are connected with it, such as the reproductions of forms [*Abbilden*] and finally, all the arts, among which is the theater.

SYMBOLS AND LOGOS

One usually calls a symbol a sign that, through signification, refers to something other than itself. In fact, the signification is always something other than itself. The signification is always something which goes beyond the sign, insofar as a sign is purely material and simply exists. Even when the perception of red is already a perception of red as precisely this red, and thereby an "intentioning," an "apprehension" [*Meinen*] goes a bit beyond this red and even goes beyond it in the direction of the formation of the general concept of red. This general concept is not at all presupposed here. There is certainly some truth in the nominalist thesis, which believes that the general concept can be formed only on the basis of a plurality of experiences in which the similar is acknowledged as similar. But the perception of "several" as similar among them already supposes that a "same" (in the strictest sense of the word), which from that point on is necessarily an ideal "same," has been recognized; thus, the most primitive experience of a red already points, in some way, through this red, to a thousand other possibilities of red—specifically, to an ideal identity of all reds. All consciousness—I cannot develop here what, with several errors concerning particularly the thinking and also the interpretation of the a priori, is already in Plato—is thus made of itself. In the very first experience of something as something, there is also necessarily the meaning of this something as "not being" (what it is not), as being "other than the other," and that is independent of all experience.

If the adjective "symbolic" has been used to designate the necessarily inherent character of every experience, whereas we ordinarily call a sign indicating something other than itself a symbol,
this special use of the word can serve to clarify what characterizes
the symbol in general. For the symbol, understood in a general
sense, does not necessarily imply the indication of something which
would be different from what it is itself, in the sense that this something could be designated in other ways, among them in a more
"direct" way. For the young French school of poetry (Aragon, for
example) and its theoreticians, it is very important that their symbols be always "symbols," but symbols of something which cannot
be said in another way. They affirm that there is no way, even if
someone claimed it to be more direct, to express otherwise what is
expressed in and through the poem itself, and that makes the poem
no less "symbolic." This was already known and said sixty years
ago, at the time of "symbolism." That poetic movement can be
traced back to Baudelaire, and one can perceive in it the clear
consciousness of affirming something which has value for all poetry,
even for all art, from the most ancient times.

In German poetry, Hugo von Hofmannsthal has said of the
poems of Stefan George that they signify—as does all poetry, he
also affirms—something which goes beyond the words as pure verbal matter, but which it would still be impossible to say otherwise.
Certainly, said Hofmannsthal, these verses "signify," but "do not
formulate" what they signify, because one cannot formulate it in
another way [*Gespräch über Gedichte*]. Around the same time,
Rudolf Kassner (in his *Moral der Musik*) dealt with the difference
between symbol and allegory, writing that the latter is a sign whose
signification indicates something which one could willingly express
otherwise, whereas the symbol doubtless also means something, but
something which could not be formulated in any other way and
which therefore must necessarily be expressed by this very symbol,
and by it alone. It remains no less a "symbol" for all that. These
views, so important for the comprehension of a work of art, have
aroused the enthusiasm of our youth and have furnished the conceptual language that we needed at the time; they have also kept

for us even till today the value of fundamental intuitions. Meantime, we have pushed the inquiry further. Still, in our eyes it is a point of first importance that the symbol, in the specific sense of the term, contains, unlike the allegory, a signification which—quite exactly—can be symbolized only by this very symbol (even though it is necessary to make some distinction of degrees here). In the present study, by insisting on the fact that there can be no consciousness unless this consciousness is of something "as something," and in terming "symbolic" the property of containing nothing which permits one to express this something in another way, we are only continuing to recognize that the symbol is specifically not an allegory. Nevertheless, seen from another angle, the notion of the symbolic in the broad sense includes in it that of the allegorical, and even certain characteristic traits of the symbolic, taken in any sense, come more clearly from the allegory than from what one must call a symbol in the strictest sense—as we have seen in the "symbol," or rather "the allegory" of the roadsign. It becomes clear in particular from this that the significations of the symbol (taken in the broadest sense and thus including in it the allegory, but also taken in the strictest sense of symbol) are something objective: the significations are such insofar as they imply in themselves the "objective logos" and are thereby even subject to objective logical laws.

But we also know a traditional way of speaking, which consists of opposing the "thing itself" to what is "only symbol." There is here, with no contradiction, something true. It is certain that the effort of the mind which tends toward a logos that is always more pure, more ample, and more elevated, also takes it farther away from the concrete, and the superiority that this gives to the mind also contains some dangers. Besides, even the concept of reality— for the consciousness that I have of it is also a pure concept—is opposed to reality, since reality is unable to take on a meaning that is not at the very most a conceptual-limit which is destructive of itself, and as such, necessary. But it remains also that symbols are signs of the objective logos.

They are so also where they symbolize the psychic, where they "signify" the expression of the psyche. And there too they only signify. If one who understands them does not notice this, it is through comprehension or even in his perception, as such, that he perceives quickly that understanding and perception are one. If the "sending" subject of signs does anything other than "express himself," if he "addresses himself" and, still more, if, without even addressing himself any more, he formulates some thoughts, he also only emits signifying signs, whether or not he wants, through signs, to indicate, notify or, above all, appeal.

Significations are objective. Nonetheless, the categories of signification cannot be opened except under subjective conditions. Nothing can ever be revealed except to a corresponding organ of apprehension. But rectification, if there is any, starts with the object, and the internal logic of the revealed frees us in great measure from submission to the subjective conditions of the revelation. It never liberates us from it completely, and there always remains the possibility of other categories of signification, quite different, which are never "opened" and perhaps never will be opened to us. Still, it is of great importance to man—even from a simply human point of view—that insofar as he is gifted with consciousness, he can never not be directed toward, not "intend," the objective logos. "Life" and "existence" lose nothing by this, no matter how the problem of rapport between logos and reality may be solved.

In the second of his *Elegies of Duino*, Rilke says:

Animals, in their instinct, see well
That we do not feel completely at home
Or secure in our interpreted world.

It is appropriate to observe—besides the fact that Rilke knew as we do that animals also live in an "interpreted" world, about which they are simply unaware that there is a problem—that man himself, who has seen the problem, the problem of signs, has also seen that the significations are objective and logical. In fact, even if this problem is not posed in all its complexity except to a small human elite, these people can find, by delving into it, a means of understanding other men, a means also of rendering justice to their "ethos"—that ethos (ethical attitude of mind) in which interest and care, for several decades and even (with some exceptions) for more than a century, have been preponderant among modern scholars. As for those who remain attached by preference to the consideration of the logos, they can still remember and reduce to their usage the word (in itself always arguable) of Plotinus: "to act is weakness."

Notes

PREFACE

1. Edward Shils, "The Study of the Primary Group," in Daniel Lerner and Harold D. Lasswell, eds., *The Policy Sciences* (Stanford: Stanford University Press, 1951), pp. 44–69.
2. Kaspar D. Naegele and Gregory P. Stone, trans. and eds., Schmalenbach, "The Sociological Category of Communion," in Talcott Parsons et al., eds., *Theories of Society* 1 (Glencoe, Ill.: The Free Press, 1961): 331–347.

INTRODUCTION

1. This is particularly true of American sociology, although one occasionally finds refreshing exceptions. Suzanne Keller, for example, has gently corrected Merton's suggested analogy between *Gemeinschaft* and *Gesellschaft* and "locals" and "cosmopolitans." See Keller, "The Planning of Communities: Anticipations and Hindsights," in Lewis A. Coser, ed., *The Idea of Social Structure: Papers in Honor of Robert K. Merton* (New York: Harcourt Brace Jovanovich, 1975), pp. 283–99, esp. pp. 291–92. Obviously, among all the frames of reference we have in mind, that of Tönnies has been most thoroughly examined by German scholars. See, for example, the special issue of the *Kölner Zeitschrift für Soziologie* 7, no. 3 (1955), edited by René König, published on the centennial of Tönnies's birth. More recently, with some reference to Schmalenbach: Werner J. Cahnman, ed., *Ferdinand Tönnies: A New Evaluation* (Leyden: Brill, 1973).
2. Otherwise, a sociological perspective could not be built. Somehow continuity (certainly not an uncritical harking back to the past, nor an inane parroting of old terms) must be reestablished. Discontinuities abound, stemming at times from ignorance, the reluctance to accept continuity when it is recognized, or an utter abandonment of concepts, where, as in the extremities of factor analysis, words and phrases are discovered, uncovered, or discarded for letters or Roman numerals.
3. For a critical assessment, see Robert S. Perinbanayagam, "The Definition of the Situation: An Analysis of the Ethnomethodological and Drama-

turgical View," *Sociological Quarterly* 25 (Autumn 1974): 521–41. Since this writing, the first volume (1976) of the *Annals of the Phenomenological Society* has appeared under the editorship of Myrtle Korenbaum. Helmut R. Wagner, "The Influence of German Phenomenology on American Sociology," in that volume, pp. 1–29, specifically points to the "trap of solipsism" that has ensnared American sociologists unfamiliar with the methodological influences of existentialism on phenomenology, particularly the neglected works of Friedrich Baerwald. See ibid., esp. pp. 8–9.

4. Stephen Toulmin, "Reasons and Causes, in Robert Borger and Frank Cioffi, eds., *Explanation in the Behavioural Sciences* (London: Cambridge University Press, 1970), p. 2; but see the entire article, pp. 1–26. For Kant's argument, see Immanuel Kant, *Prolegomena zu einer jeden künftigen Metaphysik* (Prolegomena to any further metaphysics) (Hamburg: Meiner, 1957), pp. 71–76.

5. Schmalenbach, *Die erste Konzeption der Metaphysik im abendländischen Denken* (The first conception of metaphysics in occidental thought) (Darmstadt: Wittich, 1909).

6. Like Simmel or Tönnies, Schmalenbach's assignment in philosophy included the field of sociology. At that time there were no separate positions for sociology in German universities. Sociology was typically pursued either in economics or in philosophy. Schmalenbach taught sociology at Basel as well—indeed, to the end of his life.

7. Robert Böhringer, *Mein Bild von Stefan George* (Zürich: Küpper, 1951).

8. Schmalenbach's status and fate in Germany may be gleaned from references to him in Kürschner's *Gelehrtenkalender*. It lists Schmalenbach in 1931 with 17 lines, in the 1935 edition with 8; he is dropped from the 1940/41 edition, only to reappear in 1950 with 15 lines. (Berlin: DeGruyter, 1931, 1935, 1941, 1950.) Paul Honigsheim, intimately familiar with the European circle of sociology between World War I and the Nazi period, checked over some early passages in the first translation of the *Bund*, to which we have referred above. In doing this, he betrayed absolutely no knowledge of Schmalenbach.

9. This influence was probably channeled through Rudolf Eucken. But Buber may also have alerted him to pragmatism. For Buber's correspondence to Pragmatism and for a context in which Schmalenbach might be explained, see Paul Pfuetze, *Self, Society, Existence* (New York: Harper, 1961).

10. Schmalenbach, "Wundt," *Sozialistische Monatshefte* 26, no. 2 (1920): 1094.

11. Schmalenbach, "Feuilletonphilosophie" (Pamphlet philosophy), *Sozialistische Monatshefte* 25, no. 2 (1919): 831–32.

12. Schmalenbach, "Das Sein des Bewusstseins" (The being of consciousness), *Philosophischer Anzeiger* 1929–30, pp. 354–452, esp. p. 404.

13. Alexius von Meinong, "Über die Erfahrungsgrundlage unseres Wissens" (On the empirical basis of our knowledge) (1906), in Meinong, *Gesamtausgabe* 5 (Graz: Akademische Verlagsanstalt, 1975): 369–481. Meinong is otherwise known in the Anglo-Saxon world because of his strong

influence on the early work of Bertrand Russell. Cf. R. M. Chisholm, *Realism and the Background of Phenomenology* (Glencoe: Free Press, 1960). The best introduction is J. N. Findlay's, *Meinong's Theory of Objects and Values* (Oxford: Clarendon Press, 1963).

14. See Joseph Leif, *La sociologie de Tönnies* (Paris: Bibliothèque de philosophie contemporaine, 1946). Pierre Thévenaz, *What Is Phenomenology?* (Chicago: Quadrangle, 1962). Also Thévenaz, "Avant-propos," in his edition *Sign et Symbole*, a special issue of *Etre et penser: Cahiers de philosophie* 15 (Neuchâtel, 1946). Raymond Aron, *German Sociology* (London, 1957).

15. Besides Schmalenbach's student and subsequent successor Hansjörg Salmony, the most important seems to be Michael Landmann. See Landmann, *Der Mensch als Schöpfer und Geschöpf der Kultur* (Man as creator and creature of culture) (Munich: Reinhardt, 1961). Also Kurt Gassen and Michael Landmann, *Buch des Dankes an Georg Simmel* (Berlin: De-Gruyter, 1958).

16. Gassen and Landmann specifically refer to Simmel's own acknowledgment of Eucken's work. Ibid.

17. For a short introduction to the work of Eucken, see W. T. Jones, *An Interpretation of Rudolf Eucken's Philosophy* (London: Black, 1912).

18. Buber mentions this in a conversation with Werner Kraft. See Kraft, *Gespräche mit Martin Buber* (Munich: Kösel, 1966), p. 1939.

19. Schmalenbach, *Geist und Sein* (Mind and being) (Basel: Haus zum Falken, 1939). Excerpts are to be found in this volume, part 3, "On Human Existence."

20. See Schmalenbach, "Die Idee der Logik als Philosophie vom Logos" (The idea of logic as philosophy of logos), *Jahrbuch der Schweizerischen Philosophischen Gesellschaft* 3 (1943): 1–18.

21. Alfred E. Emerson, "Homeostasis and the Comparison of Systems," in Roy R. Grinker, Sr., ed., *Towards a Unified Theory of Human Behavior: An Introduction to General Systems Theory* (New York: Basic Books, 1956), pp. 147–63.

22. Talcott Parsons, "The Present Status of 'Structural-Functional' Theory in Sociology," in Coser (see note 1 above), pp. 76–77.

23. Schmalenbach, "Simmel," *Sozialistische Monatshefte* 25, no. 1 (1919): 283–88.

24. Cf. Georg Simmel, *Über soziale Differenzierung: Logische und psychologische Untersuchungen* (On social differentiation: Logical and psychological investigations) (Leipzig: Duncker und Humblot, 1890), pp. 1–20.

25. Kant, *Prolegomena* (see note 4 above), p. 94.

26. See Perinbanayagam (note 3 above).

27. For the distinction between subjective (individualistic) pragmatism and social pragmatism, see Gregory P. Stone and Harvey A. Farberman, "On the Edge of Rapprochement: Was Durkheim Moving toward the Perspective of Symbolic Interaction?" *Sociological Quarterly* 8 (Spring 1967): 149–64. This also explains in part Schmalenbach's difficulty with Durkheim's "sociologism." See also H. S. Thayer, *Meaning and Action* (Indianapolis: Bobbs-Merrill, 1973), esp. pp. 206–10.

28. See Martin E. Spencer, "Images of Groups," in *European Journal of Sociology* 16 (1975): 194–214, citing, vice versa, the tendency in newspaper reporting to assign individual characteristics to nations.

29. Herman Schmalenbach, "Kant und die Philosophie der Gegenwart" (Kant and modern philosophy), *Österreichische Rundschau* 20, no. 1 (1924): 445–68.

30. Schmalenbach, "Leibniz: Gestalt und geisteswissenschaftliche Stellung" (Leibniz: Gestalt and its position in the humanities), *Österreichische Rundschau* 18 (1922): 9–25. See also his *Leibniz* (Munich: Drei Masken Verlag, 1921).

31. Rene König, "Zur Soziologie der zwanziger Jahre" (Sociology of the twenties), in Leonhard Reinisch, ed., *Die Zeit ohne Eigenschaften* (Time without characteristics) (Stuttgart: Kohlhammer, 1961), p. 82.

32. Hans Freyer, "Gegenwartsaufgaben der deutschen Soziologie," *Zeitschrift für die gesamte Staatswissenschaft* 95 (1934–35): 116–44.

33. Hans Freyer, *Revolution von Rechts* (Revolution from the right) (Jena: Diederichs, 1931).

34. In Felix Krueger, ed., *Philosophie der Gemeinschaft* (Community philosophy) (Berlin: Junker und Dünnhaupt, 1929), in an elaboration between pp. 143 and 168.

35. Hans Naumann, *Deutsche Nation in Gefahr* (German nation in danger) (Stuttgart, 1932).

36. Schmalenbach, "Macht und Recht: Platons Absage an die Politik" (Power and law: Plato's rejection of politics), in H. Barth and W. Rüegg, eds., *Natur und Geist: Festschrift für Fritz Medicus* (Erlenbach-Zürich: Rentsch, 1946), pp. 183–209.

37. See Michael Landmann, *Das Ende des Individuums* (The end of the individual) (Stuttgart: Klett, 1971), pp. 131 ff.

38. For a related treatment, see Peter L. Berger and Thomas Luckmann, *The Social Construction of Reality* (Garden City, N.Y.: Doubleday, 1966).

39. Theodore Abel, "The Operation Called Verstehen," *American Journal of Sociology* 54 (1948): 211–18.

40. The most recent attempt to revive an interest in Tönnies's sociology, Cahnman (see note 1 above), specifically emphasizes the dialectical conceptualization (pp. 109, 112). The dialectic was implied much earlier in what is still the most concise and complete orientation to the work of Tönnies available in English, Rudolf Heberle, "The Sociological System of Ferdinand Tönnies," in Harry Elmer Barnes, ed., *An Introduction to the History of Sociology* (Chicago: University of Chicago Press, 1948), pp. 227–48. In particular, Heberle notes the antinominal relationship of community and society. For him, the concepts are "not unreservedly antithetical." To a certain extent, this aspect of Tönnies's work reflected the influence of Marx, an influence stressed by Albert Salomon. See Salomon, "German Sociology," in Georges Gurvitch and Wilbert E. Moore, eds., *Twentieth Century Sociology* (New York: The Philosophical Library, 1945), pp. 593–94. However, there is little doubt that romanticism played a part. The dialectic permitted Tönnies to maintain the dream of a return to *Gemeinschaft*.

41. This, the best known of Tönnies's works, has been translated and supplemented by Charles P. Loomis as *Fundamental Concepts of Sociology* (New York: American Book Company, 1940). All references are to this translation.

42. Ibid., p. 18.

43. Ibid., p. 17.

44. "Human will" was for Tönnies the fundamental basis of social relations, and the resultant blurring of analytical distinctions between individual and social phenomena accounts in large part for the difficulty he has apparently had in communicating his theory. Tönnies himself was aware of this shortcoming, for he noted in a later edition of *Gemeinschaft und Gesellschaft* that, "since this book starts from individual psychology, there is lacking the complementary but opposing view which describes how *Gemeinschaft* develops and fosters natural will, on the one hand, and, on the other, binds and hinders rational will. The approach does not describe how *Gesellschaft* not only frees rational will but also recognizes and furthers it, even makes its unscrupulous use in competition into a condition of the maintenance of the individual, thus destroying the flowers and fruits of natural will." Ibid., pp. 194–95. The terms "natural" and "rational" will are Loomis's translations of *Wesenwille* and *Kürwille* respectively.

45. Ibid., p. 57.

46. In this sense, Schmalenbach's discussion of Tönnies's concepts is more sociologically encompassing than the concepts were intended to be. See this volume, part 1, "Communion—a Sociological Category."

47. It would seem that, just as the primary group derives from and in turn conditions those primary ideals which constitute *human nature*, so community is characterized as a natural relationship. See Charles H. Cooley, *Social Organization* (New York: Scribner, 1902), pp. 23–31. Wirth has also noted the parallel between Tönnies's *Gemeinschaft* and Cooley's primary group: "The community (*Gemeinschaft*), as Tönnies sees it, has a great deal in common with the primary group of Cooley, for it includes all those relationships which are familiar and intimate, spontaneous, direct, and exclusive (although apparently Tönnies is unfamiliar with Cooley's work and his concepts have a different setting from those of the American sociologist)" Wirth, "The Sociology of Ferdinand Tönnies," *American Journal of Sociology* 32 (November 1926): 419–20. To the contrary, we have drawn on Cooley's conception of "communion" to apprehend Schmalenbach's critique of *Gemeinschaft*.

48. Tönnies (see note 41 above), p. 49.

49. This phrase seems more accurately to render Tönnies's meaning than the translated "authority based on power or force." See ibid., pp. 47–53, esp. pp. 47 and 51.

50. Ibid., p. 55.

51. Ibid., p. 54. The parallel to Cooley's conception of sympathy is striking.

52. Ibid., p. 55.

53. Ibid., p. 74.

54. Ibid., p. 74.

55. "Before and outside of the convention and also before and outside of each separate contract, the relation of all to all may therefore be conceived as a potential hostility or latent war." Ibid., p. 88.

56. Tönnies constructed his concept of society logically rather than analogically as in the case of community. Consequently, given this mixed methodology, it is simpler to present his discussion of these relations by treating the "pure types" *as if* they had empirical reference. Schmalenbach clearly overcomes this problem.

57. Tönnies (see note 41 above), pp. 95–96. For a poignant statement and exemplification of Tönnies's assessment of his own position with reference to that of Paulsen and Lasalle, see Arthur Mitzman, *Sociology and Estrangement* (New York: Knopf, 1973), pp. 50–112. These passages also discuss the sources of the concepts "community" and "society."

58. Tönnies, p. 81. In contrast, consider the anomalous miser.

59. Ibid., p. 86.

60. Ibid., p. 79. Compare the "invisible hand" metaphor of classical economics. There are many parallels, and Marx, of course, drew extensively on Ricardian economics.

61. Ibid., p. 102.

62. Tönnies (see note 41 above), p. 18.

63. Elton Mayo, *The Social Problems of an Industrial Civilization* (Boston: Division of Research, Graduate School of Business Administration, Harvard University, 1945), p. 40.

64. In this sense, the concepts of natural will and rational will which are discussed here are "residual," as Parsons uses the term, since they operate logically to close Tönnies's theoretical system. The fact that Tönnies later stated that both types of will were conditioned by the social relationships in which they occurred does not alter this conclusion, because Tönnies's observation was not taken into account in his own theoretical system. See Talcott Parsons, *The Structure of Social Action* (Glencoe, Ill.: Free Press, 1949), pp. 16–20.

65. Tönnies (see note 41 above), p. 119.

66. Ibid., p. 162.

67. Ibid., p. 222.

68. Sir Henry Sumner Maine, *Ancient Law* (London: John Murray, 1870), esp. p. 170. See also his *Village Communities in the East and West* (New York: Holt, 1889).

69. While this is understandable in terms of a universal phenomenological methodology, nowhere in his discussion of communion does Schmalenbach convincingly demonstrate Durkheim's inadequacies. It is not enough simply to dismiss Durkheim's theory of the elementary forms by labeling it "sociologistic," for Durkheim, over the course of his career, may not have been as sociologistic as Schmalenbach maintained. See Stone and Farberman (note 27 above).

70. The counterarguments, for the most part, are to be found in Edward A. Shils and Henry A. Finch, eds. and trans., *Max Weber on the Methodology of the Social Sciences* (Glencoe, Ill.: Free Press, 1959).

71. Precisely reminiscent of Maine's distinction among law based on Themistes, customary law, and codified law. See Maine (note 68 above).

72. Rudolf Heberle, "Zur Theorie der Herrschaftsverhältnisse bei Tönnies," *Kölner Vierteljahrshefte für Soziologie* 5 (1925–26): 51–61.

73. For an introduction to Husserl, see Thévenaz *Phenomenology* (note 14 above). Also Herbert Spiegelberg, *The Phenomenological Movement* (The Hague: Nijhoff, 1960), vol. 1.

74. Peter Winch, *The Idea of a Social Science* (London: Routledge and Kegan Paul, 1958), p. 145. As a good example of the recent critique, see W. G. Runciman. *A Critique of Max Weber's Philosophy of Social Science* (Cambridge: The University Press, 1972).

75. Max Weber, "Knies und das Irrationalitätsproblem" (Knies and the problem of irrationality), in Weber, *Gesammelte Aufsätze zur Wissenschaftslehre* (Tübingen: Mohr, 1922), p. 76.

76. See, for example, R. H. Tawney, *Religion and the Rise of Capitalism* (New York: Penguin Books, 1947), from the Holland Memorial Lectures, 1922, pp. 261–63. Ironically, the conventional response to such criticisms is that Weber was not trying to explain but to understand. Certainly, Weber did not construe his analysis as anti-Marxist but as a necessary supplement, extension, and reformulation of Marx.

77. *Das Mittelalter: Sein Begriff und Wesen* (Leipzig: Quelle und Meyer, 1926).

78. "Individualität und Individualismus," *Kant-Studien* 24 (1919–20): 365–88.

79. Ibid., p. 370. See also the discussion in "On Lonesomeness," this volume, part 2.

80. "Individualität und Individualismus" (see note 78 above), p. 371.

81. Hans Linde, *Sachdominanz in Sozialstrukturen* (Dominance of property in social structures) (Tübingen: Mohr, 1972), p. 82.

82. Ibid., p. 62.

83. Ibid., p. 36.

84. Claude Lévi-Strauss, *Structural Anthropology* (New York: Basic Books, 1963), pp. 232–41, 277–323.

85. Roman Ingarden, *Über die kausale Struktur der reinen Welt* (On the causal structure of the pure world) (Tübingen: Niemeyer, 1974).

86. Alfred Schütz and Thomas Luckmann, *Strukturen der Lebenswelt* (Structures of the world of life) (Neuwied: Luchterhand, 1975). For an assessment and sense of impact of Schütz in the United States, see, inter alia, Jack D. Douglas, ed., *Understanding Everyday Life* (Chicago: Aldine, 1970).

87. Alfred Schütz, "Concept and Theory Formation," in his *Collected Papers* 1 (The Hague: Nijhoff, 1973): 48–66.

88. Charles H. Cooley, *Human Nature and the Social Order* (New York: Scribner, 1902), p. 73.

89. Ibid., pp. 86, 87.

90. Ibid., p. 87.

91. Ibid., p. 103.

92. See the review by James S. Coleman of Harold Garfinkel's *Studies in Ethnomethodology* (Englewood Cliffs: Prentice-Hall, 1967), in *American Sociological Review* 30 (February 1968): 126–30, esp. pp. 128–29. At this writing, ethnomethodologists have become much more "hard-nosed."

93. George H. Mead, "Cooley's Contribution to American Social Thought," *American Journal of Sociology* 35 (March 1930): 693–706.

94. Herbert Blumer, *Symbolic Interactionism: Perspective and Method* (Englewood Cliffs: Prentice-Hall, 1969), includes Blumer's earlier essay "Science without Concepts." See ibid., pp. 153–70.

95. Ibid., p. 168.

96. Ibid.

97. Ibid., pp. 138–39.

98. Specifically, ibid., pp. 59–60, and throughout Schmalenbach's writings.

99. Robert E. Park and Ernest W. Burgess, *Introduction to the Science of Sociology*, 2d ed. (Chicago: University of Chicago Press, 1924), p. 16.

100. For a summary of these developments in American sociology, see, inter alia, David A. Karp, Gregory P. Stone, and William C. Yoels, *Being Urban* (Lexington, Mass.: Heath, 1977).

101. For instance, Edward A. Tiryakian, in a review of an approach that is essentially that of Schmalenbach, makes no mention of him. See Tiryakian, "Existential Phenomenology and the Sociological Tradition," *American Sociological Review* 30, no. 5 (1965): 674–88. Despite Irving M. Zeitlin's strong inclination toward phenomenology, the same holds for him. See his *Rethinking Sociology* (Englewood Cliffs: Prentice-Hall, 1973).

102. Ferdinand Tönnies, "Gemeinschaft und Gesellschaft," in *Handwörterbuch der Soziologie* (Stuttgart: Enke, 1932), pp. 180–91. Upon his own assertion, Tönnies did not feel close to phenomenology, claiming little knowledge and understanding of such an approach. See his "Selbstdarstellung" (Self-portrait), in *Die Philosophie der Gegenwart in Selbstdarstellungen* (Modern philosophy in self-portraits) (Leipzig: Meiner, 1923), pp. 203–44. Werner Cahnman (see note 1 above) sees Tönnies nevertheless as essentially a phenomenological sociologist.

103. Heberle (see note 72 above). In a later article on Tönnies (see note 40 above) he makes no mention of Schmalenbach.

104. See also René König, "Die Begriffe Gemeinschaft und Gesellschaft bei Ferdinand Tönnies" (The concepts "community" and "society" in the work of Ferdinand Tönnies), *Kölner Zeitschrift für Soziologie* 7, no. 3 (1955): 348–420.

105. Theodor Geiger, "Gemeinschaft," in *Handwörterbuch der Soziologie* (see note 102 above), pp. 173–80.

106. Linde (see note 81 above).

107. Schmalenbach, "Das soziale Prestige der Lebensalter" (Social prestige of age groups), in G. Albrecht, ed., *Reine und angewandte Soziologie: Festgabe für Ferdinand Tönnies* (Pure and applied sociology: Essays in honor of Ferdinand Tönnies) (Leipzig: Buske, 1936), pp. 258–62.

108. See Hans Lenk and Günther Lüschen, "Epistemological Problems and the Personality and Social System," *Theory and Decision* 6, no. 3

(1975): 333–55, for a pledge to further empirical research in the context of general action theory.

109. For a general assessment of the recent interest in phenomenological sociology, see John Rex, ed., *Approaches to Sociology* (London: Routledge and Kegan Paul, 1974), pp. 5, 125–44.

THE COMMUNION—A SOCIOLOGICAL CATEGORY

1. See my essay "Individualität und Individualismus." *Kant-Studien* 24 (1919–20); also my *Leibniz* (Munich, 1921).

2. *Gemeinschaft und Gesellschaft* 1.6. Also see the erratic discussion in 1.18: "All original public worship is familistic, hence appears most rebust as domestic worship where hearth and altar are the same." It would seem that these families—monogamous and patrimonial—originally cultlike, should therefore have been conceived as communions. See below, for example. Tönnies had already remarked (1.7) that "pure spiritual brotherhood, after many experiences, can only endure physical living together up to a certain point." Nevertheless, he is acquainted with religious phenomena only in the explicit sense of the "later" forms of comparable community. Understandably, then, the omission of the communion from consideration follows from this, as does Tönnies's psychological construct *Wesenwille*, the rich profundity of which has obscured many things.

3. *Grundriss der Sozialökonomie* 3. See *Wirtschaft und Gesellschaft* 9, par. 2. "Within society there is the distinction—also, indeed, a duality—between *Wertrational* [value-rational] and *Zweckrational* [goal-rational]." I concur with Max Weber's formulation.

4. Most assuredly Max Weber considered blood ties, in consequence of his methodological delimitation (see below), not as social but only as "biological" phenomena.

5. Of these there are many and diverse factors. Obviously it is not my intention to present a fully developed theory of community here; I am employing only as many of those factors as are necessary to throw into relief the distinctive peculiarities of the "communion." Moreover, I do not believe at this time that a comprehensive classification of all the principal factors that contribute to the emergence of community will be possible. Nor, of course, do I see any interest in it. The examples that have been offered here serve merely as illustrations. They should in no way permit the inference that the areas represented in them exhaust the entire area. I shall make an additional remark only to show that this area can be extended in still another direction. Namely, when two professional colleagues meet, they share the objective qualifications of their profession. Although a profession is something individually achieved and perhaps entered fairly recently, so that there may be a complementarity between the professional and the momentary situation, only the objective "conditions" are operative and lend a community-like character to the relationship between colleagues.

6. According to this argument, the conscious and the unconscious seem not to be opposites. Actually there are two conceptions of consciousness. Actual knowledge, as knowledge about something, is always only knowledge of "circumstances." (I know that . . .) The circumstances are "there" (phenomenologically), and the "existential" is known at the same time without affecting it in any way. Thus there is an unmediated, directly perceived apprehension of the conditions of existence itself, and, beyond such objective circumstances, lies the question of the relation of knowledge to them, insofar as the existence of knowledge as a phenomenon of its own kind has not been considered. Knowledge may or may not affect the "unconscious." It remains real. The matter of "consciousness," then, is raised along with "the unconscious." This too, of course, can become an object of knowing (though useful, the expression is certainly awkward). However, this is not essential; the expression "unconscious consciousness"—"unknown consciousness" is probably better—is not nonsense. One can live predominantly in "the bright light of awareness" without ever being aware, for example, of that fact. Moreover, someone else may be very much aware of the many peculiarities of such a person's "unconscious." For the most part, "ignorance" belongs to the "unknown consciousness," as do those things that have readily disappeared from consciousness while being preserved in the "unconscious," or, in any case, functioning there, but they are then, indeed, something quite different. On the whole, the conscious is more closely related to the process of knowing than is the "unconscious," since knowing is a function of the conscious, although occasionally knowing may affect the unconscious. (Only as a function of consciousness can knowing destroy the unconscious. The impact of the unconscious upon knowing and upon the conscious is highly problematical and complicated, in any case.) I believe that these remarks are needed here. Perhaps I should also have emphasized that the unconscious, if you will, is a phenomenon of consciousness or, better, something directly known as well as something that may be revealed.

8. Unnoticed feelings are no more to be considered unconscious events than perceived unconscious events are phenomena of consciousness.

9. *Gemeinschaft und Gesellschaft*, 3d ed., 1.7.

10. The Brentano-Husserl insight into the intended nature of "feelings" (of many "feelings") was not known to Rudolf Otto when he undertook an analysis of *The Idea of the Holy* (London: Oxford University Press, 1925) and of its development in experience.

11. Translators' note: "I give so that you may give" (i.e., "You scratch my back, and I'll scratch yours").

12. Heinrich Schurtz, *Altersklassen und Männerbünde* (Berlin: Reimer, 1902).

13. Naturally and justly, I need not be concerned primarily with the mischief that that man of letters, Hans Blüher, has perpetrated on the basis of his interpretation of Schurtz.

14. *Gemeinschaft und Gesellschaft* 1.1, 2.6.

15. *Wirtschaft und Gesellschaft*, chap. 1.1., 1.2.

16. Translators' note: We have been dissatisfied for some time with the Parsonian translation of *Herrschaft* as "leadership." Cohen, Hazelrigg, and

Pope have recently suggested "domination." See Jere Cohen, Lawrence E. Hazelrigg, and Whitney Pope, "De-Parsonizing Weber: A Critique of Parsons' Interpretation of Weber's Sociology," *American Sociological Review* 40 (April 1975): 229–41, esp. 237–59. "Governance" seems more precisely to render Weber's meaning.

17. Weber, *Wirtschaft und Gesellschaft*, chap. 3.2, 3.10, 3.11 ff. In 3.10.4 there is an excellent discussion of the "distance between economic enterprise" and "pure charisma" (except for an absurd sentence about the "circle of Stefan George"). In 3.12.1: "Charisma is the typical emergent phase of religious (prophetic) or political (imperialistic) governance." In 3.11 (and 12a) see the discussion concerning the "driving motive" of "day-to-day routinization" which is also, to be sure, very rationalistic. Besides, it is clear that such juxtapositions are found scattered throughout the entire book and are not limited to the sociology of "governance," such as the one already quoted from chap. 1.1.9: "All traditional action and large aspects of charisma . . . [are neither wholly nor only separately comprehensible]."

PROPERTY, OWNERSHIP, AND COALESCENCE

1. George Simmel, *Soziologie: Untersuchungen über die Formen der Vergesellschaftung* (Leipzig: Duncker und Humblot, 1908), p. 135.

ON LONESOMENESS

1. Translators' note: see "Individualität und Individualismus," *Kant-Studien* 24 (1919–20): 365–88, not included in these selections because most of the ideas appear and are elaborated in other essays included here.

SOUL—THE EMERGENCE OF THE CONCEPT

1. Above all, Alfred Crawley, *The Idea of the Soul* (London, 1909), provides an excellent survey of such conceptual usage. Of course, many observations had already been made by Edward B. Tylor in his *Primitive Culture* (London, 1872). Further reports are found in Wilhelm Wundt, *Völkerpsychologie II: Mythen und Religion* (Leipzig, 1905–9). Just as we can find much about the general area in James G. Frazer, *The Golden Bough* (1900), so we can find still more in numerous articles in *Hastings Encyclopedia*. [Schmalenbach continues to cite works, including those of Durkheim, Levy-Bruhl, and Söderblom.—Eds.]

2. The discrepancy in the Aristotelian psychology was incisively recognized by Werner Jäger [*Aristotle: Fundamentals of the History of His Development* (1924; Oxford, 1934)]. The doctrine of transitory immortality was inherited from Plato and contradicted Aristotle's own biological ap-

proach. According to Jäger, the development of Aristotle led ever further away from biology, although the elder Aristotle never entirely repudiated that teaching. [Schmalenbach here makes some comments on Plato's understanding of the soul.]

3. Wilhelm Schmidt, *The Origin and Growth of Religion: Facts and Theories* (New York: Lincoln MacVeagh, 1931).

4. Robert Marrett, *The Threshold of Religion* (London: Methuen, 1909).

5. Rudolf Otto, *The Idea of the Holy* (London: Oxford University Press, 1925).

6. Hans Plischke, *Von den Barbaren zu den Primitiven* (Leipzig: Brockhaus, 1926), observes the development of concepts among primitives, but only in a substantively satisfactory way.

7. The seemingly corresponding assertion of Lucretius, "Primus in orbe deos fecit timor" [In the beginning, fear made the gods in the world] is of course quite different. Burkhardt's statement is not a systematic construction. It is a creation of the historical eye.

8. Even the sporadic attempt to compare the state of mind of the primitives with modern forms of mental illness does not necessarily mitigate the emphasis on "paradise." The idea as such has been clearly set forth by Carus, Nietzsche, and Freud. More recently Alfred Storch, *The Primitive Archaic Forms of Inner Experiences and Thought in Schizophrenics* (New York: Nervous and Mental Disease Publishing, 1924), tried to lend more precision to it. Much still needs to be added. But there are remarkable parallels. One may consider it plausible, at least, that nature could have accomplished the immense daring of human creation only by risking tremendous danger. Also, schizophrenics do demonstrate, so to speak, a certain fluidity of experience, even in their deepest melancholy or stupor.

9. The subsequent character of the purposive relation in all magic is excellently interpreted by H. Hubert and Marcel Mauss in their "Esquisse d'une théorie générale de la magie," *Année sociologique* 1902–3. [Schmalenbach goes on to cite works of Marrett, Durkheim, and Söderblom on the relation of magic and religion, and makes some speculations of his own on "purposive conduct."]

10. The emergence of the "totem" has to be seen in an analogous way. Social effects are of course secondary. Durkheim's absolute sociologism distorts the problem. There is no question that sociality is deeply obliged to the religious. As early as 1864, Fustel de Coulanges, in his *The Ancient City*, trans. Willard Small (Boston: Lee and Shepard), put the matter correctly.

11. Particularly Levy-Bruhl's *How Natives Think* (New York: Washington Square Press, 1966), but as early as his *Les fonctions mentales dans les sociétés inférieures* (Paris: Alcan, 1910). [Schmalenbach enlarges upon Levy-Bruhl's thesis]. . . . But to point up the major problem, the "survivals" of primitive prehistory persist and leave numerous traces in the lower layers of all higher cultures.

12. The etymological origin of the word "soul" is unknown. Older theories have been lost. Psyche, experience, animation, spirit, or humanity designate life, breath, whisper, or wind.

13. An exception is Durkheim, whose thesis, "The idea of the soul derives from the idea of mana" (*Elementary Forms of the Religious Life* [Glencoe: Free Press, 1947], p. 381), would be a clear statement and proper insight, if Durkheim had not been so hopelessly mired in his sociologism. [Further comments on Durkheim, Söderblom, and Marrett follow.]

14. Cf. Herbert Spencer, *Principles of Sociology* 1:179.

15. Albertus C. Kruyt, *Het animisme in den Indischen Archipel* (The Hague: Nijhoff, 1906).

16. N. Söderblom, *Das Werden des Gottesglaubens* (Leipzig: Heinrichs, 1916), p. 14.

17. Walter F. Otto, *Die Manen: Von den Urformen des Totenglaubens* (Berlin, 1923).

18. Cf. above, pp. 174–76.

19. Cf. above, pp. 182–85.

20. Ibid.

21. Furthermore, the relationship between fertilization and birth is not comprehended by most primitives. The phallus is therefore a most important "symbol." See Edwin S. Hartland, *Primitive Paternity* (London: Nutt, 1909–10).

22. See Erich Becher, *Die fremddienliche Zweckmässigkeit der Pflanzengallen und die Hypothese überindividuellen Seelischen* (Leipzig: Veit, 1917).

23. Translators' note: Schmalenbach's use of the term *Geist* (as in Hegel) covers both the English "mind" and "spirit." "Spirit" is used most frequently in this translation, but it should always suggest to the reader a dimension of "mind."

ON HUMAN EXISTENCE: REALITY, PLAY, AND SERIOUSNESS

1. Translators' note: The German verb *meinen* and the noun *das Meinen* used by Schmalenbach are translated as "apprehend" and "apprehension." A more precise rendering may be the verb "opine," as defined in the unabridged *Oxford English Dictionary*, i.e., supposing something (albeit vaguely), and not only in the meaning of holding or giving an opinion. "Opine," however, is presently obsolescent but sometimes found in philosophical discussions. As Suzanne Langer might have put it, its conventional meaning has faded. Consequently, we have turned to "apprehend," preferring lively imprecision to deathly precision. Finally, the active dimension of "apprehend" is emphasized rather than the receptive dimension.

2. Translators' note: Schmalenbach uses these terms in a special sense. See "Phenomenology of the Sign," below, part 3.

3. See my discussion, *Das Gewissen* ["Conscience"] in the *Festschrift für Karl Joël* (Basel: Helbing und Lichterhahn, 1934), pp. 202–39.

4. Ibid.

5. Ibid.

6. See my discussion of faithfulness or fidelity in "Communion—A Sociological Category," part 1.

PHENOMENOLOGY OF THE SIGN

1. I have developed these at greater length in the second part of my book, *Geist und Sein* (Basel, 1939), but since then I have reached some new conclusions that also fit into the present study. Besides Husserl, one must also mention Ferdinand de Saussure. But de Saussure has implicitly limited his research to the explanation of the phenomenon of language, just as Husserl has not noticed that his new views were applicable to the comprehension of signs in general. Besides, the inexactitudes that one finds in Husserl, especially the comprehension of the sign starting from the single "sender" subject, have also not been avoided by de Saussure and his school. See Charles Bally, "Qu'est-ce qu'un signe?" [What is a sign?] *Journal de Psychologie* 36 (1939): 161–74.

2. Godet's note: The words "notify," "notifying," etc., to translate *Kundgabe* are rather makeshift here, and too objective in meaning. It is a question of a subject which is manifested or expressed in one way or another and—to this extent at least—"makes something known" (*kundgibt*) without necessarily "applying" to someone.

3. Soares's note: *Faire* also means "make."

4. Editors' note: *Erlebnis* has been left untranslated in the French version by Godet. We have translated it as "experience." The reader should be able to understand from its context the importance of this central concept in Schmalenbach. Godet also left *Einfühlung* untranslated in the French. That term can be aptly translated as "empathy."

5. I dealt with this problem nearly twenty years ago in my work "Die Entstehung des Seelenbegriffes," *Logos* 16 (1927): 311–55. [See "Soul—The Emergence of the Concept," part 2.] There I maintain the thesis that the specific concept of the soul comes from a basis of impressions and representations which are religious, which cannot be derived in their turn (as the animist theory would have it) from a primitive belief in souls; that, quite the opposite, it is the primordial feeling of the noumenon which is then specifically tied to a noumenon of psychic nature. I am still of this opinion. I believe, however, as far as the psyches of others, in a general sense, are concerned, that it is not necessary to pass through the experience of the noumenon to reach them. Besides at that time, I had already described exactly the phenomena which are involved in our present problem, except that I had not then perceived the differentiations to be made and which have become clear to me today. I also held the erroneous view that the experiences studied here can be presented only in connection with the feeling of the noumenon, although they also exist as "profane," even if the feeling of the noumenon must be presupposed as the origin of notions of the soul.

6. The special signification that I give to the word *Ansprache* prevents me from using it, as I do in *Geist und Sein*, in the sense of an appeal in general.

Bibliography of the Work of Herman Schmalenbach

As accurately as publications could be verified in American and European libraries, this is a complete bibliography of the work of Herman Schmalenbach. Insofar as they are relevant to his philosophical and sociological work, the bibliography also lists a number of articles in magazines and major newspapers. Works translated in the present volume are marked with an asterisk.

Die erste Konzeption der Metaphysik im abendländischen Denken [The first conception of metaphysics in western thought]. Darmstadt: Wittich, 1909.

"Henri Bergson." *Die Hilfe* 1913.

G. W. Leibniz, *Ausgewählte philosophische Schriften im Originaltext* [Selected philosophical writings in original text]. Edited and with an introduction by Herman Schmalenbach. Leipzig: Meiner, vol. 1, 1914; vol. 2, 1915.

"Simmel." *Sozialistische Monatshefte*, 25 (1919): 283–88.

"Leben. Nietzsche. Chronik. Literatur." *Sozialistische Monatshefte*, 25 (1919): 482–86.

"Geschichte. Neuausgaben. Chronik." *Sozialistische Monatshefte*, 25 (1919): 658–60.

"Feuilletonphilosophie. Neuausgaben. Totenliste. Kurze Chronik. Literatur." *Sozialistische Monatshefte*, 25 (1919): 831–34.

"Naturphilosophie. Geschichtsmorphologie. Kurze Chronik." *Sozialistische Monatshefte*, 25 (1919): 1177–78.

* "Die Genealogie der Einsamkeit" [Genealogy of lonesomeness]. *Logos* 8 (1919): 62–96.

"Logik. Kurze Chronik." *Sozialistische Monatshefte*, 26 (1920): 361–63.

"Ethik. Praktische Philosophie. Rechtsphilosophie. Totenliste. Literatur." *Sozialistische Monatshefte* 26 (1920): 200–204.

"Individualität und Individualismus," *Kantstudien,* 24 (1920): 365–88.

"Hegel." *Sozialistische Monatshefte,* 26 (1920): 1094.

"Wundt." *Sozialistische Monatshefte,* 26 (1920): 1094–95.

"Judentum." *Sozialistische Monatshefte,* 26 (1920): 1095–96.

"Totenliste. Kurze Chronik. Literatur." *Sozialistische Monatshefte,* 26 (1920): 1096–97.

Leibniz. Munich: Drei Masken, 1921.

* *Die soziologische Kategorie des Bundes* [Communion—a sociological category]. *Die Dioskuren,* 2 (1922): 35–105.

"Neues zum Problem der Phänomenologie." *Deutsche Literaturzeitung,* 43/44 (1922): 969–981. 45 (1922): 993–99.

"Leibniz. Gestalt und geistesgeschichtliche Stellung" [Leibniz. His stature and position in history of thought]. *Österreichische Rundschau,* 18 (1922): 9–25.

Thomas Hobbes. *Das Naturreich des Menschen.* Edited and with an introduction by Herman Schmalenbach. Stuttgart: Frommann, 1923.

"Erlebnis und Leben" [Experience and life]. *Frankfurter Zeitung,* June 26, 1923.

"Kant und die Philosophie der Gegenwart" [Kant and modern philosophy]. *Österreichische Rundschau,* 20 (1924): 445–68.

"Die Objektivität," *Essener Allgemeine Zeitung,* June 20, 1924.

* "Soziologische Systematik" [Systematic sociology], *Weltwirtschaftliches Archiv* (B. Harms, ed.), 23 (1926): 1–15.

Das Mittelalter. Sein Begriff und Wesen. [The Middle Ages. Their conception and essence]. Leipzig: Quelle und Meyer, 1926.

Die Kantische Philosophie und die Religion. Göttingen: , 1926.

"Die religiösen Hintergründe der kantischen Philosophie" [The religious background of Kantian philosophy]. *Blätter für deutsche Philosophie,* 1 (1927): 29–60.

* "Die Entstehung des Seelenbegriffes" [The emergence of the concept of soul]. *Logos* 16 (1927): 311–55.

"Das Metaphysische in Kant." *Pädagogische Warte,* 34 (1927): 621–27.

* "Soziologie der Sachverhältnisse" [Sociology of property]. *Jahrbuch für Soziologie,* vol. 3. Karlsruhe: Braun, 1927.

"Das letzte Wort des Sokrates." *Aus unbekannten Schriften.* Festgabe für Martin Buber. Berlin: Lambert Schneider, 1928.

Kants Religion. 1. Sonderheft, Deutsche Philosophische Gesellschaft. Berlin: Duncker und Humblot, 1929.

"Die Stellung der Philosophie der Gegenwart zur Religion" [The position of modern philosophy toward religion]. *Theologische Blätter,* 39 (1929): 248.

"Das Sein des Bewusstseins" [The being of consciousness]. *Philosophischer Anzeiger*, 4 (1929/30); 359–432.

"Kunst." Schriften der Deutschen Gesellschaft für Soziologie. *Verhandlungen des 7. Deutschen Soziologentages*. Tübingen: Mohr, 1931.

Das Ethos und die Idee des Erkennens. [Ethos and the idea of cognition]. Entrance lecture at University of Basel, 1932. Tübingen: Mohr, 1933.

"Das Gewissen" [Conscience]. *Festschrift für Karl Joël*. Basel: Helbing und Lichterhahn, 1934.

"Zum 70. Geburtstag Karl Joëls," *Basler Nachrichten*, March 26, 1934.

"Nachruf auf Karl Joël [Obituary for Karl Joël]. *Der Morgen* (Berlin, 1934); 366–70.

"Das soziale Prestige der Lebensalter" [Social prestige of age groups]. *Reine und angewandte Soziologie*. Festgabe für Ferdinand Tönnies. Leipzig: Buske, 1936.

"Philosophie in der Lehrerbildung" [Philosophy in teacher education]. *Basler Schulfragen*, 1 (1939).

* *Geist und Sein*. [Mind and being]. Basel: Haus zum Falken, 1939.

"Die Idee der Logik als Philosophie vom Logos," *Jahrbuch der Schweizerischen Philosophischen Gesellschaft*, 3 (1943): 1–18.

* "Phénoménologie du signe" [Phenomenology of the sign], *Etre et Penser: Cahiers de Philosophie*, 15 (Neuchâtel, April 1946): 49–103.

"Macht und Recht. Platons Absage an die Politik." *Natur und Geist*. Festschrift für Fritz Medicus. Zürich: Walter, 1946.

Obituaries

Landmann, Michael. "Herman Schmalenbach 1885–1950." *Studia Philosophica*, 10. Basel: Verlag für Recht und Gesellschaft, 1950, pp. 1–4.

Salmony, Hansjörg A. "Professor Dr. Herman Schmalenbach zum Gedächtnis." *Basler Studentschaft*, 32, December 1950, pp. 28–30.

Name Index

Abel, Theodore, 16, 252
Achilles, 144
Aeschylus, 144
Albrecht, G., 256
Alcibiades, 144
Alexander (the Great), 122
Alkaios, 144
Alkmaion, 173
Antigone, 145, 147
Aragon, Louis, 245
Aristotle, 145, 146, 157–59, 168, 173, 259, 260
Aron, Raymond, 251

Baerwald, Friedrich, 250
Bally, Charles, 262
Barnes, Harry Elmer, 252
Barth, Heinrich, 252
Baudelaire, Charles, 245
Becher, Erich, 261
Berger, Peter L., 252
Bergson, Henri, 5, 7, 12, 263
Berkeley, George, 141, 152
Birnbaum, Immanuel, viii
Bloch, Ernst, 6
Blüher, Hans, 258
Blumer, Herbert, 39, 256
Bohringer, Robert, 250
Bonaparte, Napoleon, 122
Borger, Robert, 250

Brentano, Franz von, 6, 68, 258
Breysig, Kurt, 120
Brosses, Charles de, 161
Buber, Martin, 4, 7, 8, 250, 251, 264
Burckhardt, Jakob Christoph, 33, 161, 260
Burgess, Ernest W., 256

Cahnman, Werner J., 249, 252, 256
Caillois, Roger, 10
Calvin, John, 33, 148
Carlyle, Thomas, 38
Carus, Titus Lucretius, 260
Cassirer, Ernst, 2
Chisholm, R. M., 251
Chomsky, Noam, 10
Christ, 146–49
Cioffi, Frank, 250
Codrington, Robert Henry, 167
Cohen, Jere, 258, 259
Coleman, James S., 256
Comte, Auguste, 49
Cooley, Charles H., 1, 2, 37–39, 253, 255, 256
Coser, Lewis A., 249, 251
Coulanges, Fustel de, 41, 260
Crawley, Alfred, 259
Cressey, Donald R., 39
Cromwell, Oliver, 68

267

Subject Index

Act (action), 10, 13, 30, 31, 34, 62, 75, 87, 110–112, 114–116, 191, 192, 196, 197, 212, 227, 238, 248, 254, 257, 259

Address, 13, 42, 191, 193, 195, 211, 226–231, 232, 233–242, 247

Affection, 81, 84, 86, 96, 102, 127, 130, 133, 143, 230

Age, 19, 70, 106, 108, 119, 163, 193, 229, 256

Alienation, 65, 123, 124, 137, 140, 143, 144, 146, 150

Animal(s), 126, 158, 161, 163, 170–172, 175, 192, 197, 198, 203, 204, 219, 230, 231, 237, 238, 241, 242, 247

Animism, 159, 160, 166, 175, 181, 262

Antagonism, 19, 26, 56, 58, 65, 78, 79, 100, 105, 107, 161, 230, 231

Anthropology, 108, 207, 255

Anxiety, 161, 177, 238, 243

Appeal, 217, 218, 222–224, 232–234, 236–239, 242, 262

Apprehension (*Meinen*), 8, 10, 12, 16, 36, 37, 38, 39, 51, 53, 77, 78, 80, 112, 174, 189, 190, 191, 192, 196, 197, 199, 201, 204, 205, 206, 207, 210, 211, 218, 219, 222, 232, 239, 244, 247, 258, 261

Aristocracy, 65, 68, 97, 101, 121, 124, 144, 153

Art, 3, 16, 33, 101, 132, 140, 152, 197, 206, 211, 244, 245

Asceticism, 30, 110, 151

Autarchy, 99, 103, 115, 117, 118, 198

Authority, 18, 19, 98, 124, 153, 154, 253

Being (*Sein*), 3, 8, 13, 16, 53, 62, 89, 130, 138, 174, 196, 208, 244, 250, 262

Biology, 9, 10, 57, 138, 157–159, 169, 173, 176–178, 184, 257, 260

Bonds (ties), 18, 22, 27–29, 65, 67, 70, 73–77, 80, 84, 87–92, 94, 96–100, 106, 107, 109, 110, 118, 123, 124, 129, 131, 140, 196

Bourgeoisie, 20, 21, 24, 25, 40, 65, 68, 101, 102, 106